Poverty in Scotland

2014

The independence referendum and beyond

Edited by: John H McKendrick, Gerry Mooney, John Dickie, Gill Scott and Peter Kelly

CPAG • 94 White Lion Street • London N1 9PF

CPAG promotes action for the prevention and relief of poverty among children and families with children. To achieve this, CPAG aims to raise awareness of the causes, extent, nature and impact of poverty, and strategies for its eradication and prevention; bring about positive policy changes for families with children in poverty; and enable those eligible for income maintenance to have access to their full entitlement. If you are not already supporting us, please consider making a donation, or ask for details of our membership schemes, training courses and publications.

Published by the Child Poverty Action Group, in association with The Open University in Scotland, Glasgow Caledonian University and the Poverty Alliance

The views expressed are those of the authors and do not necessarily represent the views of the Child Poverty Action Group.

94 White Lion Street
London N1 9PF
Tel: 020 7837 7979
staff@cpag.org.uk
www.cpag.org.uk

© Child Poverty Action Group/The Open University in Scotland/Glasgow Caledonian University/the Poverty Alliance 2014

A CIP record for this book is available from the British Library

ISBN: 978 1 906076 94 8

Child Poverty Action Group is a charity registered in England and Wales (registration number 294841) and in Scotland (registration number SC039339), and is a company limited by guarantee, registered in England (registration number 1993854). VAT number: 690 808117

Cover design by Devious Designs
(based on an original design by John Gahagan)
Typeset by Devious Designs
Printed in the UK by Russell Press
Cover photos by Paul Box/Reportdigital; Jess Hurd/Reportdigital

About the editors

John Dickie is Head of CPAG in Scotland. He is responsible for promoting policies that will contribute to eradicating child poverty, as well as overseeing the strategic development of second-tier welfare rights services that ensure frontline agencies are able to support families to receive the financial support to which they are entitled. He previously worked at the Scottish Council for Single Homeless and before that directly with young people experiencing homelessness. Visit: www.cpag.org.uk/scotland.

Peter Kelly has been Director of the Poverty Alliance since 2004, having joined the organisation as Policy Manager in 2002. He represents the Alliance on a wide range of forums, including the European Anti-Poverty Network. He has served on a number of advisory forums, for both the Scottish and UK governments, and currently chairs the Scottish Living Wage Campaign. Before joining the Poverty Alliance, Peter worked at the Scottish Low Pay Unit. Visit: www.povertyalliance.org.

John McKendrick is Senior Lecturer in the Glasgow School for Business and Society at Glasgow Caledonian University. His research is primarily concerned to inform the work of practitioners and campaigners beyond the academy who seek to tackle poverty in Scotland. In recent years, he has completed research for the STV Appeal (attitudes toward child poverty in Scotland) and Save the Children (survey of local authority work on tackling child poverty locally). He has published several guides and briefings for practitioners in Scotland, and drafted much of the text for the Scottish government's online guide to tackling child poverty locally. Visit: www.gcu.ac.uk/gsbs/staff/drjohnhollandmckendrick.

Gerry Mooney is Senior Lecturer in Social Policy and Criminology in the Faculty of Social Sciences at The Open University in Scotland. He has written widely on social policy, devolution, poverty and inequality, social divisions in the urban context, class divisions, and the sociology of work. Among other publications, together with Gill Scott, he edited *Social Justice and Social Policy in Scotland* (Policy Press, 2012) and, together with Hazel Croall and Mary Munro, he edited *Criminal Justice in Scotland*

(Willan, 2010). Visit: www.open.ac.uk/socialsciences/staff/peopleprofile. php?name=gerry_mooney.

Gerry's Open University online materials can be accessed at: www.open. edu/openlearn/profiles/gcm8.

Gill Scott is Emeritus Professor of Social Inclusion and Equality at Glasgow Caledonian University. Gill was Founding Director of the Scottish Poverty Information Unit, which she led until she retired. She was external adviser to the Scottish government from 2003 to 2006 on poverty issues and Lead Expert for URBACT European Network Women, Employment and Enterprise from 2008 to 2011. Visit: http://gcal.academia.edu/gillscott.

About the contributors

Stephen Boyd is Assistant Secretary of the Scottish Trades Union Congress, with responsibility for economic and industrial policy, the environment, utilities, transport, and arts and culture. He is a member of the First Minister's Energy Advisory Board, the Aerospace, Defence and Marine Industry Advisory Group, the National Textiles Forum, the Highland Economic Forum, the Scottish Council for Development and Industry's Executive Committee, the Scottish government's Public Procurement Advisory Group and the Scottish government's Regulatory Review Group.

Bea Cantillon is Professor of Social Policy and Director of the Herman Deleeck Centre for Social Policy at the University of Antwerp, Belgium. She has published widely and internationally on a wide range of issues relating to poverty, social policy, social security, the welfare state and gender.

Mike Danson is Professor of Enterprise Policy at Heriot-Watt University. He has advised and been commissioned by governments, trade unions, community groups, the OECD, the European Commission and others on such issues as employability, regional development, volunteering, Gaelic, enterprise and ageing.

Fernando Fantova has worked in the social policy and intervention sectors for more than thirty years. He has worked with people with disabilities and for community development in the third sector in Spain and Latin America. He has held the position of Deputy Minister of Social Affairs in the Basque government, and is currently working as an independent consultant. The majority of his written work is available for consultation at: http://fantova.net.

Miquel Fernández is Assistant Professor of Social Anthropology at the University of Barcelona and Professor of Sociology at the Autonomous University of Barcelona. Among other work, he has recently written around issues of symbolic and systemic violence in relation to urban transformation and urban life in Barcelona.

Cailean Gallagher is a researcher at Yes Scotland. He is involved with Trade Unionists for Yes, Mair Nor a Roch Wind, and is a member of the Labour Party and Unite. He has worked with openDemocracy, co-editing the *Restating Scotland* debate and *Fight Back! A Reader on the Winter of Protest*, and was founding editor of the *Oxford Left Review*.

Jim Gallagher was Director General for devolution in the UK government, Senior Adviser to the Prime Minister on devolution strategy (2007–2010) and Secretary of the Calman Commission. Jim is currently a fellow at Nuffield College, Oxford and Visiting Professor of Government at Glasgow University, and is also currently an adviser to the pro-UK 'Better Together' campaign.

Lisa Hauschel is a graduate from Humboldt University, Berlin, where she completed a Masters in British Studies and wrote her dissertation on the politics of child poverty in Scotland and the UK. She currently works for a Member of the Scottish Parliament.

Fiona McHardy is Research Officer at the Poverty Alliance and most recently worked on the Big Lottery-funded project, Evidence, Participation, Change. Prior to joining the Poverty Alliance, she worked as Research Assistant in the Scottish Poverty Information Unit at Glasgow Caledonian University.

Carlo Morelli is Senior Lecturer in Business and Economic History in Economic Studies at the School of Business at Dundee University. His research focuses on the distribution of income, child poverty and devolution.

Gareth Mulvey is currently Lord Kelvin Adam Smith Fellow (Sociology) at the University of Glasgow and previously worked as Researcher at the Scottish Refugee Council.

Mary P Murphy is Lecturer in Irish Politics and Society in the Department of Sociology at the National University of Ireland, Maynooth. She has research interests in gender and social security, globalisation and welfare states, the politics of redistribution, and power and civil society. She is an active advocate for social justice and gender equality and a Commissioner Designate of the Irish Human Rights and Equality Commission.

Angela O'Hagan is Research Fellow at the Institute for Society and Social Justice Research at Glasgow Caledonian University. She is also Convenor of the Scottish Women's Budget Group and from 2007 to 2013 was a member of the statutory Scotland Committee of the Equality and Human Rights Commission.

Paul Seaman is Lecturer in Economics in Economic Studies at the School of Business at Dundee University. His research focuses on the economics of welfare reform and labour economics.

Stephen Sinclair is Reader in Sociology and Social Policy at Glasgow Caledonian University, where he undertakes research in the Yunus Centre for Social Business and Health.

Carolina Stiberg is originally from Gothenberg in Sweden, but is currently living and working in Edinburgh. She has a degree in modern languages from Gothenburg University, and a Masters in British Studies from Humboldt University in Berlin. As part of her Masters degree, she worked as an intern for a Member of the Scottish Parliament. She subsequently graduated from Humboldt in March 2012.

Robin Tennant is Fieldwork Manager with the Poverty Alliance. He is responsible for overseeing the development of its community engagement work and poverty awareness training programme.

About the organisations

CPAG in Scotland is part of the Child Poverty Action Group. It promotes action for the prevention and relief of poverty among children and families with children. To achieve this, CPAG aims to: raise awareness of the causes, extent, nature and impact of poverty, and strategies for its eradication and prevention; bring about positive policy changes for families with children in poverty; and enable those eligible for income maintenance to have access to their full entitlement. If you are not already supporting us, please consider making a donation, or ask for details of membership schemes, training courses and publications. For further information, please visit www.cpag.org.uk/scotland.

With over 15,000 students across Scotland, **The Open University in Scotland** is one of Scotland's leading providers of higher education. It is committed to widening access to higher education and has an open admissions policy. As a result, no previous qualifications are necessary to study at degree level. Many of its students are on a low income and receive help towards the cost of their course fees. For further information, contact The Open University in Scotland on 0131 226 3851, scotland@open.ac.uk or visit www.open.ac.uk/scotland. Learning resources are also available on the Open University's OpenLearn website (www.open.edu/openlearn), YouTube platform (www.youtube.com/user/OUlearn), and ITunes library (www.open.edu/itunes/). Together, these offer a wide range of resources relating to different aspects of poverty in Scotland, the UK and beyond.

Established in 1992, the **Poverty Alliance** is the national anti-poverty network in Scotland. It works with a range of community, voluntary and statutory organisations to find better solutions to the problems of poverty in Scotland. The Alliance attempts to influence anti-poverty policy by lobbying and campaigning, organising seminars and conferences, producing briefing papers and other information. A key goal for the Alliance is to have the voices of people experiencing poverty heard in policy processes. For further information, please visit: www.povertyalliance.org.

The Scottish Povorty Information Unit of **Glasgow Caledonian University** was the driving force behind the first edition of *Poverty in Scotland*. The study of poverty in Scotland remains a focus within Glasgow Caledonian University and Emeritus Professor Gill Scott and Dr John H McKendrick continue its long-standing association with this publication. A commitment to engage with practitioners beyond the academy is the hallmark of much of the applied poverty research undertaken within the Glasgow School for Business and Society at the university.

The **Scottish Council for Voluntary Organisations** (SCVO) is the membership organisation for Scotland's charities, voluntary organisations and social enterprises. SCVO has helped fund this publication because it believes poverty is now the biggest crisis ever to hit Scotland, and the recent economic and financial crisis has proved that it could land at anyone's doorstep. In a country as rich as Scotland, this is a disgrace. SCVO works with its members to shine a light on the scale and impact of the poverty crisis, and wants people in Scotland to take action and work with the third sector to help alleviate the impact of poverty. For more information about SCVO and its work, see www.scvo.org.uk.

Acknowledgements

We are very grateful to all the people who contributed to this book. Their enthusiasm for tackling poverty and highlighting the major issues that must be addressed in Scotland at the current time was much appreciated.

Gerry Mooney is grateful to Diane Morris in the Open Media Unit at the Open University, Milton Keynes, and Una Bartley, Louise Davison and Kate Signorini at The Open University in Scotland, Edinburgh, for their support with this publication.

We very much appreciate the financial support from the Scottish Council for Voluntary Organisations and the Educational Institute of Scotlane that has helped make publication of this book possible.

Finally, the editors would like to thank colleagues in Glasgow Caledonian University, the Poverty Alliance, Child Poverty Action Group and The Open University in Scotland for their support.

Contents

Section One
Introduction

One
Poverty, 'austerity' and Scotland's constitutional future

Gerry Mooney

2014: a momentous year

2014 will be a momentous year, not only for Scotland but for the entire UK. On 18 September 2014, voters in Scotland will be asked to give their verdict on independence for Scotland or staying in the United Kingdom. While at the time of writing, in late 2013, the opinion polls are pointing to a 'No' to independence vote, irrespective of the outcome of the ballot, Scotland – and consequently the rest of the UK – will be a very different place. This latest edition in the *Poverty in Scotland* series is out of sequence with the previous volumes in that it has not been produced ahead of a Scottish Parliament election campaign. In the 2002, 2007 and 2011 editions, we were aiming to locate the exploration of poverty and anti-poverty policy within the context of devolution, and to centre the issue of poverty and social welfare more generally at the heart of the then forthcoming electoral debates in Scotland. This remains the committed aim of this volume too, but the sub-title, 'The independence referendum and beyond', immediately points to a rapidly changing political landscape in Scotland, one that has undergone profound transformation since the introduction of devolution in 1999. Few could have argued that within 15 years of devolution, a ballot would be held on independence for Scotland. However, along with change there are continuities: this is a landscape which remains profoundly disfigured by poverty, disadvantage and, of course, by inequality. The constitutional question and the poverty/inequality question have become crucially interlinked. This has also been reflected in the independence debate itself as it has unfolded during the course of 2013 and into 2014. In some ways, different ways, this goes to the very heart of the kind of society we wish Scotland to become – irrespective of the outcome of the referendum. But it is also important that we recognise from the outset that social policy issues and, in particular, issues around poverty and welfare, have been pivotal to the discussion of Scottish devolution since 1999, not least that the Scottish Parliament is largely a social policy-making body.[1]

This book as a whole is neutral on the question of Scotland's constitutional future, though the editors and contributors have different views on this.[2] In **Section Four** you will encounter contributions from the two main sides of the debate – from the 'Yes' (to independence) campaign and from the 'Better Together' (in the UK) camp. While the different contributors to this book have their own particular views and perspectives on independence, all of us as editors, as contributors, and in the organisations represented, think the issues of poverty and social welfare should be central to the constitutional debate.

The constitutional question aside, *Poverty in Scotland 2014* carries on with other traditions that have become established as central to the series: providing an accessible account and overview of the evidence base on poverty in Scotland, exploring its main dimensions, dynamics, and its uneven social and geographical impacts. In similar fashion, it reviews a range of different anti-poverty policies and, again as with previous editions, offers a wide range of different thematic essays that focus on particular aspects of poverty and inequality in Scotland today or which advance particular arguments for addressing such issues. However, to the goal of looking forward and offering new insights, this edition departs from the previous ones in that it includes a series of essays that consider poverty and anti-poverty policy making in other countries and national contexts (see **Section Six**).

'Austerity' UK, 'austerity' Scotland

By any measure, Scotland remains a society that continues to be scarred by poverty. The 'headline' poverty statistics from 2013 show us that:

* 870,000 people in Scotland still live in poverty (17 per cent of the population);[3]
* 200,000 children in Scotland still live in poverty (20 per cent of all children).

Poverty in Scotland, and across the UK, is significantly higher than in many other European countries. In Denmark and Norway, for example, 10 per cent of children or fewer live in poverty, while the Netherlands has an over-all poverty rate of 11 per cent.[4]

Poverty exists across Scotland. Nearly all local authorities in Scotland have council wards where over 20 per cent of their children live in poverty.[5]

Real progress had been made in reducing the numbers of people living in poverty, specifically among children (down by 160,000 since 1996/97) and pensioners (down by nearly two-thirds since 1996/97). These trends follow dramatic increases in poverty between 1979 and the mid-1990s.

However, recent independent modelling forecasts that, as a result of current UK coalition government tax and benefit policies, there will be massive rises in child poverty in the coming years.[6] In Scotland alone, fore-cast trends suggest around 65,000 more children being pushed into poverty by 2020.[7]

While child poverty has further declined since 2010, this is because the median income, against which is it is measured, had itself fallen.[8] However, investment in, and uprating of, family benefits in line with rising prices until 2011/12 protected low-income families' incomes (to some extent) as the median fell. This protection has now been removed as a result of UK government social security cuts and the 1 per cent cap on benefit uprating, leading in large part to the forecast explosion in child poverty referred to above.

Any discussion of poverty in Scotland must acknowledge from the outset that the patterns, distribution and depth of poverty and disadvan-tage are shaped in no small part by a policy-making agenda that takes place outside Scotland (that is, at the UK Parliament in London), policies that are working to erode social protection. While the devolution of more powers to Scotland is the stated position of the four main political parties, albeit to varying degrees, at present it is the UK government that largely determines the social welfare landscape of Scotland. In previous issues, we have discussed the role of reserved (to the UK government) and devolved (to the Scottish government) powers and possible tensions between these, and it is understood that work and employment policy, welfare benefits and pensions, the minimum wage, most taxation and trade union legislation remain within the policy remit of the UK govern-ment. In Chapter 1 of *Poverty in Scotland 2011* we highlighted that, in 2011, the political and policy-making landscape had undergone a signifi-cant shift from the early days of devolution in the late 1990s.[9] The UK gov-ernment, a Conservative/Liberal Democrat coalition, administers key areas of social welfare and benefits in Scotland, a Scotland governed by an SNP-led majority government in a Parliament in which the two UK governing parties lie a distant third and fourth in terms of votes and seats. The Labour Party is the main opposition party in both Parliaments, a far cry from its dominance in UK and Scottish politics in the early years of devolution.[10]

In 2011, the coalition partners in London had been in government for a year, and already there were indications of the direction of travel in relation to policy towards social welfare, benefits, work and employment. In what was referred to by Conservative leader David Cameron as 'the new age of austerity', large-scale cuts in public expenditure had already been announced.[11] Yet relatively few could have predicted with any degree of certainty just how far the UK government would be prepared to go in a new era of, to use the heavily worn phrase, 'welfare reform'. A total £22 billion of cuts to the annual value of UK benefits and tax credit support will have been made by 2014/15. It is estimated that between £1.6 billion (around £480 for every adult of working age)[12] and £2 billion[13] will be cut from Scottish household incomes.[14] The Scottish government estimates that the cumulative impact of UK government welfare reforms over the five years to 2014/15 could result in the welfare bill for Scotland being reduced by over £4.5 billion.[15]

The idea of 'austerity' has entered political, popular and media discourse as a shorthand way of capturing the period of economic and financial crisis that engulfs much of the UK today. It is presented and represented almost as a technical term, devoid of any political basis, seemingly neutral in that the main Westminster political parties all saw 'austerity' cuts as offering the only way to economic growth and financial health. The only issue of contention was the timescale for rolling out cuts in public expenditure. Alongside the idea of austerity, other phrases came to be popularised: 'sharing the pain' and 'we are all in this together' were among the most notable of a plethora of terms deployed in an effort to convince us all that everyone should suffer in largely equal measures.[16]

Yet if we approach the notion of 'austerity' with a more critical eye, we can see that it was never going to be 'equal' or 'fair' in its impact – nor was it intended to be. Austerity for the contributors to this book is, at its most basic, a government strategy to reduce a budget deficit by slashing public spending, public services and, significantly, pensions and other welfare benefits. These cuts impact most adversely on those who are already among the most disadvantaged in society, but also have a disproportionate impact on women, both as public sector workers and as users of publicly provided services that are now being reduced.[17]

However, this Is still a largely superficial understanding of what austerity denotes. It is also about an assault on the very social contract that was held by successive generations of people in the UK to be a core part of UK citizenship. Across the UK and elsewhere in Europe, notably in Greece, Portugal and Spain, austerity programmes have dismantled or are dismantling not only benefits and services, but also the mechanisms and structures that work to reduce inequality and enhance equity.[18] Cutting wages, in-work and out-of-work benefits, pensions and the social wage more generally (that is, the range of public services) is also about restoring conditions for profit and wealth accumulation. It is clear from the UK Treasury's own analysis that, aside from the very richest quintile, the cumulative effect of the coaltion's spending decisions on tax, benefits and services is highly regressive.[19]

Through this more critical, indeed deeper, understanding of austerity, we can see that it is not a neutral or technical strategy. On 1 April 2013, in a leading article entitled 'The day Britain changes: welfare reforms and coalition cuts take effect', *Guardian* journalist Patrick Wintour highlighted the range of measures taking effect from that day which heralded a far-reaching and hard to reverse change to the UK social security system.[20] Among the most notable of UK-wide measures was the scrapping of what was termed the 'under-occupancy charge' (or 'spare-room subsidy'). Now popularly known as the 'bedroom tax', this aimed to cut the levels of housing benefit. Disability living allowance was abolished to be replaced by a personal independence payment, the change of label significant in denoting that it is no longer based on an individual's condition but on how that condition affects her or his independence – and that means her/his ability to work. For the first time ever, welfare benefits and tax credits will not rise in line with inflation, but between 2013 and 2016 will rise by only 1 per cent per year, amounting to a cut in their real value. The introduction of universal credit replaces most working-age means-tested benefits for those in and out of work. But behind this administrative change lies a much greater range of sanctions aimed at forcing the recalcitrant 'workless' into employment.

'Benefit bashing' has become the order of the day for the UK coalition and its supporters in some sections of the media. What seems an endless supply of shock stories about 'welfare scroungers' or benefits claimants living in mansions (even better if they are recent immigrants) works to secure the narrative ground and to legitimise UK government welfare reforms, an issue that we return to later.

Amidst the various welfare reforms introduced by the UK coalition government, it is the 'bedroom tax' which stands out for many as capturing the punitive thrust of much government policy. In September 2013, the 'bedroom tax' hit the headlines with a United Nations official arguing that the UK government should 'suspend immediately' its introduction, as it could represent a violation of the human right to adequate housing.[21] While widely attacked by Conservative politicians and commentators, these claims sat alongside figures showing that over 50,000 people faced eviction from their social housing as the UK government's under-occupancy charge kicked in, within only four months of its being introduced.[22]

Insecurities, risk and uncertainties

Austerity is working in other ways to change the social fabric of the UK. 'Social security' is steadily being diminished for an increasing proportion of the population across Britain, and this includes larger numbers of people who are in some form of paid employment. Insecure and low-paid employment is increasingly prevalent,[23] as is the phenomenon of labour market 'churning' – that is, a working life characterised by episodic low-paid, low-quality work and then a period of unemployment.[24] The growth and spread of 'poor work' across many areas of the UK lays the lie that 'economic recovery' is benefiting everyone. Indeed, for many there is a degradation of work as hard-fought wages and conditions are eroded in an atmosphere in which having a job is seen as better than having no job at all – irrespective of pay or security. The spread of low pay is one of the hallmarks of this latest period of austerity. For the Resolution Foundation, the economic crisis has pushed a further 1.4 million workers below the living wage, the rate seen as necessary for a basic standard of living. In its *Low Pay Britain 2013* report, the Foundation highlights that 4.8 million workers in Britain (20 per cent of all employees) earn below the living wage – a leap from 3.4 million (14 per cent) in 2009, at the height of the recession.[25] Further, such figures can hide the uneven impact of the growth of poor work on particular sections of the population. Young workers are hit particularly hard, with one in three young workers (those aged 16–30, some 2.4 million people) active in some form of low-paid and low-skilled employment. In 2013, 37 per cent of new employees entered part-time work, with a further 32 per cent taking temporary work (an issue which is discussed by Stephen Boyd in Chapter 16 of this book).[26] In 2013, 58 per cent of low-paid workers (2.9 million people) worked part time – up from under 30 per cent in 1975. And there is a very clear gender dimension to this, with women accounting for almost 66 per cent of the five million workers of all ages living in poverty. Further, the precarious labour market position of many recent immigrants and refugees is also noteworthy here (see Chapter 18).

Such inequalities are reflected across Scotland too. Here, between 2008 and 2013, the numbers in in-work poverty increased from 255,000 to 280,000.[27] Alongside this, the number of people in part-time work but seeking full-time employment increased by 50,000 over the same period.[28]

UK government policies have worked to reduce expectations of a secure working life, not only for many young workers but also for many of those who have decades or more of work ahead of them. The provision of good quality pensions remains a diminishing hope for more and more workers, while the erosion of other long and hard-fought terms and conditions promises a working life – if fortunate enough to have a working life – of hardship and insecurity, accompanied by personal and familial risk and uncertainty. UK government policies may also have detrimental health outcomes for working-age people in receipt of benefits, as well as for their families.[29]

The insecurities of working life in Britain in 2014 have been laid bare by the growth and spread of zero-hours contracts. TUC figures published in mid-2013 estimated that over 300,000 workers in the care sector alone are employed on zero-hours contracts, with such contracts prevalent in other areas of the public sector, including in further and higher education, and elsewhere across the economy.[30] That the care sector in particular is highlighted here as an area of the labour market where such work is prevalent also serves as a reminder that in our society it is all too often the most socially necessary or socially valuable work that is poorly paid and characterised by poor-quality conditions of employment. That this is also an area of the labour market where women workers are found in particularly high numbers also serves to remind us again that occupational segregation remains a feature of employment and that female workers are often among the most vulnerable sections of the labour force, such vulnerability compounded by the negative effects of welfare reforms on women's role as carers of children.[31]

However, with 30 per cent of working families in the UK having at least one parent employed in the public sector, the TUC reports that the impact of the decline in real public sector wages as a result of pay freezes, combined with benefit changes, will see an additional 180,000 children with at least one parent employed in the public sector ending up in poverty as a result of UK coalition government policies by 2015.[32] Many public sector jobs are far removed from the image of generously rewarded, cossetted and financially secure work as presented by sections of the media and some politicians in recent years.

Highly insecure forms of employment not only contribute to the rise in the proportion of the working population who are in poor work, but also lead to a significant deterioration in the quality of service provided, services that are already heavily relied on by the poorest and most disadvantaged groups in the population.

The inequalities that characterise working life, namely low income, low-quality work and low expectations, alongside working patterns that are disruptive of family and other areas of life – income-poor and time-poor – impact on people in many other ways. Health, both physical and psychological, can be affected as can people's general sense of wellbeing, which is undermined by stress and feelings of marginalisation and alienation. Low income and poor-quality work is associated with personal debt and exclusion from forms of consumption that are considered socially acceptable and desirable.[33]

Returning to the assertion that we are, in some vague way 'all in this together', the 2013 edition of the *Sunday Times* 'Rich List' recorded a massive increase in wealth for the super-rich in the United Kingdom.[34] The number of billionaires stands at a record 88 – up from 77 in 2012. The combined wealth of the richest 1,000 UK residents has reached £450 billion, a total increase of £35 billion on the 2012 figure. The wealth of the top 200 richest residents in Britain and Ireland amounts to £320 billion, an eight-fold increase on the £38 billion held by the richest recorded in the first 'Rich List' in 1989.

Scotland remains one of the most unequal countries in the Western world. According to figures from the Office for National Statistics, the UK government's own agency, the most affluent households in Scotland are 273 times richer than the poorest households.[35] Further, in 2012, the richest 100 men and women in Scotland saw their combined wealth increase from £18 billion in 2011 to £21 billion in 2013.[36] The problem is, therefore, not an overall shortage of resources as such – more the uneven distribution of private wealth.

Challenging disrespect, stigma and punitive approaches to poverty

That Scotland and the rest of the UK are increasingly unequal places now almost passes without comment. 'Fairness' and 'equality' have come to be among the most contested notions in relation to the impact of austerity policy making. While voices are frequently heard about fairer taxation, alongside protests against tax evasion by large corporations and the wealthy, there is at a political and policy-making level little sign that the wealthy should be contributing much more to society or that rising inequality is shameful. 'Shame' is something that seems to be reserved for those who are worse off, much worse off.

While the significant rise in low-paid and low-quality work (the 'poor work' detailed earlier) stands in sharp contrast to and counters historic, long-standing and dominant myths about a Britain engulfed by hordes of 'workless' families, often trapped in 'welfare ghettos', such myths remain hugely potent, arguably more so than in a long time.[37] Austerity has also carried with it punitivism against people experiencing poverty and disadvantage.

Under New Labour and now under the UK Conservative/Liberal Democrat coalition, welfare reforms have been driven by: the themes of 'worklessness', reflecting a lack of individual responsibility; that there exists a pervasive 'culture of dependency' that is personally and socially corrupting and fuelled by over-generous state support; and that such state-invoked personal failure is a primary cause of unemployment, a refusal to work and poverty in general – alongside a lengthy list of other social ills ranging from illegitimacy, family breakdown, addiction and educational failure through to indebtedness, crime and deviancy. Both the Green Paper, *21st Century Welfare*,[38] and the White Paper, *Universal Credit: welfare that works*,[39] reflect these themes of a 'broken society' characterised by welfare dependency and worklessness – in particular, 'inter-generational' worklessness.[40] Here, worklessness is understood as natural and cultural, produced and transmitted across families. In some senses there is little that is new here in that it reflects long-held beliefs that there is a segment of the population that is feckless, undeserving and an 'underclass'.

Austerity and welfare reform have invoked a much harsher language and a more punitive attitude to poverty.[41] A language of 'workless families', 'welfare dependency', 'worklessness' reflects the belief that welfare ben-

efits are a 'lifestyle choice'.[42] This is an image of a 'broken Britain' populated by problem groups who are a drain on hard-pressed resources in a
time of economic crisis. Notable among such groups are the '120,000
troubled families' who require particular intervention – or sanctions – to
force a turnaround in their lives.[43] Again, the familiar themes of 'dysfunctional' and unstable family structures, inter-generational transmission and
generally dysfunctional and destructive behaviour are to the fore here.
Elsewhere, UK government politicians and their supporters point to a
landscape where 'welfare ghettos' house such 'troubled' families and
other problem populations.[44]

   These ways of thinking – while dominant – do not go unchallenged
by those labelled activists, by campaigning groups and by some politicians,
academics and researchers. While this negative and punitive language is
overwhelmingly associated with the Conservatives and UK government
politicians and policy makers, and is markedly less evident in Scotland
where the Scottish government has generally avoided the punitive language that has come to characterise UK government welfare reform rhetoric, it is a mistake to think that such ways of thinking, the view that people
experiencing poverty and disadvantage are in some ways culpable for
their own predicament, is not to be found in Scotland (see Chapter 2).

   Once more though, there is resistance to such representations – the
misrepresentation of poverty and the disrespect of those experiencing
poverty and marginalisation. In recent years, a range of campaigns has
emerged that seek to challenge discrimination and hostility against people
experiencing poverty. The Scottish Campaign on Welfare Reform has
advocated a different kind of 'reform' to the welfare system – one that
sharply contrasts with successive UK governments' notions of 'reform'
(reform here deployed as a euphemism for cuts in benefits, increasing
conditionality and reduced entitlements).[45] In challenging inaccurate and
discriminating media stories which demonise or stereotype benefit
claimants, the Campaign is one of a number of campaigning organisations
that seek to shift the emphasis away from blaming individuals, families and
indeed entire communities to a renewed focus on wider societal and
structural issues, such as the lack of good quality and well-paid employment. The 'Stick Your Labels' campaign and Child Poverty Action Group's
initiative, 'People Like Us' strive to highlight 'the shocking news' that people receiving benefits 'are just like us'.[46] Re-emphasising that benefit
claimants are real people, real families and real children is central to challenging the many myths that surround poverty and people in poverty.
'Myth busting' has taken on a renewed importance in the context of aus-

terity and UK government welfare reforms.[47] A further report in 2013 saw a number of church organisations come together to challenge the myths and lies surrounding the discussion of poverty.[48]

Poverty remains then a hugely contentious and contested area of investigation, reporting and policy making. The contributors to this edition of *Poverty in Scotland* share a commitment to challenging the myths and lies that unfortunately continue to inform its discussion.

The Scottish government 2011 and poverty policy

The headline poverty figures provided earlier show in very stark terms the extent of poverty in Scotland today – and the challenges that face both the Scottish and UK governments. In its *Annual Report for the Child Poverty Strategy for Scotland 2013*, the Scottish government laid bare the extent of child poverty in Scotland and its debilitating and unequal impact on young people across Scottish society.[49] The report, which the Scottish government must publish each year, in accordance with the UK Child Poverty Act 2010, showing how it will contribute to meeting UK targets, charts progress towards the eradication of child poverty by 2020. While this report shows a reduction of two percentage points in relative child poverty since 2011 (before housing costs are taken into account), massive increases in child poverty are forecast – in part as a consequence of wider economic changes and rising unemployment, but also as a result of UK government policy measures and the downward pressure on budgets and deepening cuts in welfare benefits and other tax changes. The challenge for the Scottish government is to address child poverty in a policy and political climate that is increasingly unfavourable as far as child poverty is concerned.[50]

It is important to reaffirm that policies do make a difference, and do have an impact, albeit perhaps less than poverty campaigners fought for, as was shown as a result of the policies introduced by the New Labour UK government, some of which have only demonstrated an impact following Labour's defeat in 2010. Between 1998/99 and 2011/12, for example, using the 'before housing costs' measure used to measure progress against statutory child poverty targets, child poverty was nearly halved in Scotland, the rate dropping from 28 per cent to 15 per cent. However, predictions for the current decade until 2020 point to a deteriorating picture. From 14.8 per cent in 2011, one estimate is that child poverty in

Scotland will have increased to 20 per cent by 2020. On a UK level, it is estimated that an additional nearly one million children will be in poverty, giving a rate of 22.5 per cent.[51]

The UK coalition government has reaffirmed its commitment to the Child Poverty Act introduced by Labour in 2010, yet with £20 billion of cuts to the social security budget by 2015/16 alone, together with cuts leading to deteriorating services, it is increasingly apparent that it will not only fall well short of the goal of a further significant reduction in child poverty by 2020, but that the rate will increase markedly.[52]

The Scottish government has the capacity to invest more ambitiously in combatting child poverty by, for instance: moving towards a more universal approach to childcare and early years provision; free school meals, enhancing access to affordable and good quality food; helping address fuel poverty; and as helping to meet the 'hidden' costs that are often associated with schooling (such as uniform and clothing costs, school trips, activities and materials), which will alleviate hard-pressed family budgets and provide young people with a better quality life, both at home and in education.

UK government welfare reform has been seized on by the SNP government and the 'Yes' campaign more generally to argue that independence would protect Scotland from such policies. In her foreword to the Scottish government's *Annual Report for the Child Poverty Strategy for Scotland 2013*, the Deputy First Minister commented:[53]

> While we are doing all we can to tackle child poverty, the actions of the UK Government will result in more than £4.5 billion being cut from Scottish households. As a devolved government we are seeking to mitigate the damage done by welfare reform. We cannot possibly mitigate all of the impacts it will continue to have on children and families in Scotland…Through our commitments on the social wage and protecting universal benefits we have already demonstrated what we can do with just some of the powers available to us… This government wants to eradicate child poverty. I believe Scotland can do better and given the full range of powers that independence will deliver, I believe we will do better.

That things will be better after independence can leave the current Scottish government vulnerable to claims that it could be doing more, within existing devolution legislation and budget choices, to address issues of poverty. There have been significant job losses in Scottish public services in recent years and, as elsewhere in the UK, public sector workers have endured pay freezes. There is then, at least potentially, a gulf between the rhetoric of what benefits independence *may* provide and the reality of the current situation in which austerity is biting as hard in Scotland as it is in many other parts of the UK.

Before 2012, however, arguments for independence rarely addressed social welfare and benefits issues, so in some way this marks a significant shift, but this was also built on the unpopularity of UK government policies among Scotland's voters, something that was given political expression in the Scottish Parliament. In December 2011, SNP and Labour MSPs voted to withhold legislative consent for the UK Welfare Reform Bill. While the Scottish Parliament in Edinburgh cannot prevent the UK government changing the benefits system, such a move meant that these reforms were out of step with Scottish laws and necessitated the Scottish Parliament introducing its own legislation. That this was the first time that the Scottish government had withheld legislative consent for a UK government bill highlights once more the increasingly central role of welfare in Scottish politics.[54] Lying behind this though is the wider question of Scotland's constitutional future.

The referendum and beyond: towards a Scottish welfare regime?

The Scottish Parliament is very much a social policy-making parliament. By that is meant that the majority of powers devolved to that Parliament relate to matters of social policy. This encompasses areas such as education, health, social work and housing, but also extends to important Scottish government interventions around equalities, anti-poverty policies and a diverse range of other powers that impact on social policy in some form. That Scotland-specific policies are developed and implemented, together with important differences in practice and governance between Scotland and other parts of the UK, has contributed to the idea that social policy making is very different in Scotland and, in turn, that this is related to what would appear to be a distinctive political arena around which such issues are debated.

However, key social policy areas, such as most taxation, social security benefits and employment policy, remain under the control of the UK government and it is the devolution of these areas, or their incorporation into a *Scottish* welfare state in the context of an independent

Scotland, which is becoming an increasing element of the debate around the creation of a 'fairer' Scotland.

The fact that the debate around social welfare in Scotland has embarked on an increasingly divergent path from that in England and is tied up with other issues relating to more powers and/or independence does point to a welfare landscape that is increasingly different to that in England (in particular), at least in important respects.

In 2011/12, total public sector expenditure for Scotland was estimated to be £64.5 billion. This was equivalent to 9.3 per cent of the comparable total UK public sector expenditure in 2011/12, so a higher proportion than Scotland's share of the UK population at around 8.38 per cent at the time of the 2011 census. This may be accounted for primarily by Scotland having more people on a lower income, a higher share of pensioners and a larger number of people with disabilities in its population. Social protection was the largest Scottish expenditure programme and, together with health expenditure, accounted for over half of total public sector expenditure for Scotland – equating to around half of Scotland's GDP. Welfare reforms and changes in the public sector are felt far and wide across Scotland and these also in no small part contribute to the ongoing political controversies around the role of social welfare in both the devolved, and a potential independent, Scotland.[55]

The political debate in Scotland around social welfare is distinctive in important respects from other areas of the UK. In part, this distinctiveness also emerges not so much from what is happening in Scotland – but from developments taking place in England. There is, for example, no widespread privatisation of the NHS in Scotland – a process that appears to be developing apace across key areas of NHS provision in England. Differences in other aspects of social policy making, in education policy, criminal justice policy and across a range of other issues means that the policy landscape of Scotland and England appear increasingly different – as do the debates to which these policy landscapes both reflect, and give rise. This is the context in which arguments around social welfare have become increasingly central, both to the independence debate and to the future of Scottish society. It is also significant that the existence of a Conservative-led government at Westminster, rather than a Labour one, has led to more vocal opposition to UK government policies and, in particular, to the further roll-out of yet another set of welfare 'reforms'.

UK government welfare reforms have been criticised by the SNP as out of step, not only with the wishes of voters in Scotland but also as seriously at odds with 'Scottish values'. Much of this is related to other claims that Scottish voters and the wider public in Scotland are in some way less hostile to people in receipt of benefit, that negative attitudes to welfare are more diluted in Scotland. While the evidence to support this view is weak, it is notable that much of the Scottish press is less prone to the moralising and punitive tone that often accompanies welfare reporting in England.

In late 2012 and in 2013, First Minister Alex Salmond and Deputy First Minister Nicola Sturgeon have repeatedly made forays into the welfare debate. At the March 2012 SNP conference in Glasgow, the Deputy First Minister argued that:[56]

'Only independence can put a stop to heartless Tory welfare reforms that will punish the vulnerable and the disabled. And only independence will give us the tools we need to rid Scotland of the poverty and deprivation that still scars our nation and create the jobs and opportunities that will get people off benefits, not for Tory reasons, but for the right reasons.'

In subsequent speeches, Sturgeon, Salmond and other Scottish ministers continued to push this line, adding themes that spoke of Scottish values and attitudes underpinning social policy and equity, promising a Scottish welfare system that would be driven by social justice and demonstrating a strong commitment to social democracy. There was now, however, an added dimension to such claims – that the UK government's welfare reforms were not only 'eroding the social fabric' of society, but they also marked a radical departure from the foundations of the post-war British welfare state. Alex Salmond had previously flagged this line of argument in his Hugo Young Lecture in London in January 2012. Clearly speaking to an English audience, Salmond claimed that:[57]

'... anyone who accepted the union partly because of the compassionate values and inclusive vision of the post-war welfare state may now be less keen on being part of a union whose government is in many respects eroding those values and destroying that vision... And looking at the problems of health reform now, I thank the heavens that Westminster's writ no longer runs in Scotland on health issues. But the looming issues of welfare reform exemplify why Scotland needs the powers to make our own policies to meet our own needs and values.'

That the SNP has been only too willing to seize on UK government welfare reforms to advance the case that only an independent Scotland with a distinctive Scottish welfare state is true to the foundations of the post-war UK welfare state leaves the nationalists open to counter-claims that independence for Scotland will further erode what is left of that welfare state, introducing competing notions of citizenship and entitlements for different parts of the UK. The claim made here is that more devolution or full independence leaves not only the population in England vulnerable to further erosions in welfare entitlement, but that it would diminish trans-UK systems of benefits and social security. These issues are considered in more depth in **Section Four**, but at this stage it is also important to acknowledge that some of the proposed alternatives to full independence also advocate the transfer of further powers over welfare spending to the Scottish government. In part, this also reflects the provisions of the Scotland Act 2012, which paved the way for the transfer of further fiscal powers to Scotland. Therefore, the future state of welfare across the UK is likely to be characterised by even more divergence and complexity, but again this is also being driven by developments in England as much as it is by proposals for further devolution to Scotland.

Issues for a Scottish welfare state

Social welfare issues are, and have been, central to other perspectives in the independence debate and around the idea of a 'fairer Scotland' more generally. 'Fairness' itself remains a key goal, but as yet undefined with little clear indication of what it might mean in a future Scotland. The controversies and arguments around social welfare in the independence debate are ongoing, and in the run up to the September 2014 referendum these issues will come to take on more significance. In the 2012 Scottish Social Attitudes Survey, almost two-thirds (64 per cent) of those polled in Scotland believed that the Scottish Parliament should make the important decisions for Scotland about the level of welfare benefits, while 56 per cent say the same about tax levels.[58] This evidence can, of course, be taken as a signal of support not only for independence but also for 'devolution max'– that is, the maximum devolution of powers to Scotland *within* the UK.

The Scottish government has yet to fully cost a Scottish welfare system and this has left the SNP open to attack by opponents. However, work has begun on developing proposals for a Scottish welfare state. Scottish government ministers have set out their vision on welfare in an independent Scotland in *Your Scotland, Your Voice* and in *Working for*

Scotland: the government's programme for Scotland 2012/13. The Deputy First Minister established an Expert Working Group on Welfare in January 2013 to review the cost of benefit payments upon independence and the delivery of those payments in an independent Scotland.[59]

In its report in May 2013, the Group rejected claims, often voiced by politicians, that Scotland was more dependent on welfare than the UK as a whole.[60] The Group noted that the overall difference between Scotland and other parts of the UK is minimal, but is also largely accounted for by key demographic differences mentioned above, notably a higher proportion of the population on incapacity benefit and severe disablement allowance. It further argued that Scotland could afford to meet its welfare commitments under independence – and that the infrastructure was already in place in the shape of UK government departments based in Scotland, which would transfer to Scotland with independence. However, it is also acknowledged that it would take several years for the benefits system of an independent Scotland and the rest of the UK (or whatever it comes to be termed) to be completely disentangled, with implications for the shaping of a new welfare system.

Important questions remain. What would a Scottish tax regime look like? How could it generate more income for Scotland on a more equitable basis? What might a Scottish welfare state look like? What sorts of social provision could be developed with a higher tax base? How could this be used to tackle poverty and promote greater equality and fairness for Scotland as a whole?

There is, as yet, from the SNP or Scottish government (or from any of the opposition parties in the Scottish Parliament, with the exception of the Greens) no argument for a major redistribution of income and wealth. Against this there are other arguments that fairness can only come about through challenging the major inequalities, and sources of inequality, that exist within Scotland itself (for example, inequalities in and at work) through improving the rights of workers and so on. This will bring challenges to all the main political parties in Scotland and it remains an issue to which they have not as yet faced up. There is considerable uncertainty over the vision for a Scottish welfare state that will emerge over the next few years. Might this be a Scandinavian model of social welfare – or a system which represents a more residualised form of welfare?

Common Weal: a new vision for welfare in a new Scotland?

The debate around what kind of welfare state Scotland should have is of course a debate around the kind of society we would wish to see Scotland become. That this debate is directly linked with the question of Scotland's constitutional future is clear. But it is not a debate that is limited by constitutional matters alone. During 2012 and 2013, the notion of 'Common Weal' as the basis of a distinctively Scottish welfare system has risen to prominence. In a series of papers published by the Jimmy Reid Foundation, proponents of the Common Weal have advocated a far-reaching vision of Scotland as a fairer, progressive and more sustainable society.[61] Looking to some of the economic and social policies in the Nordic countries, it places an attack on entrenched inequality and wealth by a completely revamped taxation system that would enable better quality, well-funded public services. Social goals would drive economic development, not the pursuit of private profit. A new set of principles would underpin a Scottish welfare state, in the form of contract between people in Scotland delivered through the state. Greater participation in all forms of governance would remove corporate political and policy-making influence. We return to these issues in the concluding Chapter 28.

That there is a debate around the future of Scotland's welfare system[62] brings into sharp focus the questions of poverty and inequality – but also wider issues about the kind of economy and society that would be necessary for the eradication of poverty. That this is leading to new thinking around new forms of welfare system is positive and to be encouraged, but at the same time the challenge is also to advance now the issue of poverty in a way that is free of stigma and disrespect. We cannot afford to wait for independence or any other future constitutional arrangement to be bedded down before rethinking poverty and anti-poverty policy.

The Structure of *Poverty in Scotland 2014*

Section Two: The nature of poverty in Scotland begins with the vexed question of how poverty is best to be understood. Here issues of definition and measurement occupy centre stage (Chapters 2 and 3). Long-standing controversies around these issues are also reflected in the discussion of the primary causes of poverty in Scotland, which are considered in Chapter 4.

Section Three: Poverty in Scotland: the evidence explores recent trends in the distribution and patterns of poverty and inequality across Scotland (Chapters 5 and 6). It also considers the ways in which poverty is impacting on particular groups within Scotland (Chapter 7) and how the day-to-day lives of a large number of people are adversely affected by the experience of living in poverty and on low income (Chapter 8).

Section Four: Poverty, social welfare and the constitutional question provides a platform for the two main opposing sides in the independence debate – the 'Better Together' ('No' to independence) campaign (Chapter 10) and the vote 'Yes' (for independence) campaign (Chapter 11) – to argue their respective cases and to offer the most suitable constitutional foundations for tacking poverty and disadvantage. Elsewhere, in Chapter 9, we provide other commentary that reflects the fact that the wider constitutional debate also encompasses arguments for the greater devolution of powers to the Scottish Parliament – while remaining within the UK.

In line with previous editions, **Section Five: Principles for a more equitable Scotland** offers a range of short and accessible themed essays (Chapters 12 to 19), which have as their common goal identifying and advancing principles for a more equitable Scotland, principles it is felt should be central to the future direction of policy on poverty, disadvantage and inequality in any future constitutional settlement. The choice of essays here span a wide range of issues and areas of interest – some of which overlap and all of which are connected in different ways. In any volume such as this, it is always a difficult task to decide which areas should be included. Our choice here was partly informed by the areas that were included in *Poverty in Scotland 2011*. We did not wish to go over the same ground, but felt safe in the knowledge that the debates and issues covered then, three to four years ago, remain as relevant today.

Section Six: Perspectives from Europe and beyond marks a new departure for the *Poverty in Scotland* series. The title of this section highlights that we are concerned about learning the lessons from the fight against poverty and the promotion of social welfare in other countries. There was a range of factors that informed our choice of countries: on the one hand, we were keen to include contributions that discussed poverty and social welfare issues in other countries where there were movements for autonomy, separation or independence – all terms that are heavily value laden – and in which similar kinds of issues to those being voiced in

Scotland were being mobilised in discussions. The inclusion of chapters from Catalonia (Chapter 21) and the Basque Country (Chapter 22) in Spain, and Belgium (Chapter 23), where there is a marked and growing divide between Flanders and Wallonia, represented obvious likely case studies from which we might be able to draw lessons for Scotland. The choice of Canada (Chapter 27) and Germany (Chapter 25) also, in part, reflected (at least in the case of Canada, where in Quebec there has long been a movement for independence) the interest with movements for autonomy. However, both countries, as different kinds of federalism, also offer other potential lessons and insights for Scotland, where possible tensions between different levels of government, federal and regional, may have consequences for anti-poverty and social welfare policy making.

The inclusion of a chapter on the experience of the Irish Republic (Chapter 26) is also important for the lessons that it can offer Scotland. As is pointed out in the chapter, Scotland can learn much from what Ireland *did not* do, and we are reminded once again that a strategy based on economic growth alone is never enough to effectively challenge poverty and disadvantage.

The decision to have an essay which considered the lessons which could be learned from the experience of Nordic states (Chapter 24) is perhaps not surprising. Scotland is not the only country where politicians and policy makers have looked to Scandinavia, often enviously, for an ideal type of welfare system, a model to be followed. However, in keeping with the critical stance and approach adopted across this book, we were keen to have a critically informed account of the 'Nordic model', an account which not only forces us to be more questioning about other welfare regimes, but also to reinforce the need for a similarly critical approach to be a feature of any discussion of a possible future welfare regime in Scotland.

Section Seven: Conclusion (Chapter 28) provides a brief overview of the main themes that have emerged from the contributions that span this book, and advances the case for social welfare, poverty and inequality (and wealth!) as key issues to be considered alongside constitutional matters.

Notes

1   For further discussion of the central role of social policy since 1999, see G Mooney and G Scott (eds), *Social Justice and Social Policy in Scotland*, Policy Press, 2012

2   For background discussion on the independence referendum and on the con-

stitutional choices facing Scotland, see I McLean, J Gallagher and G Lodge, *Scotland's Choices*, Edinburgh University Press, 2013 and I Macwhirter, *Road to Referendum*, Cargo Publishing, 2013. A range of learning materials on the independence debate are also available from OpenLearn at http://www.open.edu/ openlearn/society/politics-policy-people/politics/the-context-the-indepedence-debate.

3   From *Poverty in Scotland Summary Briefing*, updated August 2013, http:// www.cpag.org.uk/sites/default/files/CPAG-scot-briefing-poverty-in-scotland-up date-August-2013.pdf

4   International comparisons are for 2011 on a 'before housing costs' basis under which 15 per cent of Scotland's children live in poverty (see Chapter 5, Figure 5.3, p90)

5   http://www.endchildpoverty.org.uk/images/ecp/Scotland_LA%20and%20ward %20data%20upload.xls

6   See http://www.ifs.org.uk/comms/comm121.pdf and www.ifs.org.uk/comms /r78.pdf

7   *Child Poverty Action Group in Scotland Response to the Local Government and Regeneration Committee Call for Evidence on 14/15 Draft Budget*, 27 September 2013

8   See H Aldridge, P Kenway and T MacInnes, M*onitoring Poverty and Social Exclusion in Scotland 2013*, Joseph Rowntree Foundation, 2013, http://www. jrf.org.uk/publications/monitoring-poverty-scotland-2013

9   J H McKendrick, G Mooney, J Dickie and P Kelly (eds), *Poverty in Scotland 2011: towards a more equal Scotland*, CPAG, 2011 is free to access from the Open University's OpenLearn website at http://www.open.edu/openlearn/society/ poverty-scotland/content-section-1

10 Even if New Labour depended on a coalition with the Liberal Democrats to form the first two Scottish governments in 1999 and 2002.

11 David Cameron, 'The age of austerity', speech at Spring Forum, 2009, http:// www.conservatives.com/News/Speeches/2009/04/The_age_of_austerity_speech _to_the_2009_Spring_Forum.aspx

12 Report by Sheffield Hallam University for Scottish Parliament Welfare Reform Committee, April 2013, http://www.scottish.parliament.uk/parliamentarybusiness/ CurrentCommittees/62069.aspx – excludes the impact of the switch from RPI to CPI for benefits uprating.

13 Scottish government analysis, March 2013, see http://www.scotland.gov.uk/ Topics/People/welfarereform/analysis/welfareexpenditurecutsn – includes the impact of the switch from RPI to CPI for benefits uprating.

14 For more detail and a discussion of the overall impact of welfare reform on families in Scotland, see http://www.cpag.org.uk/content/welfare-reform-impact-

families-scotland and a CPAG factsheet at http://www.cpag.org.uk/sites/default/files/CPAG_Scot_factsheet_WR_families_April13.pdf

15 Scottish government, *UK Government Cuts to Welfare Expenditure in Scotland: welfare analysis*, 2013, http://www.scotland.gov.uk/Resource/0041/00417011.pdf

16 See 'Themed Issue on Social Policy in an Age of Austerity', *Critical Social Policy*, 32, 2012, p3

17 See G Mooney, 'Scotland, the CSR and Public Sector Cuts', in *In Defence of Welfare: the impacts of the Spending Review*, Social Policy Association, 2011, http://www.social-policy.org.uk/downloads/idow.pdf

18 Oxfam, *A Cautionary Tale: the true cost of austerity and inequality in Europe*, 2013

19 See S Lansley and J Mack, *A More Unequal Country?*, 2013, http://www.poverty.ac.uk/editorial/more-unequal-country; J Hills, J Cunliffe, L Gambaro and P Obolenskaya, *Winners and Losers in the Crisis: the changing anatomy of economic inequality in the UK 2007–2010*; R Lupton, *Social Policy in a Cold Climate*, Research Report No.2, London School of Economics and Political Science Centre for Analysis of Social Exclusion, June 2013, http://sticerd.lse.ac.uk/dps/ case/spcc/rr02.pdf; HM Treasury, *Impact on Households: distributional analysis to accompany Autumn Statement 2013*, December 2013

20 P Wintour, 'The day Britain changes: welfare reforms and coalition cuts take effect', the *Guardian*, 1 April 2013

21 A Gentleman, '"Shocking" bedroom tax should be axed, says UN investigator', the *Guardian*, 11 September 2013

22 See E Dugan, '50,000 people now facing eviction after bedroom tax', *The Independent*, 19 September 2013; and False Economy, 'Our research in *The Independent*: bedroom tax: 50,000 people face eviction', 2013, http://falseeconomy.org.uk/blog/our-research-in-the-independent-bedroom-tax-50000-people-face-eviction

23 See J Plunkett and J P Pessoa, *A Polarising Crisis? The changing shape of the UK and US labour markets from 2008 to 2012*, Resolution Foundation, 2013, http://www.scribd.com/doc/183978630/A-Polarising-Crisis-The-changing-shape-of-the-UK-and-US-labour-markets-from-2008-to-2012

24 See T Shildrick, R MacDonald, C Webster and K Garthwaite (eds), *Poverty and Insecurity*, Policy Press, 2012

25 Resolution Foundation, *Low Pay Britain 2013*, 2013

26 See note 25

27 See K Trebeck and S Francis, *Our Economy: towards a new prosperity*, Oxfam, 2013, http://policy-practice.oxfam.org.uk/publications/our-economy-towards-a-new-prosperity-294239

28 See note 8

29 See G McCartney and others, *Making a Bad Situation Worse? The impact of welfare reform and the economic recession on health and health Inequalities in Scotland (Baseline Report)*, NHS Health Scotland, 2013, http://www.scotpho.org.uk/publications/reports-and-papers/1109-making-a-bad-situation-worse

30 'Rise in zero-hour contracts a "worrying trend"', TUC Press Release, 3 July 2013, http://www.tuc.org.uk/workplace/tuc-22328-f0.cfm

31 See Scottish government, *The Gender Impact of Welfare Reform: equality and tackling poverty analysis*, 2013, http://www.scotland.gov.uk/Resource/0043/00432337.pdf

32 '180,000 children with a parent working in the public sector to be pushed into poverty by 2015', Trades Union Congress, 24 June 2013, http://www.tuc.org.uk/economic-issues/economic-analysis/180000-children-parent-working-public-sector-be-pushed-poverty

33 See note 27

34 'Rich List 2013', *Sunday Times*, 21 April 2013

35 T Peterkin, 'Britain's wealthiest families 500 times richer than the poorest', *The Scotsman*, 13 July 2012

36 F MacGregor, 'Rich List: fortunes soar 60% for wealthiest Scots', *The Scotsman*, 12 April 2013

37 See for example, Centre for Social Justice, *Signed On, Written Off: an inquiry into welfare dependency in Britain*, 2013

38 Department for Work and Pensions, *21st Century Welfare*, 2010

39 Department for Work and Pensions, *Universal Credit: welfare that works*, 2010

40 See L Hancock and G Mooney, '"Welfare ghettos" and the "Broken Society": territorial stigmatization in the contemporary UK', *Housing, Theory and Society*, 30:1, 2013, pp46–64; and G Mooney, 'The "Broken Society" Election: class hatred and the politics of poverty and place in Glasgow East', *Social Policy and Society*, 8, 4, 2009, pp1–14

41 Department for Work and Pensions, *Social Justice: transforming lives*, The Stationery Office, 2012; HM Government, *State of The Nation Report: poverty, worklessness and welfare dependency in the UK*, 2010

42 G Osborne, in G Wintour, 'George Osborne to cut £4b more from benefits', the *Guardian*, 9 September 2010

43 L Casey, *Listening to Troubled Families: a report by Louise Casey CB*, Department for Communities and Local Government, 2012. The Poverty and Social Exclusion website contains a number of critical essays and contributions around the notion of 'troubled families' at http://www.poverty.ac.uk/.

44 See Centre for Social Justice, *Signed On, Written Off: an inquiry into welfare dependency in Britain*, 2013, http://www.centreforsocialjustice.org.uk/UserStorage/pdf/Pdf%20reports/CSJ_Signed_On_Written_Off_full_report-WEB-2-(2).pdf

45 Scottish Campaign for Welfare Reform, *A Manifesto for Change*, Scottish Campaign for Welfare Reform/Poverty Alliance/CPAG Scotland, 2013

46 Poverty Alliance, 'Stick your Labels', Poverty Alliance, 2010, http://poverty alliance.org/userfiles/files/StigmastatementsOct2010.pdf; CPAG, 'People Like Us', 2013, http://www.cpag.org.uk/people-like-us

47 *New Statesman*/Webb Memorial Trust, *Bursting the Poverty Myths*, 2013, http://www.webbmemorialtrust.org.uk/download/publications_&_reports/New% 20Statesman%20Povety%20Supplement.pdf

48 Foremost here are the myths that 'they' (people experiencing poverty) 'are lazy and just don't want to work'; that 'they' are addicted to drink and drugs; that 'they' are not really poor, they just don't manage their money properly; that 'they' are on the fiddle; that 'they' have an easy life on benefits; and that 'they' caused the financial deficit. See *The Lies We Tell Ourselves: ending comfortable myths about poverty, a report from the Baptist Union of Great Britain, the Methodist Church, the Church of Scotland and the United Reformed Church*, Methodist Publishing, 2013, http://www.jointpublicissues.org.uk/wp-content/ uploads/2013/02/Truth-And-Lies-Report-smaller.pdf

49 Available from the Scottish government at http://www.scotland.gov.uk/Resource/ 0043/00432470.pdf

50 See also J McCormick, *A Review of Devolved Approaches to Child Poverty*, Joseph Rowntree Foundation, 2013, http://www.jrf.org.uk/publications/devolved-approaches-child-poverty

51 Figures available from J Browne, A Hood and R Joyce, *Child and Working-age Poverty in Northern Ireland Over the Next Decade: an update*, Institute for Fiscal Studies, 2013, Appendix A: Table A.1 for UK figures and Table B.2 for Scottish figures.

52 See L Judge, *Ending Child Poverty by 2020*, CPAG, 2013

53 N Sturgeon, Deputy First Minister, *Annual Report for the Child Poverty Strategy for Scotland, 2013*, Scottish government, 2013, http://www.scotland.gov.uk/ Publications/2013/09/2212

54 See G Scott and S Wright, 'Devolution, Social Democratic Visions and Policy Reality in Scotland', *Critical Social Policy*, 32(3), 2012, pp440–53

55 Scottish government, *Government Expenditure and Revenue Scotland 2011–2012*, 2013, http://www.scotland.gov.uk/Resource/0041/00415871.pdf

56 This lecture is available from http://www.snp.org/blog/post/2012/mar/dfm-nicola-sturgeons-address-conference.

57 Alex Salmond's Hugo Young lecture can be found at http://www.theguardian. com/politics/2012/jan/25/alex-salmond-hugo-young-lecture

58 http://www.scotcen.org.uk/media/1021490/ssa12briefing.pdf

59 Scottish government, *The Expert Group on Welfare*, 2013

60 Scottish Parliament, *The Impact of Welfare Reform on Scotland*, Welfare Reform Committee 2nd Report, 2013 (Session 4), 2013

61 Publications from the Jimmy Reid Foundation and relating to the Common Weal project are at www.reidfoundation.org and www.scottishcommonweal.org.

62 See for instance, Scottish Council for Voluntary Organisations, *A Better State: inclusive principles for Scottish welfare*, 2013, http://www.scvo.org.uk/wp-content/uploads/2013/09/Future-of-welfare-principles-discussion-paper.pdf; M Danson and K Trebeck (eds), *Whose Economy? An introduction*, Oxfam, 2011, http://policy-practice.oxfam.org.uk/publications/whose-economy-seminar-papers-complete-series-188809; and the Scottish Campaign on Welfare Reform at http://www.cpag.org.uk/scotland/SCoWR

Section Two
The nature of poverty in Scotland

Two
What is poverty?

John H McKendrick

Chapter summary

- Poverty is about not having enough. Typically, 'poverty' is understood to be a lack of resources. It can also mean inadequate outcomes or a lack of opportunities.
- Poverty is multi-dimensional and a wide range of resources may be lacked – for example, housing, fuel, education, health and money.
- Income is the primary resource that is lacking for people living in poverty. Insufficient personal or household income has a central role to play in creating or sustaining poverty in many areas of life.
- 'Income poverty' has also been of central importance in anti-poverty activity, debate and policy in Scotland. Thus, for practical purposes in Scotland, 'not having enough' is understood to be a point below which people have insufficient disposable income to purchase what it is reasonable to expect that the majority of the UK population should be able to afford.
- In Scotland (and the UK), income poverty tends to be understood in one of three main ways – absolute poverty, relative poverty and persistent poverty. The interpretation that is used most is relative poverty.
- Poverty is not the same as wellbeing, income inequality, social exclusion, social justice, multiple deprivation or material deprivation. However, poverty is closely related to each of these issues.
- Attitude surveys suggest that the wider Scottish public is not, as yet, fully supportive of the idea of poverty that underpins anti-poverty activity in Scotland.

Poverty: a deceptively simple idea

The heart of the matter is that poverty is about 'not having enough'. However, this straightforward idea is quickly complicated as attempts to define and measure poverty more precisely invariably become overly technical and theoretical, written by academics and statisticians for 'people like them'. This can be off-putting. However, the way in which we understand and define poverty has far-reaching implications on anti-poverty activity, debate and policy. It determines the number of people who are counted as living in poverty, and it can have a major influence on the policy solutions that are developed to address 'the problem'. Therefore, we must all be concerned about how poverty is defined and measured. Of course, definition and measurement are inter-linked; how we measure poverty depends on how it is defined. Yet, definition is essentially about ideas and measurement is essentially a technical challenge. Hence, in this chapter we consider how poverty in Scotland is defined; in the following chapter, we consider how poverty in Scotland is measured.

There is little doubt that ideas about poverty are complex, occasionally contradictory, and influenced by factors such as personal experiences, value judgements and belief systems. Consequently, definitions of poverty are also contested. There is no single, universally accepted, definition of poverty. In this opening section, we explain what we mean by poverty, and we describe how poverty is related to ideas of wellbeing, income inequality, material deprivation, multiple deprivation, social exclusion and social justice. We end by considering the extent to which the wider Scottish public agrees with three different ways of defining poverty.

Poverty as not having enough

It is not sufficient to state that poverty is about 'not having enough'. It begs the question: 'enough of what?' Broadly speaking, poverty might be understood as either inadequate outcomes (such as not being adequately clothed), inadequate opportunities (such as not having access to an adequate education) or inadequate resources (such as not having enough disposable income to purchase what is necessary to maintain an adequate standard of living).

Furthermore, in each case, it is possible to consider poverty as a whole, or to consider one particular dimension of poverty. For example, rather than define poverty as a bundle of poor outcomes in aggregate (using a multi-dimensional measure such as material deprivation), it is possible to measure particular dimensions, such as 'food poverty' or 'fuel poverty'. Campaigning organisations often adopt a narrower focus on a particular dimension of poverty. For example, Shelter Scotland is concerned with poor housing conditions in Scotland (what we might describe as 'housing poverty') and has used the Scottish House Condition Survey data published in 2012 to report that 348,000 homes in Scotland are affected by dampness and condensation, and 36,000 families with children are among the 59,000 households in Scotland living in overcrowded conditions.[1]

The idea of poverty as having inadequate opportunities focuses on the root cause of the problem. One example of this is the 'capability approach' that is most closely associated with the work of Amartya Sen.[2] Sen uses this idea to promote the understanding that development is about more than economic output (our equivalent would be that poverty is about more than income deprivation). However, in our consumer society, we must acknowledge that living life on a low income might be one of the reasons why people are deprived of 'capabilities' (opportunities to achieve an adequate life). For example, 'bodily health' is one capability that is associated with Sen's theory. It is widely accepted that income poverty, at least in part, has a negative impact on people's health – for example, having insufficient income to adequately heat a home may lead to dampness going unchecked, which in turn might exacerbate respiratory conditions.[3]

It is also pertinent to note that achieving fulfilment might be viewed as a worthier outcome than possessing an adequate income. Indeed, the UK government now generates national estimates of life satisfaction, sense of worth in life, happiness and anxiousness.[4] Similarly, Oxfam UK has developed a Humankind Index to provide intelligence on the things that 'really matter to the people of Scotland'.[5] At present, progressive social policy finds it easier to focus on 'lack of resources' than 'lack of personal fulfilment'. However, further development of this work may open up the possibility for a policy-driven approach to improve national wellbeing, happiness or 'the good life' in the future. However, measuring poverty or measuring fulfilment should not be viewed as two options over which a choice must be made. In the same way that a focus on 'capabilities' need not mean ignoring income deprivation, poverty should not be ignored when we focus on 'fulfilment'. Although they are different ideas, inadequate income and fulfilment are inextricably linked. On the one hand, living life on a low income is argued by many to be a contributory factor towards not achieving happiness.[6] On the other hand, there is undoubtedly the need to accord more importance to psychological wellbeing in understanding poverty.[7]

Thus, lack of resources (and lack of income in particular) has a role to play in directly producing inadequate outcomes (material and immaterial) and in making it more difficult to achieve adequate outcomes (by compromising the 'capabilities' that are needed to achieve them). Pragmatically, measures of income poverty are also easier to digest and utilise than measures of capability deprivation or fulfilment. However, there is a more significant reason for an income poverty focus in *Poverty in Scotland 2014*. It is also a fundamental right that people should have adequate resources to enable them to participate in society; in a consumer economy, adequate resources means adequate income. It must also be acknowledged that 'income poverty' has been the pre-eminent focus of anti-poverty activity, debate and policy in Scotland and the UK. Hence, in the first two sections of this book, 'income poverty' is the point of entry to this wider poverty debate.

For clarification, 'not having enough' income in the context of poverty as a lack of resources does not refer to the likes of a billionaire's insatiable thirst for Dom Perignon champagne. Rather, it refers to realities of life for almost one million people in Scotland who have insufficient income to be able to afford what the majority of people in Scotland would agree that the majority of people in Scotland should be able to afford.

Understanding income poverty

Absolute poverty

Absolute poverty refers to the level of resources needed to sustain physical survival. People are poor if they cannot feed, clothe or house themselves and their dependants. This is a definition of poverty that is only about subsistence, the amount needed to keep body and soul together. As Ruth Lister points out, absolute definitions of poverty are closely linked to nutrition, whereby a person or family can be considered to be poor if they do not have sufficient resources to feed themselves.[8] This conception of poverty is one that tends not to be associated with contemporary

Scotland, based on attitudes such as 'there is real poverty in Malawi, but not here', or 'we used to have poverty in Scotland, but not any more'. However, the proliferation of food banks in Scotland in recent years may lead us to question whether Scotland has truly rid itself of absolute poverty.[9]

In this absolute definition of poverty, income is central to the way we conceptualise poverty, as poverty is not having enough income to buy life's necessities. However, the definition of 'necessity' must be based on some assessment of need and our understanding of what is an essential need varies over time and across place. For this reason, few serious analysts, and none of the major political parties, would use an absolute measure alone to understand poverty in Scotland in the twenty-first century. It should be acknowledged that the measure of 'absolute income poverty' defined in the Child Poverty Act is not strictly a measure of 'absolute poverty' in the way that is outlined here.

Relative poverty

Relative poverty is defined in relation to the standards of living in a society at a particular time. People live in poverty when they are denied an income sufficient for their material needs, and when these circumstances exclude them from taking part in activities that are an accepted part of daily life in that society. However, there are issues with this approach. In times of economic growth, people may be reclassified as being poor, even when their material standard of living is improving (the decade following the mid-1990s in Scotland). On the other hand, it is possible that, in times of recession, people may be considered to have stopped being poor, when their material standard of living is falling – for example, since 2009/10 in Scotland. These apparent 'anomalies' arise because people are considered to be poor, relative to the norm, and are not only based on what their personal circumstances happen to be.

Despite the obvious shortcomings, in this book we primarily use the relative measure of poverty, believing that poverty should be defined by the standards of society as it is today. By using a relative measure, we arrive at an understanding of poverty that is fit for purpose in the twenty-first century:[10]

> ... an understanding based on a measure that has the lack of income at its heart, but which acknowledges that poverty is about what that lack of

income implies – the inability to obtain the types of diet, participate in the activities and have the living conditions and amenities which are customary... in the societies to which they [the poor] belong.

As is discussed in the following chapter, it is important to take account of the wider economic context when interpreting data on relative poverty.

Persistent poverty

There are also limitations to only using moment-in-time measures of poverty, as the population experiencing poverty is not static. Poverty dynamics research has shown that poverty can be transient (a condition experienced only for a short period of time) or recurrent (a condition into which households repeatedly enter and leave at different points in time).[11] Persistent poverty is defined over time. Where attempts have been made to measure persistent poverty in the UK, the approach that has been used is to define persistent poverty as that which occurs when relative income poverty is experienced by a household in three of the preceding four years. At the time of writing, the UK government had not confirmed that this was the way in which persistent poverty was to be measured for the 2010 Child Poverty Act.

Poverty and related ideas

Poverty and income inequality

The SNP-led Scottish government has set itself apart from earlier Scottish governments and the current UK government by asserting its intention to tackle income inequality, while retaining a focus on reducing income poverty. Through the Solidarity Purpose Target, the Scottish government aims to 'increase overall income and the proportion of income earned by the three lowest income deciles as a group by 2017'. More generally, growing interest in income inequality in the UK has followed the publication of *The Spirit Level* by Kate Pickett and Richard Wilkinson, in which they use international evidence to demonstrate that societies with higher levels of income inequality have excessively high negative social outcomes – ie, inequality *per se* contributes directly to social problems.[12] These shifts in political and academic thinking also reflect concerns in wider society at the current time. In light of the international banking crisis, subsequent global economic slowdown and austerity cuts, growing levels of discontent have been expressed at what are increasingly deemed to be excessive levels of pay (and non-waged income) that is enjoyed by bankers, business elites and high-ranking officers in the public service.

There is a close relationship between income inequality and income poverty and all too often they appear to be used interchangeably, in particular when relative poverty is discussed. The confusion is understandable, although it should be avoided. Income inequality is not a measure of income inadequacy; rather, it is a measure of the way in which income is distributed across a population. In contrast, income poverty specifies a level below which income is deemed to be inadequate. Of course, it is highly likely that where there is income inequality, there will be income poverty and that the eradication of poverty will require action to tackle income inequality. However, income inequality does not provide us with an estimate of how many people exist on an inadequate income. Although we consider the question of income inequality in Chapter 6, in this book we are primarily focused on the character and experiences of those who do not have sufficient income (income poverty).

Poverty and material deprivation

Deprivation is used to describe the lack of access to, or possession of, particular goods or services. Deprivation is not entirely dependent on income. Thus, a rich woman and a poor man would both be judged to be 'housing deprived' if they did not have access to adequate housing conditions (the former perhaps as a result of the difficulties involved in maintaining an older heirloom property to an adequate standard, the latter perhaps a result of not earning or receiving an adequate income). Housing, education and employment are among the issues for which deprivation is most commonly measured.

The OECD offers a helpful definition of material deprivation when it describes it as 'the inability of individuals or households to afford consumption goods and activities that are typical in the society of which they are part'.[13] Material deprivation might be described as an 'output' measure of poverty, in that it describes whether an adequate standard of living has been achieved (through direct public service provision and independent purchases using disposable income). In contrast, income poverty might be described as an 'input' measure of poverty, in that it is based on the financial resources that are available to secure an adequate standard of living. Thus, government has a role to play in material deprivation through service provision and by ensuring that citizens have an adequate disposable income.

Clearly, it would be expected that there is a close association between income poverty and material deprivation; those with fewer financial resources will be less able to provide for their material needs. However, intervening factors mean that it cannot be assumed that people living with income poverty will be materially deprived. For example, people who are 'income poor' may receive support in kind from members of the wider family, which prevents them from experiencing material deprivation, or they may have recently lost a well-paid job, have an income below the poverty line but many material possessions bought on their previous higher income. On the other hand, people who have recently escaped income poverty may find themselves materially deprived for some time thereafter, particularly if their increased level of disposable income is to be used to service debts that accumulated when they were living in poverty.

Poverty and multiple deprivation

As the name suggests, multiple deprivation is used to describe the situation when individuals, households or collections of people in small geographical areas are deprived of a range of conditions at the same time – for example, they are deprived of adequate housing, education and employment. In Scotland, multiple deprivation is most closely associated with small geographical areas through the Scottish Index of Multiple Deprivation. Areas of multiple deprivation in Scotland are currently identified using 38 indicators spread across seven domains (see Chapter 3). Multiply deprived areas are defined relatively; most typically, 15 per cent is used as the threshold for defining a multiply deprived area – ie, of the 6,505 data zones in Scotland, those whose deprivation score is ranked 1 to 975 (the bottom 15 per cent) are described as 'multiply deprived' areas.

While multiple deprivation in Scotland tends to be used as an area measure, not all people residing in multiply deprived areas will live in poverty. Similarly, many people living in poverty will not be residing in multiply deprived areas. However, intuitively we would expect that people living with income poverty would be more likely to live in the most deprived areas.

Poverty, social inclusion and social exclusion

The idea of social exclusion – and the Scottish variant of social inclusion – had been prominent in the anti-poverty work associated with New Labour in both Scotland and the UK as a whole. Changes in the political land-scape at Holyrood and Westminster have heralded a less prominent posi-tion for the concepts of social exclusion/inclusion in recent years.

Definitions of social exclusion usually describe how and why it occurs, as well as its implications. The European Union notes that social exclusion occurs when people cannot fully participate or contribute to society because of '… the denial of civil, political, social, economic and cultural rights'.[14] This is very similar to the thinking behind relative poverty in that relative poverty is based on the understanding that low income is significant as it prevents participation in wider society at a level all would be expected to enjoy. Thus, social exclusion can result from 'income poverty'. The idea of social exclusion remains important in understanding poverty in Scotland, even if the concept is used less often than before.

Of course, it must be clarified that social exclusion is viewed as resulting from combinations of linked problems, only one of which may be low income. For example, other causes of social exclusion include dis-crimination, unemployment, poor skills, poor housing, bad health and family breakdown. Social exclusion and income poverty are related – one may result from the other – but they can also exist independently of each other (people living in poverty may not be socially excluded, and the non-poor may be socially excluded) and should not be used interchangeably.

Poverty and social justice

As with social exclusion, the prominence of the use of the description 'social justice' in public circles has fluctuated through time. It was partic-ularly prominent in the early years of the Scottish Executive when its anti-poverty strategy was focused around social justice milestones. When social justice milestones were replaced with the Closing the Opportunity Gap approach,[15] the use of the term 'social justice' became less promi-nent. Social justice is a broad and contested term and definitions vary across the political spectrum. They include ideas of distributive justice, util-itarianism, equality, and libertarian ideas of 'governance'. Fundamentally, social justice is to pursue the belief:[16]

... that society can be reshaped – its major social and political institutions changed – so that each person gets a fair share of the benefits, and carries a fair share of the responsibilities, of living together in a community.

Ideas of social justice underpin our thinking about poverty in Scotland, even if they are not to the fore in contemporary debate. Indeed, it might be considered that the emphasis placed on understanding poverty as a human rights issue – such as the right of children not to live life in poverty[17] – is a way in which Scotland's concern about tackling the social injustice of poverty finds expression in contemporary times.

Poverty, happiness and wellbeing

As noted above, government and the third sector have recently promoted the importance of ideas about 'the good society'. These ideas have a broader focus than poverty, but it might be argued that this is, at least in part, a reaction to the prominence afforded to the relative income poverty measure. However, as with each of the other ideas discussed above, the issue is not one of making a choice to determine which is the 'best' measure. The challenge is to acknowledge the importance of all aspects of what makes for a 'good society' and to better understand how a lack of income contributes toward lower levels of happiness, wellbeing and the like for people in Scotland.

How people in Scotland define poverty

To this point, we have considered what professional experts working in the anti-poverty field (from academia, the third sector and government) mean when they talk about poverty. It cannot be assumed that the wider public agree with these definitions of poverty. Indeed, social attitudes research tends to suggest that there is a gap between public and professional thinking (Figure 2.1).

Figure 2.1 shows public support, in Scotland and in the UK as a whole, for three different definitions of poverty. The public were asked whether they agreed or not with each definition of poverty. Least support is given for a definition whereby 'someone in Britain is in poverty if they have enough to buy the things they really need, but not enough to buy the

Figure 2.1:

Public support for different definitions of poverty, Scotland and the UK, 2010

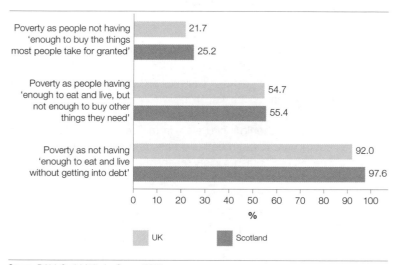

Source: British Social Attitudes Survey, 2010

Notes:
1. UK totals include Scotland.
2. See text for explanations of definitions.

things most people take for granted'. A small majority support a conception of poverty as people having 'enough to eat and live, but not enough to buy other things they need'. On the other hand, there is almost universal support for the idea that 'someone in Britain is in poverty if they have not got enough to eat and live without getting into debt'.

Although there is evidence of marginally more support in Scotland than in the UK as a whole for each definition of poverty, it is the similarities between Scotland and the rest of the UK that are most evident. Of particular concern is that the definition that might be seen by some as closest to the one used most often to measure poverty in the UK (the first in Figure 2.1 perhaps resonates with the thinking that underpins relative poverty) has minority public support in Scotland. Work remains to be done in Scotland (and the UK) by anti-poverty activists in academia, government and the third sector to gain wider public support for an understanding that poverty is about more than the basic requirements for existence and survival.

Conclusion

We would argue that poverty in Scotland can perhaps best be understood in terms of Peter Townsend's definition that:[18]

> Individuals, families and groups in the population can be said to be in poverty when they lack the resources to obtain the types of diet, participate in the activities and have the living conditions and amenities which are customary, or are at least widely encouraged and approved, in the societies in which they belong.

Several key issues should be drawn from Townsend's ideas. First, resources can accrue through both incomes and services. However, the marketised nature of Scottish society means that income must be central to discussions about poverty. Second, poverty is relative to the needs and wants of the wider society. This means that poverty in Scotland is qualitatively different to that experienced in the global South (or in earlier historical periods in Scotland). Third, poverty in the twenty-first century is not only about survival and minimum subsistence to avoid starvation; it is about a standard of living that allows adequate participation within society. Finally, work remains to be done to convince the wider public in Scotland that this is a definition of the problem of poverty that befits contemporary Scotland.

Notes

1   Shelter Scotland, *National Housing Statistics*, http://scotland.shelter.org.uk/housing_issues/research_and_statistics/key_statistics/the_facts_about_scotlands_housing

2   A Sen, *Commodities and Capabilities*, Oxford University Press, 1985

3   C McCormack, *The Wee Yellow Butterfly*, Argyll, 2008

4   See http://www.ons.gov.uk/ons/guide-method/user-guidance/well-being/index.html and http://www.ons.gov.uk/about/consultations/measuring-national-well-being/index.html

5   See http://policy-practice.oxfam.org.uk/our-work/poverty-in-the-uk/humankind-index

6   D Walsh, M Taulbut and P Hanlon, *The Aftershock of Deindustrialisation: trends in mortality in Scotland and other parts of post-industrial Europe*, Glasgow Centre for Population Health, 2008

7   C Craig, 'Ringing the Bell', in *Tears That Made the Clyde: well-being in Glasgow*, Argyll, 2010, pp356–78

8   R Lister, *Poverty*, Polity Press, 2004

9   See http://www.trusselltrust.org/map

10 P Townsend, *Poverty in the United Kingdom*, Penguin, 1979

11 N Smith and S Middleton, *Poverty Dynamics Research in the UK*, Joseph Rowntree Foundation, 2007

12 R Wilkinson and K Pickett, *The Spirit Level: why more equal societies almost always do better*, Penguin, 2009

13 See http://stats.oecd.org/glossary/detail.asp?ID=7326

14 C Oppenheim and L Harker, *Poverty: the facts*, Child Poverty Action Group, 1996

15 N Smith, N Branosky, J H McKendrick and G Scott, *Closing the Opportunity Gap: scoping work for design of impact assessment*, Scottish Executive Social Research, 2007

16 D Miller, 'What is Social Justice?', in N Pearce and W Paxton (eds), *Social Justice: building a fairer Britain*, Politicos, 2005

17 Scottish government, *Do the Right Thing: progress report 2012*, p61, www.scotland.gov.uk/Resource/0039/00392997.pdf

18 See note 10

Three
How do we measure poverty?

John H McKendrick

Summary

- In Scotland, the UK and across Europe, household income is used to estimate poverty – those with a low household income are considered to be living in poverty.
- A consensus has emerged – poverty is considered to be present when a household's income is below 60 per cent of the median national income.
- In the UK, the government's official targets for reducing child poverty use measures of poverty that are based on household income *before* housing costs are deducted. This is common in Europe and allows international comparisons to be made. CPAG and many poverty experts argue that poverty should be estimated based on household income *after* housing costs have been deducted, as this gives a better indication of disposable income, which is a clearer indication of the lived experience of poverty.
- Measuring poverty is far from straightforward. Challenges are faced in getting accurate income data in the first instance and then there are a series of technical issues that must be addressed by experts before poverty can be estimated from household income data.
- In recent years, alternative ways of estimating poverty have been developed.
- In 2013, the Social Mobility and Child Poverty Commission responded to the UK government's proposal for a new 'multi-dimensional approach' to measuring child poverty, concluding that any new measure should supplement, rather than replace, the way in which child poverty is measured (according to the terms of the Child Poverty Act 2010).

A measurement consensus... of sorts

There is a broad consensus among politicians, government and expert analysts that household income can be used to estimate poverty (when poverty is defined as a lack of resources). Having a very low income indicates poverty. Typically, this approach involves asking people for information about their household's income and composition, and then using this data to find out if that household's income is below a threshold income value that defines the point below which that particular household should be considered to be living in poverty. The threshold value that is most commonly used is 60 per cent of the median income for similar households. In monetary terms, in 2011/12 this was equivalent to a weekly income, after housing costs were deducted, of less than £357 for a couple with two children aged five and 14.[1] The use of a 60 per cent threshold value is the main way in which poverty is measured in Scotland (the UK and Europe).

Box 3.1:
Measuring poverty *before* housing costs or *after* housing costs?

Many poverty analysts argue that it is more accurate to determine whether a household is living in poverty *after* housing costs have been deducted from total household income, as this better reflects the actual disposable incomes of low-income households (housing being a fixed cost over which people living in poverty have little control). In contrast, the UK government targets for tackling child poverty use a *before* housing costs estimate. The difference this makes is explained in this chapter. For clarification, the *after* housing costs approach is used throughout this book, unless specific reference is made to the UK government's targets.

For a variety of reasons, measuring poverty is far from straightforward. This chapter's review of how poverty is measured in Scotland first explains how the 'expert measurement consensus' was reached. Although there is agreement on the key point that income should be used to measure poverty, there are technical issues to consider (some of which divide expert opinion), other challenges to overcome and limitations that must be acknowledged. Box 3.1 flags up one of these issues. All are considered in more detail, before attention is turned to how poverty is measured for local areas within Scotland. Some alternatives to using household income to measure poverty are considered at the end of the chapter, including a proposal from the UK government that favours the use of a 'multi-dimensional' approach to measure child poverty.

How the measurement consensus was reached

No measurement carries the status of the single official government measure of poverty for Scotland (and the UK). Even so, incremental steps have brought us to the point of consensus, in effect a *de facto* national measure of income poverty for Scotland and the UK.

First published in 1988, *Households Below Average Income* (HBAI) is an annual review of the UK income distribution compiled by the Department for Work and Pensions (DWP) (previously the Department of Social Security) using data collected in the Family Resources Survey.[2] It is a major source of information on people living on low incomes and provides '… an explicitly relative measure which looks at how people at the bottom of the income distribution have fared in relation to the average.'[3] HBAI provides official figures on low income. It is based on a survey of 26,000 households in the UK (including 4,500 households in Scotland), but is sufficiently well designed to allow robust national estimates to be made from these data.

In the same year that HBAI was being introduced, the Statistical Programme Committee of the European Union decided that 60 per cent of *median* income (before housing costs are deducted) should be used as the measure of income poverty when making international comparisons.[4] UK government desire to tackle child poverty was the primary driver of the rise to prominence of the 60 per cent income threshold measure in Scotland and the UK. In 1999, the UK government committed itself to eradicating child poverty within a generation, a vision that is shared by the Scottish government and which was re-affirmed in 2010 with the passing of the Child Poverty Act.[5]

Following a user consultation between 2002 and 2003, the DWP, in conjunction with HM Treasury, initially devised a three-tier measure of child poverty, which consisted of measures of absolute low income, relative low income, and material deprivation and low income combined (Table 3.1).[6] A fourth tier – persistent low income – was added as part of the Child Poverty Act 2010. Where poverty is to be measured by low income alone, the threshold of 60 per cent median income is used. The baseline year for absolute low income was redefined in the Child Poverty Act 2010 from 1998/99 to 2010/11.

Table 3.1:
UK government's four-tier measure of child poverty

Tier 1: Absolute low income

Number and proportion of children in households whose equivalised income before housing costs is below 60 per cent of inflation-adjusted UK median income in 2010/11. This is a measure of whether the poorest families are seeing their incomes rise in real terms. Success is defined as when less than 5 per cent of children live in households with absolute low income.

Tier 2: Relative low income

Number and proportion of children in households whose equivalised income before housing costs is below 60 per cent of UK median income in the same year. This is a measure of whether the poorest families are keeping pace with the growth of incomes in the economy as a whole. Success is defined as when less than 10 per cent of children live in households with relative low income.

Tier 3: Material deprivation and low income combined

Number and proportion of children that are both materially deprived and are in households whose equivalised income before housing costs is less than 70 per cent of the UK median in the current year. This is to provide a wider measure of children's living standards. Success is defined as when less than 5 per cent of children live in households with material deprivation and low income combined.

Tier 4: Persistent low income

Number and proportion of children in households whose equivalised income before housing costs is below 60 per cent of UK median income in the same year for three of the previous four years. This is a measure of whether or not families are consistently in a position that their income keeps pace with the growth of incomes in the economy as a whole. At the time of writing, three years on from the introduction of the Child Poverty Act 2010, the level of persistent low income that defines success has not been defined.

The Child Poverty Act 2010 formalised targets to reduce child poverty by 2020 using these measures. Although child poverty has been the driver of the measurement consensus in the UK, in Scotland annual updates on 'income poverty' are also presented for adults of working age and pensioners. Data on 'income poverty' in Scotland is routinely published as part of the HBAI annual report (Scotland can be compared to other UK nations and regions in England in all tables comparing Government Office regions).[7] Furthermore, the Scottish government publishes a shorter annual report on income inequality and income poverty that focuses exclusively on Scotland as a whole.[8] Income poverty (and the 60 per cent income threshold) is also central to how poverty is measured in the

European Union and the UK is party to the Europe 2020 target to reduce by 20 million the number of people living in poverty in the European Union.[9] Previously, the European Union developed a suite of 18 different indicators to enable it to reach a comprehensive understanding of poverty across the European Union.[10]

However, in Europe, other thresholds (for example, 40, 50 and 70 per cent of the median) are also used when considering poverty, in order to obtain the fullest picture. Some of these alternative thresholds are used in the UK. The 70 per cent median income is used as an element in the UK combined child poverty measure of material deprivation and low income. More recently, the UK government has used the 50 per cent median income threshold (in conjunction with the material deprivation measure) to define what is described as 'severe poverty'.[11] This estimates that a small proportion of children are living in severe child poverty (for 2011/12, HBAI suggests that 3 per cent live in severe poverty, whereas 17 per cent live in relative income poverty[12]). The UK government is using a more exacting measure of deprivation than that of Save the Children when it proposed a measure of severe child poverty in 2010.[13]

Using household income to estimate poverty

There is no single monetary value that defines the level below which all households in Scotland would be deemed to be living in poverty; a whole range of monetary values must be used as threshold levels of 'income poverty' in order to compare fairly household income across different household types. After all, a couple with four children will require a higher level of income to maintain the same standard of living as one adult living alone and, therefore, the 'poverty threshold' must be higher for the larger household.

Table 3.2 describes the key poverty threshold values for 2011/12 for four common household types. In addition to describing the mean and median weekly household income for each household type, the final two columns of this table specify the 'income poverty thresholds'.

This adjustment of household income to account for household composition is known as 'equivalisation'. From 2005/06, the HBAI series has used the modified OECD equivalisation scale. The Scottish government has published online guidance to aid understanding of how equivalisation works.[14]

Table 3.2:

Weekly income (after housing costs) and income-based poverty lines (before and after housing costs), including the self-employed, for different household types, UK, 2011/12

	Weekly income (after housing costs) £		Weekly income-based poverty lines (60% median) £	
Family household type	**Mean**	**Median**	**Before housing costs**	**After housing costs**
Single with no children	266	213	172	128
Couple with no children	459	367	256	220
Single with two children (aged 5 and 14)	550	440	308	264
Couple with two children (aged 5 and 14)	743	594	392	357

Source: Department for Work and Pensions, *Households Below Average Income: an analysis of the income distribution 1994/95–2011/12*, Information Directorate of DWP, 2010, Table 2.4ts

Note: Poverty would be defined at an income below the figures listed in columns 4 and 5 of this table.

Second, a much more controversial issue among poverty analysts is whether poverty should be measured before housing costs or after housing costs have been deducted (see Box 3.1). Although this seems a mundane and technical issue, its impact is significant. The number of people considered to be living in poverty in Scotland is much higher using an after housing costs measure – 870,000 in Scotland in 2011/12, compared with 710,000 using a before housing costs measure.[15]

Furthermore, the risk rate of poverty changes dramatically for different groups. Poverty rates are lower for those groups whose direct housing costs are lower (such as those owning their homes outright, but living on a low income) if an after housing costs measure is used. The impact this difference makes is most marked by comparing children and pensioners. Using a before housing costs measure suggests that the number of children living in poverty in Scotland is lower (150,000, compared with 200,000 with an after housing costs measure), whereas the level of poverty among pensioners is higher with a before housing costs measure (140,000, compared with 110,000 with an after housing costs measure).[16]

Many poverty analysts would argue that the after housing costs measure should be used, as housing costs represent a fixed budget item over which low-income families have little choice. This is particularly important when comparing across Government Office regions and national regions, as it smoothes out the distorting effect of the marked variations in housing costs across the UK. It is argued that discounting housing costs from calculations of low income ensures that we are better able to compare what low-income families across different regions have at their disposal to spend. However, in line with practice in Europe, official government measures for tracking progress on poverty tend to be based on measuring poverty before housing costs, as do the definitions used for the targets set by the Child Poverty Act 2010. HBAI and the annual Scottish report on poverty and income inequality provide poverty estimates using both the before housing costs and after housing costs approaches. For the reasons outlined in Box 3.1, of this book tends to present data using an after housing costs measure. This avoids the risk of underestimating the number of children living in poverty in Scotland that comes with using a before housing costs measure.

Third, far more consensus has been reached about the technical challenge of whether household income should be calculated using the mean or median. Mean and median refer to different ways of measuring the average. Although the *mean* is most commonly used as the way of measuring an average, the favoured way of measuring poverty and low income is to use the median. Mean income is found by adding all the incomes of households and dividing the total by the number of households. Mean income can be easily distorted by very low or very high income. The *median* refers to the mid-point of an ordered range of data. The median measure of average income is less susceptible to distortions, in particular from those on high incomes, and hence is a more appropriate measure of what constitutes a typical income.

A fourth and final technical challenge is whether 'income poverty' should be considered as 'absolute low income' or 'relative low income'. Until the Child Poverty Act 2010, absolute low income in relation to the HBAI figures referred to those households with less than 60 per cent of 1998/99 UK median income before housing costs were deducted. This threshold was adjusted by inflation for each subsequent year. More recently, the base year against which absolute low income has been set has been changed from 1998/99 to 2010/11. According to the DWP, absolute low income '... is important to measure whether the poorest families are seeing their incomes rise in real terms'.[17] Relative low income in relation to the HBAI figures refers to the number and proportion of households with below 60 per cent of UK median income before housing costs were deducted for each year. The threshold is, therefore, recalculated every year to account for increases in median incomes, rather than simply being fixed for the base year then adjusted to account for inflation. This measure allows us to consider whether those on low incomes are keeping up with the rest of society.

As the absolute and relative figures for low income are measured in different ways, it is necessary to be clear about what these figures may mean. 'Relative low income' is a useful way of assessing whether government policies are specifically ensuring that those at the bottom of the income distribution are seeing their incomes improve. 'Absolute low income' indicates whether overall conditions have improved or worsened through time. Most sense can be made of these data when the results are set against each other at the same point in time (see Chapter 5).

HBAI and the annual Scottish report on poverty and income inequality provide poverty estimates using both the absolute and relative measures. Something that neither measure is able to do is to tell us anything about the standard of living that anyone living below the threshold experiences.

Getting accurate household income data in the first instance

Income is a sensitive issue and questions on household income are often not included in social surveys in the UK. Experience has shown that having been asked to provide details on household income, survey respondents have expressed concern at the detail that is required to generate accurate data, the personal nature of income data, and the perceived uses to which the data would be put.[18] The Family Resources Survey is exceptional in that it asks very detailed questions on household income.

The Family Resources Survey is subject to robust data quality checks to increase the reliability of its data. These checks are not always feasible in smaller scale social surveys and, consequently, the reliability of household income data from smaller scale social surveys should not always be assumed. There are many reasons for regarding cautiously any unofficial poverty estimate based on household income: the complex earning patterns of those with irregular sources of income; the challenge of collating household income data when several members of the household contribute to the total and when income is not pooled for the household; and the likelihood that those who do not return an accurate tax return or submit an accurate social security claim will also be unlikely to state an accurate household income in a social survey. The robust data quality procedures used by the Family Resources Survey mean that we can have greater confidence in Family Resources Survey income data, which carry the Office for National Statistics stamp of approval.

Limitations of household analysis

Poverty based on household income is, by definition, a measure of poverty for private households. Thus, the main measure of poverty used in Scotland does not claim to measure whether those living in communal establishments are living in poverty. For example, almost 1,500 looked-after children in Scotland live in 'residential establishments'[19] and the prison population in custody in Scotland is almost 7,900 adults.[20] National poverty statistics do not relate to such groups.

Furthermore, a household income does not necessarily imply that all members of that household will have equal access to this income resource. Gender-sensitive analysis has demonstrated that women in Scotland, in particular, are prone to foregoing their household share for the benefit of other household members.[21] On the other hand, due to the dependency of their parents, children of substance abusers, for example, may not have access to the level of resource that household income suggests.[22]

A national estimate of *household* poverty is not designed to account for poverty in institutions (or intra-household inequities in terms of how this household income is utilised); a fuller understanding of poverty in the UK would require data or studies that are complementary to HBAI data.

Limitations of disposable household income as a measure of poverty

All things being equal, disposable household income – gross income, net of tax and national insurance and housing costs – should provide a measure of how much income households have available to meet their living needs. If that level of income falls below a benchmark, the household is considered to be living in poverty. However, disposable household income is not always an accurate indicator of the extent to which households are able to meet their daily living needs.

For example, disposable household income does not adequately reflect the income that is actually available to meet daily living needs for all households. Specifically, households with individuals who have a high level of debt to service may have less income to use (and therefore a lower standard of living) than others who earn less, but have no debts. These debt problems may be compounded for those on the lowest incomes by the greater likelihood that they will be using financial service providers who charge a relatively higher fee for their service.

Even if disposable net income adequately reflects the income that is available to meet daily living needs, it may not adequately reflect what some groups are able to purchase with it – ie, some groups face higher costs of living. For example, there has been longstanding concern that the additional social security payments that supplement the income of families with disabled people are insufficient to meet the additional costs of living with disability.[23] Similarly, costs of living vary across place. The Joseph Rowntree Foundation acknowledges this and has used research-based evidence to adapt its minimum income calculator to account for the higher cost of rural living, which it estimates at between 10 per cent and 20 per cent more than in urban areas.[24]

Sources of information for household income

As might be expected, household income data that is available to measure poverty is more readily available for Scotland as a whole than for local areas within Scotland. However, the range and quality of local poverty data sources in Scotland has continued to improve in recent years.

Scotland

There are four regular sources of household income data that can be used to estimate poverty for Scotland as a whole. The first source has been referred to earlier in this chapter and is the standard against which other sources are judged. The HBAI dataset is derived from the Family Resources Survey, in which a representative sample of the UK population is asked a series of detailed questions in order to accurately determine household income. Results from the HBAI are readily available, widely used, and often discussed in the media. Two free-to-download publications provide access to results for Scotland. The main *Households Below Average Income* report, published annually in June, while focused on the UK as a whole, provides data through which Scotland can be compared to other Government Office regions in the UK.[25] The shorter *Poverty and Income Inequality in Scotland* report, published annually in May/June by the Scottish government, focuses exclusively on Scotland.[26]

From 2005, the Scottish government-funded Growing Up in Scotland study has been able to use aggregate household income data to estimate poverty for very young children in Scotland.[27] As this has a longitudinal design (returning in later years to the families of the same children), it is also possible to use Growing Up in Scotland to estimate the persistence of poverty among young children in Scotland.[28] However, these 'possibilities' are not always fully realised. Data on household income is provided from a single question asked to the mother (or main carer) of the child; respondents classify their annual income according to one of 17 income bands. Although the loss in accuracy is considered not to be 'catastrophic',[29] Growing Up in Scotland does require some complex manipulation in order to derive a relative poverty measure and the results tend to produce a slightly higher estimate of child poverty in Scotland, relative to HBAI. Perhaps for these reasons, Growing Up in Scotland reports tend to use round number thresholds for 'low income' (most typically, defining as low-income households, those with the lowest 20 per cent of equivalised income), rather than measures of relative poverty, when exploring how living life on a low income impacts on young children in Scotland. This low income classification of households tends to be close to, but not to match exactly, households that would be classified as living in poverty using the official definition of relative income poverty.

Since 1999, the Scottish Household Survey has been collecting and publishing information on household income in Scotland.[30] This was designed to provide data at the level of each of the 32 local authorities biennially, and thus has the potential to provide regular sub-national estimates of poverty. Unlike Growing Up in Scotland, a series of questions are asked to collect income information from the head of household, her/his partner and a random adult. However, income data are missing for many households in the Scottish Household Survey.[31] Nevertheless, with caution, Scottish Household Survey data on household income can be used to understand the significance of living life on a low income, as many of the survey's tables compare life experiences of those with lower and higher household incomes. However, and as with Growing Up in Scotland, it would be far more helpful if household income were converted into a measure of household poverty. Although in 2010, for the first time, the Scottish government published a paper that provided estimates of poverty in Scotland using Scottish Household Survey data,[32] this was described as 'data being developed' and today Scottish Household Survey data are used no more widely to estimate poverty in Scotland.

Understanding Society, the UK household longitudinal study, started in 2009 (incorporating and enhancing the long-established British Household Panel Survey) and collects information from 4,000 Scottish households annually, as part of a very large UK sample.[33] It is a key source of information on poverty and low income dynamics and provides unique insight into persistent poverty. Although a very rich and robust source of information on income poverty in Scotland, results are less readily available than those of the HBAI, Growing Up in Scotland and the Scottish Household Survey, and the complexity of the data means that this has been a resource that has been underutilised to date. Through time, it will become an important source of information for understanding Scottish poverty.

Local

HBAI, Growing Up in Scotland and Understanding Society have not been designed, and do not have sufficient sample sizes, to measure poverty directly using household income for local areas within Scotland. However, the prospects for local estimates of poverty in Scotland based on household income have improved in recent years.

First, as noted above, the Scottish government has produced an estimate of poverty using the Scottish Household Survey. Although only using a before housing costs approach, this provided estimates for Scotland's 32 local authorities, as well as the national estimate for Scotland as a whole.[34]

Second, a proxy measure for relative income poverty is now available which provides estimates of local child poverty for larger sub-national areas (such as local authorities) and very small sub-national areas (such as for each of the 6,505 data zones in Scotland).[35] Previously known as 'national indicator 116' and the 'revised local child poverty measure', this has recently been re-named as the 'children in low-income families local measure'. The change of wording is significant and acknowledges that this measure is an estimate (albeit a very good one), rather than a local equivalent of the national measure. This highly localised estimate of child poverty is based on UK government analysis of data drawn securely from

HM Revenue and Customs and the DWP. It estimates the proportion of children living in poverty as being the proportion of all children living in the area who are either: (a) living in families in receipt of out-of-work benefits or (b) living in families receiving tax credits whose reported income is less than 60 per cent median income, before housing costs have been deducted. Donald Hirsch has produced similar information for End Child Poverty.[36]

Finally, a research project completed in 2013 for the Improvement Service has generated 28 measures of low income and poverty for data zones (intermediate zones and local authorities) in Scotland.[37] Using readily available survey evidence (Scottish Household Survey, Family Resources Survey and Understanding Society), this data modelling exercise has delivered 'robust and transparent estimates of household income and poverty for local and small areas in Scotland', to generate 'a range of measures which can be used for a range of purposes.' Although there are no immediate plans to refresh this modelling exercise on a regular basis, the work has: shed useful insight into the complexity of local poverty in Scotland; established the possibility of producing useful local estimates; and developed models that make use of existing data and which could be repeated (or enhanced) at a later date.

Measuring poverty without household income

Although poverty tends to be measured using household income, and although (as discussed earlier) the range and quality of household income data sources for Scotland continues to improve, it is acknowledged that household income alone (and even household income combined with material deprivation) cannot fully capture the ways in which poverty impacts on people's lives. For this reason, it is worth acknowledging five of the main ways that poverty in Scotland is represented without household income.

Benefits and administrative data

Given that social security aims to provide claimants and their dependants with social protection, there is some merit in using information on benefit claimants to estimate poverty. As discussed earlier for the 'children in low-income families local measure', benefits data can be particularly effective at providing local estimates of child poverty, if it is used in conjunction with income-based tax credit data. More generally, welfare statistics are accessible, updated regularly and are available for the smallest geographical areas (data zones in Scotland).

However, limitations must be acknowledged in using social security statistics to estimate poverty. First, benefit and tax credit levels are very often inadequate in protecting households from poverty (for example, out-of-work benefits for a couple with one child aged less than 11 amount to only 66 per cent of the relative income poverty threshold discussed earlier).[38] Therefore, using out-of-work benefit statistics alone will dramatically underestimate the extent of poverty as, by definition, they will not provide estimates of in-work poverty. Second, in times of flux, changes to entitlement rules mean that social security statistics are less useful for tracking changes in levels of poverty through time.

The proportion of those eligible for local welfare benefits – such as free school meals,[39] school clothing grants or an education maintenance allowance[40] – are also useful as proxies for local poverty (particularly when the goal is to profile poverty for school populations). Clearly, consideration has to be given to conditions of eligibility, administration and service uptake in appraising their utility as a proxy measure for local poverty.[41]

Necessities and material deprivation

Material deprivation is a measure of the impact of poverty or, more accurately, the extent to which poverty impacts on a population. Indeed 'reducing children's deprivation' is a goal that is measured by one of the 50 national indicators of the Scottish government.[42] Typically, material deprivation is evidenced by respondents wanting, but not being able to afford, a threshold number of material goods, leisure activities and social activities from a pre-determined list. The possibility of in-kind support from the wider family (for example, a grandparent buying a winter coat) or from the wider community (for example, a local sports clubs subsidising the costs of participation) means that low income may be ameliorated and does not necessarily lead to material deprivation. For this reason, there is merit in considering, in tandem, both income poverty and material deprivation.

As mentioned earlier in the chapter, data on material deprivation is used alongside household income in one of the four government measures of child poverty (see Table 3.1, tier 3). For this child poverty indicator,

using Family Resources Survey data in the HBAI series, material deprivation is when a child lives in a family that has a deprivation score of 25 or
more on a scale ranging from 0 to 100, based on list of 21 adult and child
items (items which the child does not have, because her/his family cannot
afford them).[43] Four of the 21 items used to indicate material deprivation
were changed in 2010/11. Pensioner material deprivation is also measured separately using a list of 15 items. These data are updated annually.

Poverty and Social Exclusion UK is a major project involving most of
the UK's leading academic poverty analysts. It uses a consensual
approach to define poverty in terms of people lacking the 'necessities of
life'.[44] It is a more detailed measure of material deprivation than HBAI, in
which a consensus position (more than 50 per cent support, with no significant variation among sub-populations) is used to specify what the UK
considers to be a 'necessity'. Further survey work then determines
whether people lack these 'necessities of life', with poverty indicated by
those who 'do not have, because they cannot afford'. The final list of
necessities comprises 20 adult items (32 were considered), five adult
activities (14 were considered), 17 child items (22 were considered) and
seven child activities (eight were considered).[45] Poverty is then calculated
using a deprivation threshold.[46]

Areas of multiple deprivation

Since its launch in 2004, the Scottish Index of Multiple Deprivation has
provided a useful comparison of relative deprivation at small area level
across Scotland.[47] The Index was last updated in 2012.[48] With 6,505 data
zones in Scotland, this micro-geography has enabled the identification of
pockets of deprivation that may have been missed in previous analyses
using larger geographical areas as the basis of comparison (for example,
council wards). In particular, residing within one of the 15 per cent 'most
deprived areas' is now a key marker of deprivation in Scotland.

Multiple deprivation is a broader concept than poverty (see Chapter 2).
Indeed, analysts have found there to be more merit in using the 'income
deprivation' domain (one of the deprivations that count towards the multiple deprivation measure) as a proxy for poverty.[49] However, both the multiple deprivation measure and the narrower income deprivation measure
are of more limited value in estimating rural poverty (and rural deprivation).
Poverty in rural Scotland is spatially dispersed and area-based measures
of deprivation tend to underestimate the scale of the problem.[50]

Minimum income standards

The minimum income standard project was launched in 2008, is uprated every year and is funded by the Joseph Rowntree Foundation.[51] The minimum income standard is the budget required by households to cover the cost of goods and services that are considered to be essential to meet a minimum socially acceptable standard of living in the UK. In this respect, it is another household income-based approach to measuring poverty. It specifies an income level below which people are considered to be unable to have a socially acceptable standard of living.

The minimum income standard approach differs from the HBAI approach to poverty measurement in two key respects. First, the minimum income standard is based on robust focus group research and expert consultation to define what the people of the UK consider to be required to achieve this minimum living standard, rather than a notional figure of 60 per cent below median income. Second, it factors in a multiplier to account for the higher costs of living in rural areas. Minimum income standard research suggests that the 60 per cent median income level used to measure poverty, whether measured before or after housing costs, is actually far below what is required as a minimum income by many household types in the UK.

Multi-dimensional indices

We have argued that poverty has wide-ranging impacts on people's lives and yet (but for good reasons) poverty tends to be measured primarily by using household income. It is therefore understandable that there is ongoing dissatisfaction among those who view poverty as a many-headed monster that the narrow approaches to measuring poverty (focusing largely on low income) have come to dominate.[52]

Some significant developments in Scotland in the last few years, which have a wider focus than poverty, might be viewed, at least in part, as a reaction against an overly narrow focus on income. Launched in 2012, Oxfam Scotland has developed its Humankind Index, which acknowledges the importance of having enough money to enjoy the good life, but also that the good life is determined by much more than this.[53] In a similar vein, NatCen Social Research has used Scottish Household Survey data to develop a multi-dimensional index of 'multiple disadvantage' in Scotland in which low income is but one of seven disadvantages that are acknowledged.[54] Both studies provide some sub-national and some sub-group data to complement the national overview for Scotland.

These measures are conceived as complementary to income-based measures of poverty in Scotland. Furth of Scotland, DEMOS has been developing similar work.[55] Using 20 indicators (including low income, lacking material goods, fuel poverty and deprived neighbourhood), it applied cluster analysis to this data (drawn from the Understanding Society dataset) to identify 15 types of poverty in the UK. However, income poverty remains central to this measure of poverty and to be classified poor, a 'poor household' must have a household income that is no more than 70 per cent below median household income.

A more direct challenge to the primacy of income-based measures of poverty was raised in June 2010 when the UK government gave notice of a Review on Poverty and Life Chances,[56] which would 'examine the case for reform to poverty measures, in particular for the inclusion of non-financial elements'. *Measuring Child Poverty: consultation on better measures of child poverty* followed in which a multi-dimensional measure of child poverty was proposed which, in addition to low income and material deprivation, would comprise information on worklessness (among adults), unmanageable debt, poor housing, parental skill level, access to quality education, parental health and family stability.[57] However, the UK government's own Social Mobility and Child Poverty Commission, in its first written piece of advice to ministers, reaffirmed the centrality of household income to any measure of child poverty.[58] Acknowledging the value of developing a multi-dimensional measure, it concluded that this should be supplementary to the existing targets (see Table 3.1).

For the foreseeable future, income poverty (and the 60 per cent income threshold) will be central to how poverty is measured in Scotland, the UK and the European Union.

Conclusion

Considerable progress has been made, and continues to be made, in how we measure poverty in Scotland. Every edition of *Poverty in Scotland* has reported on new developments and better data. Although data is by no means perfect, and further work should be undertaken to refine and improve our poverty measures, Scotland is now fairly well served with information to inform anti-poverty activity. Perhaps the immediate priority for Scotland is to make better use of the array of resources that are now available to measure poverty, particularly at the sub-national scales of data zones, neighbourhoods and local authority areas.

Notes

1 Department for Work and Pensions, *Households Below Average Income: an analysis of the income distribution 1994/95–2011/12*, Information Directorate, 2013, Table 2.4ts

2 See https://www.gov.uk/government/organisations/department-for-work-pensions/series/households-below-average-income-hbai–2

3 C Oppenheim and L Harker, *Poverty: the facts*, Child Poverty Action Group, 1996

4 Eurostat Task Force, 'Recommendations on Social Exclusion and Poverty Statistics', Paper presented to the 26–27 November meeting of the EU Statistical Programme Committee, 1998

5 *Child Poverty Act 2010*, HMSO, 2010

6 Department for Work and Pensions, *Opportunity for All: eighth annual report*, 2006, http://www.bris.ac.uk/poverty/downloads/keyofficialdocuments/Opportunity%20for%20All%202006.pdf

7 See note 1

8 Scottish government, *Poverty and Income Inequality in Scotland, 2011/12*, 2013

9 See http://epp.eurostat.ec.europa.eu/portal/page/portal/europe_2020_indicators/headline_indicators

10 See note 4

11 HM Government, *A New Approach to Child Poverty: tackling the causes of disadvantage and transforming families' lives*, 2013

12 Department for Work and Pensions, *Households Below Average Income: an analysis of the income distribution 1994/95–2011/12*, Information Directorate, 2013

13 C Telfer, *Measuring Severe Child Poverty in Scotland*, Save the Children, 2010

14 See http://www.Scotland.gov.uk/Topics/Statistics/Browse/Social-Welfare/IncomePoverty/Methodology#a3

15 See note 8, Table A1

16 See note 8, Table A1

17 Department for Work and Pensions, *Measuring Child Poverty*, 2003, www.dwp.gov.uk/ofa/related/final_conclusions.pdf

18 A Teague, *Income Data for Small Areas: summary of response to consultation*, Census Advisory and Working Groups, National Statistics, 1999; J Collins, D Elliot, S Walker, J Watson and M M dos Santos, *2007 Census Test: the effects of including questions on income and implications for the 2011 Census*, Office for National Statistics, 2007

19 Scottish government, *Children's Social Work Statistics 2011/12*, 2013, Table 1.1

20 Scottish Prison Service, 'Prisoner population', Scottish Prisoner Population as at Friday 27 September 2013, http://www.sps.gov.uk/Publications/Scottish PrisonPopulation.aspx

21 J H McKendrick, S Cunningham-Burley and K Backett-Milburn, *Life in Low-income Families in Scotland*, Scottish Executive, 2003

22 M Barnard and N McKeganey, 'The Impact of Parental Problem Drug Use on Children: what is the problem and what can be done to help?', *Addiction*, Vol. 99,5, pp552–59, 2004

23 N Smith, S Middleton, K Ashton-Brooks, L Cox, B Dobson and L Reith, *Disabled People's Costs of Living*, Joseph Rowntree Foundation, 2004

24 N Smith, A Davis and D Hirsch, *A Minimum Income Standard for Rural Households*, Commission for Rural Areas and the Joseph Rowntree Foundation, 2010

25 See note 1

26 See note 8

27 See www.growingupinscotland.org.uk

28 M Barnes, J Chanfreau and W Tomaszewski, *The Circumstances of Persistently Poor Children*, GUS Topic Findings 2010/11, Scottish government, 2010

29 See note 28, p10, following J Micklewright, and S V Schnepf, *How Reliable are Income Data Collected with a Single Question?*, Applications and Policy Working Paper A07/08, Southampton Statistical Sciences Research Institute, 2007

30 See www.scotland.gov.uk/Topics/Statistics/16002/SurveyOverview/

31 S Hope and I Nava-Ledezma, *Scottish Household Survey: methodology and fieldwork outcomes 2011*, Ipsos-Mori, 2013

32 Scottish government, *Relative Poverty Across Scottish Local Authorities*, 2010

33 See https://www.understandingsociety.ac.uk

34 See note 32

35 See http://www.hmrc.gov.uk/statistics/child-poverty-stats.htm

36 See http://www.endchildpoverty.org.uk/why-end-child-poverty/poverty-in-your-area

37 G Bramley and D Watkins, *Local Incomes and Poverty in Scotland: developing local and small area estimates and exploring patterns of income distribution, poverty and deprivation*, Report of Research for the Improvement Service, 2013, www.improvementservice.org.uk/income-modelling-project

38 See http://www.poverty.org.uk/12/index.shtml?2, Graph 3

39 See http://www.scotland.gov.uk/Topics/Statistics/Browse/School-Education/ SchoolMealsDatasets

40 Scottish government, *Educational Maintenance Allowances 2011/12*, 2013, http://www.scotland.gov.uk/Resource/0041/00413124.pdf

41 Short Life Working Group, *Review of Identification and Registration of Those*

Eligible for Free School Meals and School Clothing Grant Provision Across Scotland, 2011, http://www.scotland.gov.uk/Resource/Doc/920/0112280.pdf

42 See http://www.scotland.gov.uk/About/Performance/scotPerforms/indicator/childdeprivation

43 See note 1, Appendix 2

44 See http://www.poverty.ac.uk

45 M Gannon and N Bailey, 'Attitudes to the "Necessities of Life" in Scotland: can a UK poverty standard be applied in Scotland?', Paper presented at the Social Policy Association Annual Conference, Sheffield, 8–10 July 2013

46 See http://www.poverty.ac.uk/definitions-poverty/consensual-method

47 See http://www.scotland.gov.uk/Topics/Statistics/SIMD

48 See http://simd.scotland.gov.uk/publication-2012/

49 See note 37

50 J H McKendrick, C Barclay, C Carr, A Clark, J Holles, E Perring and L Stien, *Our Rural Numbers Are Not Enough: an independent position statement and recommendations to improve the identification of poverty, income inequality and deprivation in rural Scotland*, Rural Poverty Indicators Action Learning Set, 2011, http://www.scotland.gov.uk/Resource/Doc/94257/0120769.pdf

51 See http://www.jrf.org.uk/topic/mis

52 HM Government, *Measuring Child Poverty: a consultation on better measures of child poverty*, Cm 8483, 2012, http://www.official-documents.gov.uk/document/cm84/8483/8483.pdf

53 See http://policy-practice.oxfam.org.uk/our-work/poverty-in-the-uk/humankind-index

54 M Barnes and C Lord, *Multiple Disadvantage in Scotland: secondary analysis of the Scottish Household Survey dataset*, Report for Quarriers and Demos, NatCen Social Research, 2012, www.natcen.ac.uk/study/multiple-disadvantage-in-scotland

55 C Wood and others, *Poverty in Perspective*, Demos, 2012, http://www.demos.co.uk

56 See http://webarchive.nationalarchives.gov.uk/20110120090128/http://povertyreview.independent.gov.uk

57 See note 52

58 Commission on Social Mobility and Child Poverty, *Measuring Child Poverty: consultation response*, 2013, https://www.gov.uk/government/publications/measuring-child-poverty-consultation-commission-response

Four
What causes poverty?

John H McKendrick

Summary

- Both the UK and Scottish governments have made firm commitments to tackle child poverty.
- Policy interventions from local, Scottish and UK governments have helped reduce, but not yet eradicate, poverty in Scotland.
- The reasons for poverty are complex and multi-faceted. The primary poverty-generating mechanisms are social, economic and political. Tackling poverty requires a sustained and long-term comprehensive strategy, rather than a quick-fix, single-issue intervention.
- The way in which poverty-inducing factors take effect is complicated. It is overly simplistic to both reduce poverty to a single cause and to ignore the intervening factors that policy solutions need to take into account.
- Over the last fifteen years concerted political will and policy action, alongside a growing economy, contributed to reductions in the level of poverty in Scotland and elsewhere in the UK, particularly among pensioners and children. Independent modelling now forecasts a reversal of that progress, with significant increases in poverty anticipated as a result of current UK government tax and benefit policies.
- A much more ambitious and focused anti-poverty strategy is now needed if poverty in Scotland is to be reduced on all key measures in the years ahead.
- The wider Scottish public are more likely to focus on 'individual factors' (when asked to explain why poverty exists).

Introduction

This chapter accounts for the causes of poverty in Scotland. This is by no means a straightforward task.

First, there are several possible reasons for why people experience poverty. Poverty is sometimes attributed to the **behaviour of individuals**. Here, consideration is given to how personal knowledge of the 'feckless poor', grounded in everyday social theorising based on stereotypes, is used to support the viewpoint that poverty results from the failings of individuals. Although such explanations have popular appeal, it is argued that this type of explanation is of limited value in accounting for poverty in Scotland. Poverty can be attributed to **social factors**, that is, characteristics that define groups of people and which place additional demands on their resources and/or make them more vulnerable to other poverty-inducing factors. Here, reference is made to the social factors that induce poverty among the groups identified as being vulnerable to poverty. Poverty in Scotland can also be attributed to **political factors**, that is, the extent to which government is prepared to intervene to tackle poverty and the effectiveness of these interventions. Of course, the core concern of *Poverty in Scotland 2014* is to reflect on the ways in which government could tackle poverty in Scotland after the referendum. In this chapter, the focus is on the types of options that are available to government (rather than the structures which might be most effective for their implementation). Finally, poverty can also be attributed to **economic factors** – for example, the strength of the macro-economy.

Second, the poverty experienced by individuals tends to result from more than one of these poverty-inducing factors. For example, the susceptibility to poverty of single adults without children, migrating to work in remote rural Scotland from Eastern Europe, might be attributed to: language barriers limiting their ability to move beyond the low-paid employment which brought them to Scotland to work in jobs that are populated with other migrants who share their cultural background (social factor); limited opportunity in the wider local labour market to earn a decent living wage (economic factor); and a lack of state intervention as rural poverty is not deemed to be a pressing priority for policy intervention (political factor). Progress in some factors may not be sufficient to counteract other persistent poverty-inducing circumstances.

Third, the factors which cause people to experience poverty are inter-related. For example, the susceptibility to poverty of lone parents might be attributed to restricted labour market options given lone parents' need to combine work with parental responsibilities (social factor), resulting in difficulties in accessing employment that pays a decent living wage (economic and political factor). Here, the social situation influences the economic possibilities, both of which contribute to the poverty experienced by the individual.

Finally, the ways in which poverty-inducing factors influence individuals can be complex, hidden and indirect. For example, and in a global context, Scotland is a small nation, with a small domestic market. Like other small European nations, the vitality of its economy is intertwined with imports, exports, global investment and inward investment. It is, therefore, susceptible to changes in the global economy and UK national economy (for better, or for worse). However, the extent to which these macro-economic forces result in poverty is dependent on a host of intervening factors, such as the economic strategies of transnational corporations, inducements and support from inward investment agencies, national social protection and pay policies, and the ability of the local economy to absorb job losses or supply workers with the skills demanded in growth sectors.

Individual factors

Many of us have anecdotal knowledge of an individual who seems to do little to arrest the poverty that s/he experiences. We may also be aware of others who would be classified as 'poor' using official data sources, but who supplement their income through the informal economy. More generally, many do not understand why people can be poor given anti-poverty mechanisms such as: state support through social security payments (for example, employment and support allowance); safeguards against low income (for example, the national minimum wage); opportunities provided in communities and by the state to enable people living in poverty to enhance their employment prospects (ie, through the many Skills Development Scotland programmes[1]); and local interventions to reduce the costs associated with living on a low income (for example, local food co-operatives sourcing quality food and selling it more cheaply than local retailers). Furthermore, public debate on poverty in Scotland often draws on deeply entrenched stereotypes, which rationalise people's life trajectories on the basis of where they live or on their social profile. For example, 'she'll be poor because she lives in [add in the name of the 'council estate' in your town]', is likely to be the 'common-sense' and everyday thought process of many Scots. In short, individuals are sometimes deemed to be the primary cause of their poverty and the large number who are described as being poor in official measures of poverty is perceived to be an overstatement of the problem. Such arguments carry some intuitive appeal and are reinforced by sensationalist or superficial media coverage.

There are five key points that critique the line of thinking that attributes poverty to the action or inaction of individuals. First, poverty experienced by children has little to do with children's own actions; the 200,000 children experiencing poverty in Scotland (Table 5.1) do so exclusively on account of chance, that is, the accident of birth, which determined the families into which they were born. Clearly, not all people experiencing poverty can be held responsible for this condition. Second, reducing explanations for poverty simply and singularly to the actions of individuals does not allow the possibility of poverty being influenced by other factors, and takes no account of the large-scale structural (social, political and economic) forces that shape people's lives. As was argued in Chapter 1, the causes of poverty are multi-faceted. Third, on closer analysis, what appear to be 'individual-level' factors often reflect underlying social and economic processes. For example, the understanding that poverty is transmitted down through generations of the same family is often perceived to be a problem of the individual, when more correctly it should be viewed as a social and economic factor. As James McCormick argued so persuasively many years ago in an earlier CPAG publication, poor places keep people poor.[2] Fourth, focusing on individual behaviour as a cause of poverty risks distracting attention from the social, economic and political factors over which it is possible for policy makers to exert influence and which, therefore, hold most potential for eradicating poverty. Finally, there is a numerical challenge to those who argue that poverty is the fault of individuals. According to the Scottish government, 870,000 people experience poverty in Scotland (Figure 5.5). There can be no credibility in the argument that one-sixth of the population in Scotland experience poverty on account of their own personal failings.

Social factors

As Chapter 7 demonstrates, the distribution of poverty in Scotland is uneven across social groups and place. This must not, however, lead to an explanation for Scotland's poverty that is based only on describing the changing composition of Scotland's population. Thus, for example, the changing composition of families in Scotland since the early 1970s – including the rise in lone parenthood – should not, *per se*, be used to explain the corresponding growth in poverty. It is more accurate to explain that the rise of poverty was down to the high risk of poverty faced by a group growing in size and the failure of policies to intervene to reduce this risk. There is clearly an association between these trends (and between the extent of poverty and other social trends), but this offers no insight into the root causes of poverty. Most problematically, this approach encourages scapegoating and a culture of blame – for example, lone parenthood causes poverty.

However, there are common shared characteristics among social groups that make some more susceptible to poverty and make the escape route from poverty more difficult than otherwise would be the case. Table 4.1 summarises some of the social factors that are experienced by some of the groups identified in Chapter 7 as being particularly susceptible to poverty.

Of course, Table 4.1 is only a summary overview of some of the main social factors that may cause or exacerbate the poverty experienced by particular groups of people in Scotland. Although space does not permit presentation of evidence that would justify the assertions made in Table 4.1, further comment is provided for two of the group-specific poverty-inducing factors.

First, suggesting that the national minimum wage is a contributory factor for young people's poverty seems counter-intuitive. After all, the introduction of the minimum wage has sought to guard against low pay since it was introduced in April 1999. In particular, the specification of a 'development rate' for workers aged 18–21 at the outset in 1999, the extension of wage protection to workers aged between 16 and 17 years old in 2004, the introduction of an apprentice minimum wage in 2010, the extension of the adult rate to 21-year-olds from 2010, and the annual uprating of the minimum wage since 1999 have each sought to protect young workers from low wages. However, on closer analysis, it could be argued that the national minimum wage could be a more effective aid in tackling poverty among young people. In effect, it justifies lower wages for young people, relative to older workers: in 2013, the main rate for workers aged 21 and over was £6.31 an hour, which is higher than the 'development' rate set for young adults between 18 and 20 years (£5.03 an hour), under-18s (£3.72 an hour) and apprentices (£2.68 an hour).[3] Thus, while the minimum wage has tackled some of its worst excesses, low pay among young people remains a major problem and the minimum wage gives credibility to lower rates of pay for younger workers.

Second, the existence of gender pay gaps is at odds with long-standing government legislation and steps to promote equal pay within local authorities and national government in Scotland. The right of women to equal pay has been enshrined in UK legislation since the Equal Pay Act in 1970 and has since been strengthened by amendments, such as that in 1984 to ensure equal pay for equivalent work. More recently, in 1999, single-status agreements were reached between the trade unions and local government in Scotland to ensure verifiable pay equality between men and women. However, by 2006, these agreements had not been implemented and the unions were concerned that single status was being implemented by imposing pay cuts and by driving down wages through job evaluation.[4] The employment status of women in Scotland is similar to that in the rest of the UK: fewer women aged 16 to 64 are economically active (73 per cent, compared with 83 per cent of men in August 2013);[5] the concentration across occupational type is highly gendered and women tend to be under-represented in the higher paying sectors and over-represented in the lower paying sectors (82 per cent of workers in 'caring, leisure and other services' occupations are women, compared with 10 per cent in skilled trades);[6] and while equivalent numbers of men and women are employed (according to the *Annual Survey of Hours and Earnings* in 2012, 1,057,000 men and 1,119,000 women in Scotland in 2012),[7] in Scotland, men are 1.4 times more likely than women to be working full time, while women are more than three times as likely as men to be employed part time.[8] While these gender patterns in work would explain why men earn more than women, as explained in Chapter 6 (Table 6.1) what is particularly disconcerting is that the pay gap between men and women is evident across every type of occupation. For full-time work in the UK, using median pay as the comparator, the gender pay gap ranges from as low as 70 per cent of male earnings for 'process, plant and machine operatives' up to a 97 per cent in customer service occupations. Across occupations, women on average earn only 82 per cent of their male counterparts.[9]

However, the gendered character of poverty should not be accepted as inevitable in the world in which we live. For example, implementation of single-status agreements should have made inroads to reduce the gender pay gap in Scotland, as should have the UK-wide gender equality duty (from April 2007). To its credit, the Scottish government is taking seriously the issue of gender pay inequality, monitoring its own gender pay gap,[10] and supporting the work of Close the Gap.[11] But, there has been no progress in closing the gender pay gap since the last edition of *Poverty in Scotland*. Clearly, more and more wide-ranging work needs to be done to close the gender pay gap in Scotland.

Table 4.1:

Social factors as a cause of poverty

Group	Factors (examples)
Lifecycle	
Children	• Limited ability to earn money to lift themselves out of poverty.
	• Poverty status is dependent on their parents or guardians.
Youth	• Lower wages for this age group, with a lower rate of the national mimum wage.
	• Benefit rates are lower for this age group, with prospects that some benefits may be removed altogether.[12]
	• Lack of opportunity to accumulate wealth that could be used to amliorate the effects of short-term bouts of poverty.
	• Poverty may be a transitional state associated with periods of education and training.
Working-age adults	• Social security system is oriented towards providing for the young and old.
Pensioners	• Many have not provided for private pensions, having been brought up believing that the state pension would provide for their needs in old age. Thus, pensioner poverty reflects the circumstances of their working lives. If they were unemployed for long periods, worked in low-paid jobs, had insecure or interrupted work histories, were ill for long periods or involved in unpaid work, they are more likely to experience poverty in old age.
	• State pension complexity results in low take-up.
	• Higher heating and fuel costs, with subsidies not meeting the full amount of these additional costs.
Families and households	
Lone parents	• Cost of childcare.
	• Availability of childcare (barrier to participation in the labour market).
	• Work-life balance (eg, mismatch between school hours and working hours).
Partnered parents	• Unequal distribution of income among householders.
	• Unequal expenditure responsibilities among householders (eg, women spending on all family members, men keeping more money to themselves).
Childless adults	• Social security system is oriented towards providing for the young, old and families with children.
	• Inadequate social security payments for single adults.

Social

Work status	• Low pay.
	• Costs associated with being part of a 'flexible' workforce (eg, higher travel costs, relative to income earned).
	• Under-employment.
Gender	• Costs associated with being primary carers of children (interrupted work histories for women).
	• Gender segregation in the labour market (over-concentration of women in lower paid jobs).
	• Gender gap in pay.
	• Intra-household distribution of income.
Ethnicity	• Pensioner poverty among immigrants (having not built up pension entitlement on account of being engaged in low-paid work and beginning to contribute in the middle of their working lives).
	• Language barriers during transitional phase for immigrants.
	• Racist harassment and victimisation; stereotyping.
	• Tendency to work in sectors of the economy in which wages are low (especially Pakistani and Bangladeshi).
Disability/illness	• Extra costs associated with managing particular disability or illness, such as medicine, housing adaption or transport costs (the majority of disabled people do not receive additional costs).
	• Higher cost of living associated with shopping locally (difficulty in accessing more distant, but cheaper, supermarkets).
	• Costs of caring.
	• Discrimination based on stereotyping.
	• Disabling environments, hampering access.

Place

Local authorities	• (Under) strength of local economy.
Rural areas	• Lack of public transport in rural areas (restricting access).
	• Additional cost of transport in rural areas (eg, the necessity of running a car).
	• Fewer public services.
	• Low pay.
	• Higher cost of living.
	• More restricted employment/career opportunities.
Local area	• By definition, these will vary across place.

Political factors

Government action – or inaction – is one of the key factors that could determine the extent and level of poverty in Scotland. To their credit, in 2010, both the UK and Scottish governments reaffirmed their commitment to eradicate child poverty within a generation and annual reports on progress have since followed.[13] However, poverty is also experienced in households without children and our governments have been less specific about setting targets to eradicate poverty for people in these households. Furthermore, the effectiveness of the strategies used by government to tackle child poverty must also be evaluated. The questions that must be answered are, 'are our governments doing enough?' and 'how effective are our government interventions?'

UK government

The UK government retained responsibility following devolution for the main levers of control over poverty in Scotland – the welfare system and taxation.

Welfare system

Social security should protect the vulnerable from the worst excesses of poverty. However, although it is undoubtedly a tool for poverty amelioration, social security is not necessarily designed to provide an income that removes households without work from poverty. Indeed, there is an ideological train of thought that welfare payments must be kept at poverty levels to act as a disincentive to individuals who are disinclined to work. Proponents of this approach would argue that the social security system could eradicate poverty by ensuring that only poverty-level incomes were available to claimants – effectively, encouraging or coercing claimants to find work and escape poverty.

    This thinking – that social security could eradicate poverty by encouraging claimants to move into paid employment – reflects the position of the current UK coalition government. 'Welfare reform', the comprehensive overhaul of the UK welfare system, aims to reduce the total cost of social security and to effect cultural change (premised on the ideological position outlined earlier).[14] Although the welfare reforms herald a much more austere future for benefit claimants, it could be argued that the ideological position is merely an extension of that held by the previous government. In recent years, social security in the UK has not aimed to remove people from poverty; rather it has sought to facilitate moves into paid work and protect people from the worst excesses of abject poverty.

There are limitations to the way in which successive UK governments have used social security as a poverty-reduction strategy. First, benefit uprating operates in ways that exacerbate poverty and income inequality. For many years, the level of benefits has been tied to prices which, although ensuring that the spending power of benefit recipients is maintained year on year, also implies that the relative value of benefits to waged income declines year on year in periods of economic growth with low inflation (when growth in prices is lower than increases in average incomes). Relatively speaking, benefit recipients become poorer compared with wage earners. This approach to uprating was characteristic of the decade that followed the mid-1990s. On the other hand, although in times of higher prices and lower wages benefit recipients should, relatively speaking, become less poor compared with wage earners, this 'gain' is often not realised, as the price rises for the necessities that are the staple of low-income families outstrip average inflation (which determines the benefit uprating). This characterises the last few years. Thus, both in times of economic growth and decline, the way in which the social security system uprates income has too often operated to make claimants relatively poorer. Although not exactly a 'progressive' system at present, the UK government is now making the system an outwardly 'regressive' one as benefits are now uprated by 1 per cent (for the 2013/14 through to the 2015/16 tax years).[15] The changes have been modelled on the expectation that inflation will outstrip 1 per cent and, thus, the effect of this change will be to increase the intensity of poverty experienced by the UK's most vulnerable people, and to increase the number of people experiencing poverty.[16]

Second, successive UK governments have subscribed to a welfare-to-work strategy through which it seeks to 'make work pay'. Although there is evidence that this approach has been successful in assisting people to escape poverty, this is an ineffective anti-poverty strategy for those who cannot work, for those for whom work is not available and for those who undertake unpaid work. The 'work not welfare' mantra has been strongly championed by the UK coalition government and is set to feature more prominently and explicitly in the coming years. Unfortunately, and unnecessarily, currently there seems to be much more focus placed on the punitive (making social security pay less in order to make work pay relatively more) than on the incentive (tangible steps to remove barriers to work, such as childcare, and increase the value of paid work, for example, through increasing the minimum wage).

Third, although UK government policies have had some beneficial effect, the use of social security to tackle child and pensioner poverty falls short of being a universal approach to overcome poverty, as social security is deployed in a more limited fashion to tackle the poverty of working-age claimants without children. It might be more accurate to assert that, until recently, the UK government has used social security as a *child* poverty reduction strategy. Even here, the progressive intervention of social security as a poverty alleviation strategy for households with children has diminished (and is set to further diminish) with the coalition government's reduction in the value of social security for children – for example, child benefit rates were frozen for three years from 6 April 2011.[17]

Fourth, the UK government has not been averse to using the social security system to effect behavioural change in a way that overrides its poverty-reduction credentials. Thus, the previous administration saw fit to withdraw some benefits from those who did not comply with its New Deal programmes and the current government continues to increase benefit sanctions at the same time as the number of conditions related to benefit entitlement is ratcheted up. Although there are differences of opinion over the moral legitimacy of using such punitive measures, they clearly demonstrate that the poverty-reducing value of social security can be overridden by other goals. Imposing severe poverty on errant claimants (and their families) by withdrawing social security is considered by government to be justified.

Taxation

Higher earners pay more tax than lower earners in absolute terms, although not, as we shall see, as a proportion of their income. For example, in 2011/12, the average annual amount paid by the richest fifth of households in the UK was £19,905 in direct taxation and £8,743 in indirect taxation. In contrast, the average amount paid by the poorest fifth of households in the UK was £1,306 in direct taxation and £3,400 in indirect taxation.[18]

It must be recognised that taxation, *per se*, does not lead to a reduction in income inequality or a reduction in poverty. Rather, both direct and indirect taxation are elements of a broader government strategy through which cash benefits (welfare support) are added to original income (for example, wages and investments) to give gross income (stage one). Gross income is then subject to direct taxation to give disposable income (stage two). In 'disposing of this income', we are liable to indirect taxation. At this point, two calculations can be made to help us understand the impact of government intervention on income. First, the sum of the indirect taxes can be deducted from the disposable income to give us a measure of post-tax income (stage three – that is, [original income + cash benefits] – [direct taxation + indirect taxation]). Finally, we can take account of the benefits in kind (fo example, education, health and social services) to give us a measure of final income. Taxation is the means through which government can redistribute earnings through cash benefits and benefits in kind.

Two criticisms can be made against the effectiveness of current taxation policy as a means to tackle income poverty. First, taxation reduces the incomes of those on already low incomes: the poorest fifth of households in the UK typically have £4,706 deducted in taxation (direct and indirect taxation) from a gross income of £12,855 (36.6 per cent of gross income is deducted in taxation).[19] In fairness, it could be argued that, to some extent, this is an administrative necessity as it would otherwise be too complex to refrain from taxing low-income groups, particularly at the point of consumption for indirect taxes. Second, although higher earners pay more in absolute sums, the lowest earning fifth of households in the UK pay a greater share of their gross income in taxation – for example, the 'tax burden' of the lowest earning fifth at 36.6 per cent is higher than that of the highest earning households (35.4 per cent of the gross income of the highest earning fifth of households is deducted in tax).[20] Indirect taxes are particularly regressive. The poorest fifth pay twice the proportion of their income on indirect taxes (26.5 per cent, compared with 10.8 per cent).[21] It should therefore come as no surprise, as will be reported in Chapter 6, that there has been little change in income inequality in Scotland in recent years.

Scottish government and local government

Although not able to dictate who receives cash benefits, the Scottish government can influence the extent and level of poverty in Scotland: through using its limited tax-varying powers; by wholesale area regeneration; by creating the conditions necessary to facilitate the labour market participation of those without work; by early intervention and improved early-years provision; by effective service delivery and intervention in the fields of education, training and health; by promoting take-up of benefits and tax credits; by ensuring people have access to advice and information on maximising their incomes; by ameliorating negative impacts of the withdrawal of UK government services and support; and by intervening to provide benefits in kind. Local government is responsible for direct provision of key services and supports people experiencing poverty (and others living on a low income) by providing an array of benefits in kind.

In recent years, the Scottish government's approach to tackling poverty in Scotland has been twofold. First, it has positioned itself against welfare reform and has sought to better understand the impact of these reforms in Scotland, and provide direct support to mitigate the impacts of these reforms. A Welfare Reform Scrutiny Group advises on welfare reform and ministers are obliged to present an annual report to the Scottish Parliament on the impact of the UK Welfare Reform Act in Scotland until 2017.[22]

Second, in partnership with Scottish local authorities, the Scottish government continues to operate its main anti-poverty programmes – ie, Achieving Our Potential (2008–) and the Child Poverty Strategy for Scotland (2011–). At the heart of both approaches is a concordat with local government through which local government has responsibility for determining and addressing local anti-poverty priorities. Although many of the drivers are conceived as local, a Ministerial Advisory Group on Child Poverty has been formed and an annual report on the Child Poverty Strategy for Scotland published.[23]

Welcome as this work is to address welfare reform and child poverty, it might be argued that relatively less focus and prominence is currently being given to the overarching Achieving Our Potential framework. Similarly, the Tackling Poverty Board that was formed to oversee and drive forward policy to tackle poverty in Scotland and the Community Regeneration and Tackling Poverty Learning Network (a community of practice for anti-poverty practitioners)[24] have been disbanded and their work subsumed by other bodies with a remit that is less focused on tackling poverty, as a whole. The demise of the Community Regeneration and Tackling Poverty Learning Network is a particular loss when so much emphasis and responsibility for tackling poverty is being devolved to the local level.

Economic factors

The performance of the macro-economy is one possible reason for the existence of poverty in Scotland. The logic is that there will be an inverse relationship between the economy and the extent and level of poverty – that is, the stronger the economy, the lower the intensity and extent of poverty. However, and for example, as was alluded to in Chapter 3 and will be discussed in Chapter 5, the contemporary reality is that the level of relative poverty (as measured by official statistics) appears to be going down significantly, at a time when the economic growth is modest.

Scottish government statistics show that the Scottish economy is recovering from the contractions that were registered in the third quarter of 2008, and persisted through to the third quarter of 2009. Although subsequent growth rates have been unremarkable, the Scottish economy has since stabilised and has registered many more quarters of modest growth than it has quarters of no growth or contraction.[25]

Gross domestic product (GDP) is a measure of the value of the goods and products being produced in a nation state in any one year, and is widely accepted as a robust measure of economic growth.[26] Prior to the economic slowdown, Scotland's economy had grown for many years, with peaks in the rate of growth in 2004 and 2007.[27] Poverty remained stubbornly high throughout this period. However, from 2007 through until the start of 2010, Scotland's economic growth first slowed down, before entering a period of increasing economic decline from the end of 2008 to the end of 2009.[28] Poverty was stable during this period. A swing in Scotland's GDP fortunes followed, with quarter-on-quarter progress starting with a reduction in the rate of GDP contraction from -3.7 per cent to -3.0 per cent to the first quarter of 2010, finally returning to growth in the third quarter of that year (0.3 per cent). This coincided with a corresponding decrease in relative poverty, but also with an increase in absolute poverty. Thereafter, Scotland's economy has been more stable, with evidence of very modest growth in most quarters.[29]

Employment (of 16–64-year-olds in Scotland) peaked at an all-time high of almost 75 per cent of the working-age population in 2007 (April to June), only to fall steadily to 70 per cent by the end of 2009.[30] Although an unwelcome trend in itself, it is notable that during this time employment rates in Scotland were the highest of all national regions in the UK. The employment rate in Scotland has since recovered to 72 per cent in the early part of 2013, although this was still lower than at any time since the end of 2002. Employment rates have remained higher than in Wales and Northern Ireland, and fluctuate around being slightly better or slightly worse than in England.

Contrary to what the public might perceive, the number and proportion of Scotland's population claiming benefits has been on a downward trend since the start of the millennium. In the middle of 1999, almost one in five adults of working age were claiming some form of benefit (615,680 or 19.6 per cent).[31] Although the numbers fluctuated, the trend was clearly downward until the middle of 2008, by which time the number of claimants had fallen to one in six (519,090). A steady increase in the number of claimants followed, peaking at 583,270 at the start of 2010. Claimant numbers have fluctuated at a level below the peak of 2010 and were estimated at 561,110 at the start of 2013.

In contrast to these economic trends, there has been a steady increase in Scotland's gross disposable household income throughout this period. This sum of all household income in Scotland suggests (using current prices) a steady year-on-year rise in household income in Scotland from £46 billion in 1997 to £82 billion in 2011.[32] The economy may have entered a period of decline, employment rates may be falling and the number drawing on social security may be rising, but overall household income continues to rise. Although it would be foolish to overstate the point (as the economic vitality of Scotland will clearly impact on household poverty), taken together, these economic trends suggest that household income is not solely determined by the economy alone. Poverty cannot be reduced to the macro-economy; economy is not the only factor explaining why people are living in poverty in Scotland.

Although not irreducible to poverty, the broader economic context sets the parameters within which distributional mechanisms will create, ameliorate or eradicate household poverty – that is, the economy determines the size of the cake that is to be shared. In times of economic growth, there is less resistance to progressive distribution. Under more stricken financial conditions, people experiencing poverty are particularly vulnerable, as those living beyond poverty seek to protect and, in the case of the better off, increase their share of overall income resource in Scotland.

What do people in Scotland think are the main reasons for poverty?

In Chapter 2, we reported a gap between public and professional opinion on what constitutes poverty. These differences of opinion, when added to the UK government's relentless assault on the poor as it seeks to justify its approach to welfare reform, and the sensationalism that often characterises how the media portrays poverty, make it interesting to consider how the wider public makes sense of poverty.

In some respects, wider public opinion in Scotland is consistent with the arguments being presented in this chapter. Using the example of child poverty, attitudinal research suggests people in Scotland acknowledge that there are multiple causes and that 'structural' factors (such an inequality in society) contribute to the problem. On the other hand, attitudinal research suggests that Scots are strongly inclined to attribute poverty to individual factors and, in particular, to individual failings. That 87 per cent of Scots think that parents' alcoholism, drug or other substance abuse contributes to child poverty and that 29 per cent of Scots apparently think this is the main cause of child poverty in Scotland suggests that the wider public in Scotland is too ready to acknowledge 'individual failing' in making sense of the poverty in Scotland.[33]

Conclusion

We have identified four broad multi-faceted factors, which account for the prevalence of poverty in Scotland. Although *some* individuals may contribute to their own poverty, structural explanations are of far greater significance in explaining the extent of Scotland's poverty. Neither are poverty trends closely aligned with economic trends. Thus, political intervention and social factors must also be considered. Between 1998 and 2010, the UK government has made commitments to tackle poverty, devised strategies and introduced policy interventions that, albeit intermittently, had an important positive impact, particularly in relation to child and pensioner poverty. Scottish government policy focus and action has also had an impact. However, the persistence of poverty for many social groups, current UK government tax and benefit policy, and the tendency for the wider public to seek explanation in ways that focus on the individual, lead to the conclusion that a positive direction of travel can no longer be assumed and that there is a need for a renewed focus to better understand and address the root causes of poverty in Scotland.

Notes

1   See http://www.skillsdevelopmentscotland.co.uk/our-services
2   C Philo and J McCormick, 'Poor Places and Beyond: summary findings and policy implications', in C Philo (ed), *Off the Map: the social geography of poverty in the UK*, CPAG, 1993, pp175–88
3   See https://www.gov.uk/national-minimum-wage-rates
4   Unison, *Single Status and Equal Pay in Local Government*, MSP Briefing 124, www.unison-scotland.org.uk/briefings/singlestatmsp.html
5   Office for National Statistics, 'Headline Indicators for Scotland (HI11)', *Regional Labour Market Statistics*, August 2013, http://www.ons.gov.uk/ons/rel/subnational-labour/regional-labour-market-statistics/august-2013/stb-regional-labour-market-august-2013.html#tab-Index-of-Tables
6   Data for April to June 2013 for the UK as a whole. Office for National Statistics, *Women in the Labour Market*, http://www.ons.gov.uk/ons/dcp171776_328352.pdf
7   *Annual Survey of Hours and Earnings*, 2012, Table 25.9a, http://www.ons.gov.uk/ons/publications/re-reference-tables.html?edition=tcm%3A77-280149
8   See note 7, Table 25.9a
9   See note 5, Table 3.1a
10   See Annex J of *Equality Outcomes and Mainstreaming Report*, http://www.scotland.gov.uk/Publications/2013/04/2397/14
11   See http://www.closethegap.org.uk
12   See http://www.bbc.co.uk/news/uk-politics-24369514
13   Scottish government, *Annual Report for the Child Poverty Strategy for Scotland, 2013*, http://www.scotland.gov.uk/Publications/2013/09/2212
14   See https://www.gov.uk/government/policies/simplifying-the-welfare-system-and-making-sure-work-pays
15   See https://www.gov.uk/government/publications/social-security-benefits-up rating-order-2013
16   *Welfare Benefits Up-rating Act 2013*, http://www.legislation.gov.uk/ukpga/2013/16/contents
17   See http://www.hmrc.gov.uk/childbenefit/payments-entitlements/payments/rates.htm
18   Office for National Statistics, *The Effects of Taxes and Benefits on Household Income 2011/12*, 2013, Table 6, http://www.ons.gov.uk/ons/dcp171778_317365.pdf
19   See note 18

20 See note 18

21 See note 18

22 See http://www.scotland.gov.uk/Topics/People/welfarereform/annualreport/ annualreport2013

23 See http://www.scotland.gov.uk/Publications/2013/09/2212

24 The work has been subsumed by the Employability in Scotland network.

25 Scottish government, *Gross Domestic Product*, Statistical Bulletin Economy Series, First Quarter 2013, http://www.scotland.gov.uk/Resource/0042/00427 797.pdf

26 One of Scotland's purpose targets is to raise Scotland's GDP growth rate to match that of the UK and small independent countries of the European Union.

27 Drawn from the economic purpose target web pages. See www.scotland.gov.uk/ About/scotPerforms/purposes/economicgrowth

28 See note 27

29 At the time of writing, poverty data were not available beyond 2011/12.

30 Scottish government, *High Level Summary of Statistics Trend: employment rate (population aged 16-64)*, 20 August 2013, http://www.scotland.gov.uk/Topics/ Statistics/Browse/Labour-Market/TrendEconomicActivity

31 All data drawn from the Department for Work and Pensions data tabulation tool at https://www.gov.uk/government/collections/dwp-statistics-tabulation-tool

32 Office for National Statistics, *Regional Household Income, Spring 2013*, NUTS1 Regional GDHI, 1997–2011 datasheet, http://www.ons.gov.uk/ons/publications/ re-reference-tables.html?edition=tcm%3A77-298694

33 JH McKendrick, *Attitudes Towards Child Poverty in Contemporary Scotland*, The Hunter Foundation, forthcoming

Section Three
Poverty in Scotland: the evidence

Five
Is poverty falling?

John H McKendrick

Summary

- The latest data, for 2011/12, show that after housing costs are taken into account, one in five of Scotland's children live in poverty (20 per cent, or 200,000 children). Almost one in ten children in Scotland live with income poverty/material deprivation combined (8 per cent).
- Official statistics suggest that relative poverty has fallen in Scotland in recent years. Between 2008/09 and 2011/12, the number of children considered to be living in relative poverty fell by 60,000. There were also 40,000 fewer working-age adults living in relative poverty (2008/09 to 2011/12) and 40,000 fewer people of pension age living in relative poverty (between 2007/08 and 2011/12).
- Scotland also experienced significant reductions in the number of children living in poverty between 1997/98 and 2004/05. The number of children living in poverty in Scotland was fairly stable from 2004/05 to 2008/09.
- For more than a decade after 1995/96, reduction in absolute poverty in Scotland was much more marked than reduction in relative poverty. This suggests that, although standards of living may have risen, many people still had an income that did not allow them to enjoy what is considered to be necessary to participate without undue restriction in Scottish society. In recent years, absolute poverty has risen while relative poverty has reduced.
- European comparisons suggest that the poverty risk in Scotland is now marginally lower than that in Europe as a whole. However, Scotland fares less favourably when compared with those European nations (for example, Scandinavian countries) against which it often seeks to compare its national performance.

Introduction

Chapter 3 described the pre-eminence of household income as a means of measuring poverty in Scotland. In this chapter, the Scottish analysis of the *Households Below Average Income* (HBAI) data is used to estimate the number of people living in poverty in Scotland and to assess whether poverty is falling, remains static or is increasing.[1] As shall become apparent, in recent years, interpretation of these data has become much more complex. In this chapter, the focus is on the total number of people living in poverty, first for children and then for the population as a whole. Estimates of the number of people living in poverty from sub-groups of the population (for example, by family type or by local authority area) are considered in the following chapter.

Figure 5.1:

Proportion of children living in absolute poverty and relative poverty (after housing costs), Scotland, 1994/95 to 2011/12

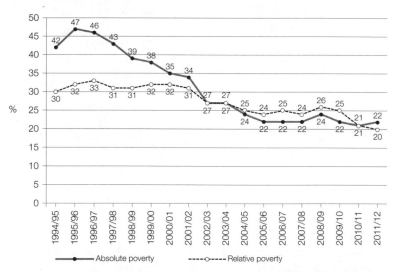

Source: Scottish government, *Poverty and Income Inequality in Scotland, 2011/12*, 2013, Tables A1 and A2

Notes:
1. Figures are derived from the Family Resources Survey.
2. The modified OECD equivalisation scales have been used in the calculations and the figures refer to income after housing costs have been deducted. See Table 2.1 for definitions of absolute poverty (low income) and relative poverty (low income).

Child poverty

There was a steady growth in child poverty in Scotland and the UK as a whole over the last few decades of the twentieth century. By 2000, it was well established that children were over-represented at the bottom of the income distribution and under-represented at the top. According to the annual HBAI report at this time:[2]

> Children are now the group most likely to be in low-income households, and most likely to remain in low-income households for a long period of time.

The UK government's historic commitment in 1999 to reduce child poverty within a generation led to actions that accelerated a trend that had started in 1996/97. From 360,000 children in Scotland living in relative poverty in 1996/97,[3] child poverty fell in five of the following eight years to reach 250,000 in Scotland in 2004/05 (after housing costs are taken into account) (Table 5.1). This was equivalent to a fall in the rate of child poverty from 33 per cent in 1996/97 to 24 per cent in 2004/05, but still meant that child poverty was far higher than it had been in the late 1970s and early 1980s.

As of 2011/12, according to these Scottish government figures, 200,000 children living in Scotland are part of households whose income is so much lower than the typical income for households in Scotland that

Table 5.1:
Number of children living in absolute poverty and relative poverty (after housing costs), Scotland, 1994/95 to 2011/12

																	Thousands
Absolute poverty	460	520	500	470	420	410	380	360	280	270	240	230	220	220	240	230	220	220
Relative poverty	330	360	360	330	330	350	340	330	280	280	250	250	250	240	260	250	220	200
	1994/95	1995/96	1996/97	1997/98	1998/99	1999/00	2000/01	2001/02	2002/03	2003/04	2004/05	2005/06	2006/07	2007/08	2008/09	2009/10	2010/11	2011/12

Source: Scottish government, *Poverty and Income Inequality in Scotland, 2011/12*, 2013, Tables A1 and A2

Notes:
1. Figures are derived from the Family Resources Survey.
2. The modified OECD equivalisation scales have been used in the calculations and the figures refer to income after housing costs have been deducted. See Table 2.1 for definitions of absolute poverty (low income) and relative poverty (low income).

they are considered to be living in poverty (ie, they live in a household with below 60 per cent of median equivalised income, after housing costs are considered). Similarly, 220,000 children in Scotland are living in households that have not experienced a sufficient real rise in income levels to lift them out of absolute (low income) poverty. In terms of proportions, and using the same Scottish government figures, one in five children in Scotland (20 per cent) live in relative poverty and slightly more than one in five children in Scotland (22 per cent) live in absolute poverty. The 'before housing costs' measure that is used, for reasons highlighted in Chapter 3, by the government when measuring progress against child poverty targets

Figure 5.2:

Children living in low-income households in Scotland, and other parts of the UK, 2011/12

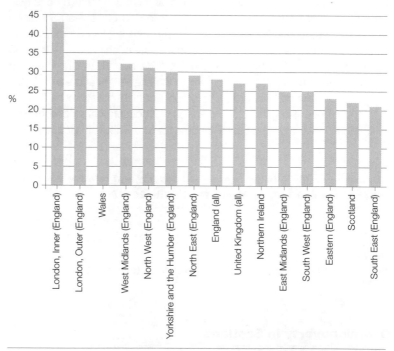

Source: Department for Work and Pensions, *Households Below Average Income 2011/12*, 2013, Table 4.6db

Notes:

1. Low household income defined as below 60 per cent UK median income, after housing costs and including self-employed.
2. The modified OECD equivalised scale has been used.

estimates that more than one in seven children in Scotland (150,000) are considered to be living in relative poverty.

Although the Scottish HBAI has now several years' worth of data on the 'tier 3' measure of child poverty (Table 3.1 in Chapter 3, measuring the combination of low household income and material deprivation), changes in the items used to measure deprivation in 2010/11 make it difficult to draw clear conclusions about rates and trends through time. However, this measure of child poverty tends to suggest that there have been reductions in poverty/material deprivation among children in Scotland in recent years. For 2011/12, using a before housing costs measure in the income component, it is estimated that 80,000 children in Scotland are living in income poverty/material deprivation combined (8 per cent of children).

As all of the figures above show, child poverty persists at a disturbingly high level in Scotland.

Figure 5.2 compares the percentage of children living in households with incomes of below 60 per cent median earnings in Scotland (relative poverty), using the after housing costs measure, with those from other Government Office regions[4] and national regions in the UK for 2011/12.

What is clear from Figure 5.2 is that a lower proportion of children live in poverty in Scotland than in any of the other national regions in the UK (Wales, Northern Ireland and England as a whole) and in most of the other Government Office regions in the UK (rates are only lower in the South East of England).

Figure 5.3 compares the percentage of children living in households with incomes of below 60 per cent median earnings in their own nation (relative poverty) across the European Union for 2011, using the before housing costs measure that is favoured by the European Union.

In contrast to the situation just a few years ago, Scotland now has a significantly lower proportion of its children living in poverty than in the European Union as a whole. Children in Scotland only fare worse than those growing up in Nordic countries, Slovenia and Cyprus.

Overall poverty in Scotland

Although children and pensioners have been the primary focus of the UK and Scottish governments' anti-poverty activity, a fuller understanding of poverty in the UK requires a more broadly-based analysis of poverty among the population as a whole.

Figure 5.3:

Children living in low-income households in European nations, 2011

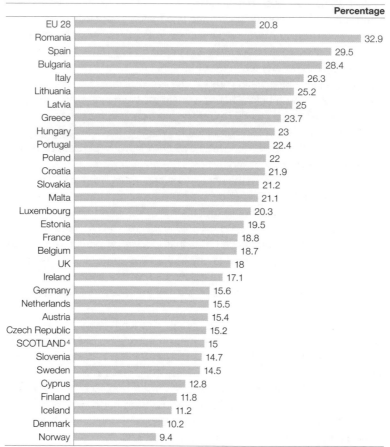

Percentage

	Percentage
EU 28	20.8
Romania	32.9
Spain	29.5
Bulgaria	28.4
Italy	26.3
Lithuania	25.2
Latvia	25
Greece	23.7
Hungary	23
Portugal	22.4
Poland	22
Croatia	21.9
Slovakia	21.2
Malta	21.1
Luxembourg	20.3
Estonia	19.5
France	18.8
Belgium	18.7
UK	18
Ireland	17.1
Germany	15.6
Netherlands	15.5
Austria	15.4
Czech Republic	15.2
SCOTLAND[4]	15
Slovenia	14.7
Sweden	14.5
Cyprus	12.8
Finland	11.8
Iceland	11.2
Denmark	10.2
Norway	9.4

Source: Eurostat, *At Risk of Poverty Rate by Detailed Age Group (less than 18 years), 2013*, tessi120

Notes:

1. Low household income is defined as below 60 per cent national median income, before housing costs and including self-employed.
2. The modified OECD equivalised scale has been used.
3. Data from 2011 are used (in preference to 2012) as 2012 data were not available for all European nations at the time of writing.
4. As is normal for international comparisons, the Eurostat UK data uses the before housing costs measure, whereas the UK data in Figure 5.2 used the after housing costs measure (see Chapter 3 for explanation).
5. Scotland data are from Scottish government, *Poverty and Income Inequality in Scotland, 2011/12*, 2013, Table A1 (before housing costs). Comparison of Scotland and European countries must be made with caution, as these are drawn from different data sources.

Figure 5.4:

Proportion of individuals living in absolute poverty and relative poverty (after housing costs), 1994/95 to 2011/12

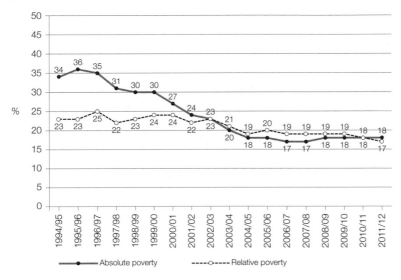

Source: Scottish government, *Poverty and Income Inequality in Scotland, 2011/12*, 2013, Tables A1 and A2

Notes:
1. Figures are derived from the Family Resources Survey.
2. The modified OECD equivalisation scales have been used in the calculations and the figures refer to income after housing costs have been deducted. See Table 2.1 for definitions of absolute poverty (low income) and relative poverty (low income).

Mirroring the presentation of evidence for child poverty, Figure 5.5 shows the number of individuals in Scotland who are living in poverty and Figure 5.4 shows the changes to the proportion of individuals living in poverty in Scotland from 1994/95.

According to these figures, 950,000 individuals are living in households regarded as experiencing 'absolute poverty' (more than 60 per cent below median equivalised household income, after housing costs have been deducted, at 2011/12 levels). 870,000 individuals in Scotland are living in households regarded as experiencing 'relative poverty' (60 per cent below median equivalised household income at current levels, after housing costs have been deducted). In terms of proportions, almost one in five individuals in Scotland live in poverty, whether defined as a relative measure (17 per cent), or an absolute measure (18 per cent).

Figure 5.5:

Proportion of individuals living in absolute poverty and relative poverty (after housing costs), 1994/95 to 2011/12

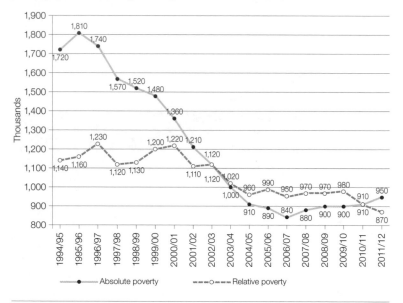

Source: Scottish government, *Poverty and Income Inequality in Scotland, 2011/12*, 2013, Tables A1 and A2

Notes:

1. Figures are derived from the Family Resources Survey.
2. The modified OECD equivalisation scales have been used in the calculations and the figures refer to income after housing costs have been deducted. See Table 2.1 for definitions of absolute poverty (low income) and relative poverty (low income).

These figures show that it is not only child poverty that is a problem in Scotland. The late 1990s and early 2000s were not characterised by the same scale of progress in reducing poverty for the population as a whole in Scotland, and there was no reduction at all in the risk of poverty for working-age adults without children. Nevertheless, some progress was evident at this time. Between 1995/96 and 2006/07, the number of individuals living in absolute poverty in Scotland fell from 1,810,000 (36 per cent) to 840,000 (17 per cent). Similarly, a fall in relative poverty can be observed from 1,230,000 (25 per cent) in 1996/97 to 950,000 (19 per cent) in 2006/07. The later years of the first decade of the twenty-first century were characterised by the same stagnation in the level of poverty that is evident for children. Similarly, in more recent years, the official statistics

Figure 5.6:

Individuals living on a low income in Scotland, and other parts of the UK, 2011/12

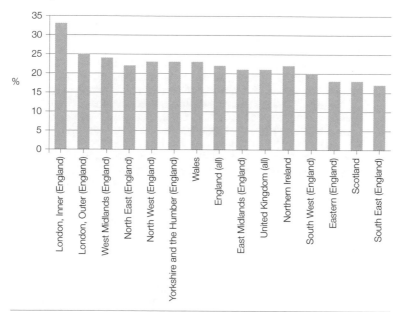

Source: Department for Work and Pensions, *Households Below Average Income 2011/12*, 2013, Table 3.6db

Notes:
1. Low household income defined as below 60 per cent UK median income, after housing costs and including self-employed.
2. The modified OECD equivalised scales have been used.

on relative poverty report a reduction in the number of people living in poverty in Scotland. Together, these figures suggest that, following a decade of fluctuations around the one million mark, the number of individuals living in relative poverty in Scotland has remained consistently below one million people in recent years (Figure 5.5).

Figure 5.6 compares the percentage of individuals living in households with incomes of below 60 per cent median earnings in Scotland, after housing costs have been deducted (relative poverty), with those from other Government Office regions and national regions in UK for 2011/12.

As for children (Figure 5.2), there is evidence to suggest that the level of poverty in Scotland compares favourably with that in other parts of the UK. Poverty in Scotland, on the whole, is lower than in Wales, England

Figure 5.7:

Individuals living in low-income households in European nations, 2011

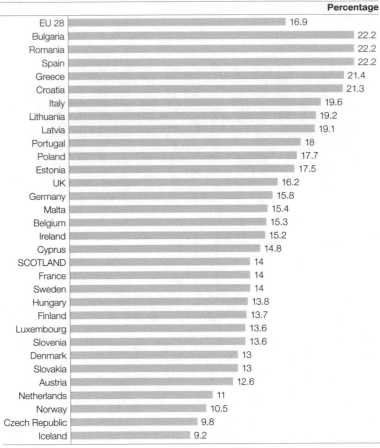

Percentage

Country	Percentage
EU 28	16.9
Bulgaria	22.2
Romania	22.2
Spain	22.2
Greece	21.4
Croatia	21.3
Italy	19.6
Lithuania	19.2
Latvia	19.1
Portugal	18
Poland	17.7
Estonia	17.5
UK	16.2
Germany	15.8
Malta	15.4
Belgium	15.3
Ireland	15.2
Cyprus	14.8
SCOTLAND	14
France	14
Sweden	14
Hungary	13.8
Finland	13.7
Luxembourg	13.6
Slovenia	13.6
Denmark	13
Slovakia	13
Austria	12.6
Netherlands	11
Norway	10.5
Czech Republic	9.8
Iceland	9.2

Source: Eurostat, *At Risk of Poverty by Detailed Age Group*, 2013, tessi 120

Notes:
1. Low household income is defined as below 60 per cent national median income, before housing costs and including self-employed.
2. The modified OECD equivalised scale has been used.
3. Data from 2011 are used (in preference to 2012), as 2012 data were not available for all European nations at the time of writing.
4. As is normal for international comparisons, the Eurostat UK data uses the before housing costs measure, whereas the UK data in Figure 5.6 used the after housing costs measure (see Chapter 3 for explanation).
5. Scotland data are from Scottish government, *Poverty and Income Inequality in Scotland, 2011/12*, 2013, Table A1 (before housing costs). Comparison of Scotland and European countries must be made with caution, as these are drawn from different data sources.

and Northern Ireland and in all English regions, except for the East of England (with which it shares the same level of poverty) and the South East.

Once again though, although UK comparative data casts Scotland in a positive light, this should not be allowed to obscure the fact that many thousands of people in Scotland are currently living in poverty – 950,000 people if the measure of absolute poverty is used, or 870,000 if we adopt the relative measure of poverty (Figure 5.5).

Figure 5.7 compares whole-population poverty across Europe using the same approach (and with the same caveats) as Figure 5.3 did for children. As for children, the last few years have witnessed a reduction of poverty in Scotland that has shifted Scotland below the European Union average. Although not quite as impressive a 'league table ranking' as was evident for child poverty, there are more countries in the European Union that have a higher incidence of overall poverty than Scotland than there are that have a lower incidence of overall poverty than Scotland.

Do these numbers make sense?

Although the number of people living in poverty remains high, there would appear to be a 'good news' story lurking within these statistics. It would appear that fewer children are now experiencing material deprivation. It would also seem that there are fewer children and adults who are not able to purchase what the typical household in Scotland can purchase. At a time when it is widely accepted that Scotland has entered an 'era of austerity' and anecdotal evidence of hard times abounds, these evidence-based claims do not seem credible. There is potentially a danger that people stop valuing these particular poverty statistics, which have been a kernel of anti-poverty activity for more than a decade.

Reaching a point where measures of child poverty are enshrined in law has been a hard-fought gain for those concerned about tackling poverty in the UK. Poverty numbers have a central role in monitoring progress and measuring success. Although, as discussed in Chapter 2, many of the 'backstage' problems have been resolved and we should have confidence in the estimates, it cannot be denied that recent HBAI analysis has generated some numbers that may not, at first reading, seem to make sense. More specifically:

• Given these times of austerity, how can 60,000 children in Scotland have been lifted out of relative poverty between 2008/09 and 2011/12?

- How can it be that a few years ago, it was estimated that 27 per cent (1,340,000) of people in Scotland were living in absolute low income poverty in 1995/96, whereas it is now estimated that 36 per cent of Scots (1,810,000) were living in absolute low income poverty at this time?
- Does it make sense that absolute poverty has increased in recent years, when relative poverty has decreased?
- If absolute poverty is worsening, how can material deprivation be improving?

It would be easy to despair at these apparent anomalies and to take the cynical view that there are 'lies, damned lies and statistics'. However, there are straightforward explanations for each of these conumdrums, and what these complexities emphasise is that there is a need for poverty intelligence to be applied when interpreting poverty data.

Falling poverty in times of austerity?

Median weekly household income in Scotland has fallen from £416 in 2009/10 to £383 in 2011/12.[5] The fall in the numbers who are counted as living in relative poverty can be attributed to the fall in the incomes of the 'squeezed middle', rather than an absolute improvement in the lot of people experiencing poverty. The UK government has highlighted this very point, although it has used this as a reason to question the utility of current measures of income poverty.[6] The fall in relative income poverty reflects the fact that the incomes of low-income households were protected, as a result of previous investment in benefits and tax credits and their uprating in line with inflation, as median incomes fell. This protection has now been removed with cuts to benefits and changes to the way in which benefits are uprated. Independent modelling now forecasts significant increases in relative income poverty as a result.[7]

Almost half a million missing poor Scots?

The Child Poverty Act 2010 set the target of reducing poverty from 2010 to 2020. It was therefore necessary to redefine the baseline year, against which future rates of absolute poverty were to be compared from 1997/98 to 2010/11. This recalibration of the baseline year makes it seem as if absolute poverty in Scotland was much higher over the last decade than had previously been reported.

Getting worse and getting better?

As noted above, the worsening position of the 'squeezed middle' gives the impression that matters are improving (relative poverty rates are falling) at the same time as other poverty statistics give the impression that matters are worsening (absolute poverty rates are rising). Together, a fuller understanding of the situation is reached – conditions have been worsening in the last few years, with the challenges being felt particularly keenly by median-income families (to the extent that the position of poorer families' relative to them, but not in absolute terms, has improved). The need for this fuller understanding is a key reason why official targets for eradicating child poverty under the Child Poverty Act 2010 use a suite of measures, including relative poverty, absolute poverty and material deprivation.

Having more with less resource?

It seems improbable that a measure of material deprivation could improve when financial resources are stretched. The most likely explanation is twofold – ie, in times of economic stress what people report that they 'would like but cannot afford' is reduced (people lower their expectations, meaning that less deprivation is recorded) and, as reported above, the income improvement of poorer households is only relative to median income and actually reflects particularly worsening conditions for the 'squeezed middle'.

The conclusion that should be drawn is that the numbers do make sense, and that the recent economic situation highlights why the full range of existing official measures are needed to monitor progress. Any current challenges in interpretation will ease soon because, unfortunately, all projections point towards a return to increasing rates of relative poverty in the years ahead. For example, the Institute for Fiscal Studies has projected that relative poverty in Scotland, after housing costs, in 2020 will be experienced by 28.4 per cent of children and 23 per cent of working-age adults – significant increases on current rates.[8]

Conclusion

The figures in this chapter have outlined the broad trends in poverty using the key measure of household income. All the data show that income poverty remains a significant problem in Scotland, although not all data point to worsening conditions. Significant falls were evident in child and pensioner poverty from 1998. More recent falls in levels of poverty from 2008/09 to 2011/12, at a time of broader economic stress, reflect the positive impact of providing social protection through inflation-linking benefit levels. However, with a decoupling of benefit uprating from inflation,and severe cuts to social security generally, including in work benefits, it seems likely that, following a period of real progress, there will now be a return to rapidly increasing rates of poverty in the years ahead. There is clearly a need to reappraise how poverty is tackled in Scotland if UK and Scottish government aims – as stated – are to reduce the numbers living in poverty. As will be shown in the chapter that follows, some groups in Scottish society are at even greater risk of poverty than these aggregate figures suggest.

Notes

1   Scottish government, *Poverty and Income Inequality in Scotland, 2011/12*, 2013
2   Department for Work and Pensions, *Households Below Average Income 2000/01*, 2001, www.dwp.gov.uk/asd/hbai.asp
3   370,000 in absolute poverty.
4   Government Offices for the English regions were abolished in 2011, having been established in 1994. However, English regional data on poverty are still published for these areas.
5   See note 1, Table A6
6   HM Government, *Measuring Child Poverty: a consultation on better measures of child poverty*, Cm 8483, 2012, http://www.official-documents.gov.uk/document/cm84/8483/8483.pdf
7   J Browne, A Hood and R Joyce, *Child and Working-age Poverty in Northern Ireland from 2010 to 2020*, Report R78, Institute for Fiscal Studies, 2013, p41, Table B.2
8   See note 7

Six
Is income inequality reducing?

John H McKendrick

Summary

- The Scottish government aims to reduce income inequality by 2017.
- Income inequality has not reduced in Scotland over the last decade. Indeed, if anything, the income share of Scotland's poorest households has been more likely to decrease, than increase, in recent years.
- Recent and projected trends for the key drivers of change for income inequality do not suggest that Scotland is moving in the right direction to tackle income inequality.
- It is unlikely that income inequality in Scotland will reduce dramatically by 2017, without substantial changes in policy, practice and strategy.

Introduction: income inequality takes centre stage

The Scottish government has set itself the target of reducing income inequality in Scotland. As discussed in Chapter 2, the high-level Solidarity Purpose Target commits Scotland 'to increase overall income and the pro-portion of income earned by the three lowest income deciles as a group by 2017'. The Scottish government's commitment to reduce income inequality (the distribution of income) is set within a commitment to increase overall income for Scotland as a whole. Thus, the aim is for the poorest Scots to receive a bigger share of a bigger cake. For the overall income component of this measure, the Scottish government uses Office for National Statistics estimates of gross disposable household income, which suggests that household income in Scotland has risen consistently year on year over the last decade, from £46.8 billion in 1997 to £82.2 billion in 2011.[1]

However, the central focus of the solidarity purpose target is the dis-tribution of household income. Not only does this imply analysis of the contemporary estimate and direction of change of income inequality in Scotland, it also involves consideration of 'direction of change' evidence for the key drivers of income inequality. According to the Scottish government, income inequality will be tackled by: the accessibility of employment opportunities, especially for those on lower incomes; opportunities for the lower paid to improve their skills; changes in the income differential between the lowest and highest paid occupations; and entitlement to, and take-up of, benefits.[2] This chapter presents evidence on the current state of income inequality in Scotland and the key drivers that may shape it toward 2017.

Income inequality: a persistent problem in Scotland

The big, bad picture in Scotland

Income inequality in Scotland is stark. The 'poorest' third of Scotland's households share only 14.1 per cent of Scotland's income.[3] Although a broader population than that which is living in poverty, this is the group that is the focus of the Scottish government's solidarity purpose target. This group's share of Scotland's total income fell in four of the last five years and has not improved over the last decade (see Figure 6.1).

However, strictly speaking, according to the Scottish government criterion, income inequality has neither reduced nor increased in Scotland in recent years. The solidarity purpose target specifies that income inequality is increasing if the income share of the poorest 30 per cent in Scotland falls by one percentage point or more (or if total income falls). Income inequality is improving if the same group increases its share of income by one percentage point or more (and total income does not fall). These targets are set against a baseline for 2006/07, when the poorest 30 per cent of individuals in Scotland shared only 13.9 per cent of income. Although the income share of this group fell for the next three years, it did not fall below 12.9 per cent (baseline minus 1 per cent) and thus income inequality is not considered to have decreased according to the definition of the solidarity purpose target. Similarly, the rise to 14.5 per cent in 2010/11 did not exceed the 14.9 per cent that would be required to denote an increase.

It is also significant that the solidarity purpose target focuses on the poorest 30 per cent in Scotland. This includes individuals who would not

Figure 6.1:

Share of total income by three lowest income groups (deciles) in Scotland, 1999/00 to 2011/12

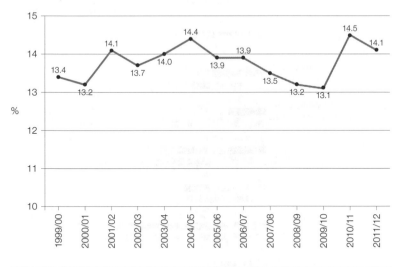

Source: Scottish government, Solidarity Purpose Target,
http://www.scotland.gov.uk/About/Performance/scotPerforms/purpose/solidarity#Chart

be defined as living in income poverty (17 per cent of all individuals using the 'before housing costs' relative income poverty measure). Figure 6.2 compares the family work status profile of different groups that are the focus of the solidarity purpose target in Scotland. In contrast to the focus on people living in poverty (largely, the population of the lowest two deciles in Figure 6.2), the Scottish government's approach to 'income inequality' (with its focus on the poorest 30 per cent) broadens the range of target groups. Contrasted with a focus on poverty, more attention is given to low-paid households.

Other ways of measuring income inequality also confirm the regressive trends of late. The Scottish government estimate of our *Gini* co-efficient (a widely used measure of overall income inequality for nations) suggests that Scotland's distribution of income has become more unequal in six of the seven years since 2004/05.[4] On the other hand, the same analysis demonstrates that Scotland has, consistently, had a more equitable distribution of income, compared to Great Britain and the UK as a whole.

Figure 6.2:
Profile of bottom three income deciles in Scotland, 2011/12

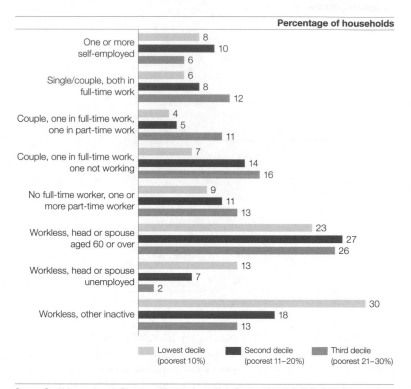

Percentage of households

One or more self-employed: 8, 10, 6

Single/couple, both in full-time work: 6, 8, 12

Couple, one in full-time work, one in part-time work: 4, 5, 11

Couple, one in full-time work, one not working: 7, 14, 16

No full-time worker, one or more part-time worker: 9, 11, 13

Workless, head or spouse aged 60 or over: 23, 27, 26

Workless, head or spouse unemployed: 13, 7, 2

Workless, other inactive: 30, 18, 13

Lowest decile (poorest 10%) | Second decile (poorest 11–20%) | Third decile (poorest 21–30%)

Source: Scottish government, *Poverty and Income Inequality in Scotland 2011/12*, 2013, Table A9

Scotland in context

In the broader European context, income inequality in both Scotland and the UK as a whole is among the worst in Europe (Figure 6.3). Using the *Gini* co-efficient estimate, and discounting the other home nations in the UK, only seven European Union nations have a more unequal distribution of income than Scotland: Latvia, Bulgaria, Portugal, Spain, Greece, Romania and Lithuania.[5]

Figure 6.3:

Income inequality in European nations, as measured by the *Gini* co-efficient, 2011

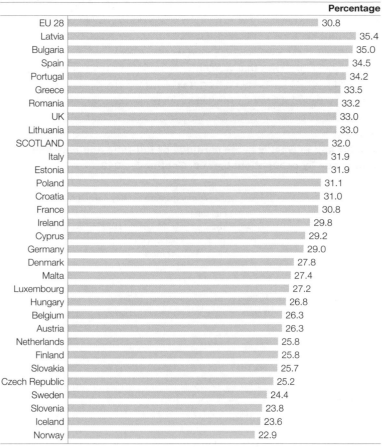

	Percentage
EU 28	30.8
Latvia	35.4
Bulgaria	35.0
Spain	34.5
Portugal	34.2
Greece	33.5
Romania	33.2
UK	33.0
Lithuania	33.0
SCOTLAND	32.0
Italy	31.9
Estonia	31.9
Poland	31.1
Croatia	31.0
France	30.8
Ireland	29.8
Cyprus	29.2
Germany	29.0
Denmark	27.8
Malta	27.4
Luxembourg	27.2
Hungary	26.8
Belgium	26.3
Austria	26.3
Netherlands	25.8
Finland	25.8
Slovakia	25.7
Czech Republic	25.2
Sweden	24.4
Slovenia	23.8
Iceland	23.6
Norway	22.9

Source:
1. EU data: European Union Statistics on Income and Living Conditions (EU-SILC) drawn from the Eurostat Data Explorer Tool. Data table with the ID [tilc_di12], 2010
2. Scottish data: drawn from Scottish government analysis of the *Households Below Average Income* dataset, http://www.scotland.gov.uk//Topics/Statistics/Browse/Social-Welfare/IncomePoverty/CoreAnalysis/ginicoefficient

Notes:
1. Higher numbers represent higher levels of income inequality.
2. Data from 2011 are used as 2012 data were missing for most European nations at the time of writing.
3. The European data are drawn from EU-SILC data.
4. Data for Scotland are drawn from the Scottish government's own analysis of *Households Below Average Income* data. In this analysis, the Great Britain *Gini* co-efficient was described as 34.0. The EU-SILC estimate for the UK is lower than this estimate. Although this may reflect Great Britain/UK differences, this may also suggest that the Scottish *Gini* co-efficient would be slightly lower if data were available through the EU-SILC.

Gender pay gap

Income inequality is measured for households, as a whole. However, income inequality in Scotland comes in different guises. Most significant of the income inequalities that exist among the population in Scotland is the gender pay gap. Regrettably, the gender pay gap has been an ever-present feature in earlier editions of *Poverty in Scotland*.

Table 6.1 shows that women working in full-time paid employment earn just over £4 for every £5 than men earn (82 per cent of men's earnings). Expressed differently, at present levels of pay, women would need

Table 6.1:

Gender gap in weekly gross earnings of full-time and part-time employees by occupational group, Scotland, 2012

	Gross median weekly earnings					
	Full time			Part time		
	Men £	Women £	Women as a % of men	Men £	Women £	Women as a % of men
Managers and senior officials	767.10	592.30*	78%	***	231.70**	***
Professional occupations	701.60	653.70	93%	243.60**	327.60	134%
Associate professional and technical	598.50	508.30	85%	121.40**	222.60*	183%
Administrative and secretarial	421.80	360.30	85%	131.90**	182.10	138%
Skilled trade	486.70	317.50*	65%	191.30**	152.50**	80%
Caring, leisure and other service	376.60	341.40	91%	173.80**	182.80	105%
Sales and customer service	330.90	295.90	89%	128.50*	131.30	102%
Process, plant and machine operatives	442.40	293.40*	66%	126.50**	***	***
Elementary	355.10	272.10	77%	123.50*	110.40	89%
All occupations	533.10	438.10	82%	141.70	168.40	119%

Source: *Annual Survey of Hours and Earnings*, 2013, Table 3.1a, http://www.ons.gov.uk/ons/publications/re-reference-tables.html?edition=tcm%3A77-280149

Notes:
1. Employees on adult rates whose pay was not affected by absence for the survey period.
2. * Treat estimate with caution
    ** Treat estimate with high caution
    *** Insufficient sample size to estimate

to work almost a 50-hour week to earn the same amount as men working a 40-hour week in Scotland. A significant gender pay gap for full-time workers is evident for all occupational groups, with women's pay falling to two-thirds of that of men's for 'skilled trades' and 'process, plant and machine operatives'.[6] The gender pay gap is more complex for part-time workers, with inequity being less marked and several examples of women appearing to be paid more than men in some occupational sectors.[7]

Through its Equality Unit, the Scottish government provides funding for a range of organisations to promote equality of opportunity for men and women in Scotland.[8] Furthermore, under the Equality Act 2010, it is a specific duty of the Scottish government to publish gender pay gap information and information on equal pay. Against a national gender pay gap of 13.9 per cent in 2012,[9] the Scottish government reported that it had a gender pay gap of 5.7 per cent for the main government, 2.1 per cent for Historic Scotland, 11.6 per cent for the Scottish Prison Service and 9.2 per cent for the Crown Office and Procurator Fiscal Service.[10]

Key drivers of change for income inequality in Scotland

In this section, we focus on the drivers of income inequality that are acknowledged by the Scottish government as areas for which, at least in part, it has responsibility. Taxation policy has the greatest power to transform income inequality in Scotland, although responsibility for that, at present, rests with the UK. Carlo Morelli and Paul Seaman consider the potential role of taxation in addressing income inequality in Chapter 17.

Employment opportunities

It is widely understood that Scotland is in the midst of a period of flux and adjustment in the Scottish labour market with the loss of public sector jobs and a consequent structural shift away from public sector employment. In terms of the anticipated impact of these changes on income inequality, all that can be said with certainty is that it is not at all clear whether the changing landscape of employment opportunities will reduce, maintain or exacerbate income inequality in the medium term.

However, at the current time and in the short term, there can be little doubt that changing employment opportunities has not been a major force in tackling income inequality in Scotland. Seasonally adjusted unemployment in Scotland over the two-year period from 2011 to 2013 fluctuated from 7.3 per cent (February to April 2013) to 8.4 per cent (May to July 2012).[11] Although unemployment has fallen steadily since, particularly for men, in recent quarters these changes are not at a rate that would impact on income inequality to any significant degree (which is also making the assumption that higher rates of employment, *per se*, would in any case reduce income inequality).

Skill development

Enhancing the skills of those traditionally at greater risk of lower income is recognised by the Scottish government as one means of tackling income inequality. Skills Development Scotland promotes a series of initiatives, each of which is designed to improve earning and employment prospects in Scotland.[12] Furthermore, in an advanced economy, one key means to improve career-earning prospects is through participation in further education and higher education.

In 2011/12, almost 257,913 students were undertaking courses at one of Scotland's colleges[13] and 281,630 students were undertaking courses at one of Scotland's universities.[14] These numbers suggest high levels of skills and personal development in Scotland. However, for the last four years, there has been a year-on-year reduction in the number of students at Scotland's colleges; the student population is two-thirds that of 2007/08, although the full-time equivalent totals are similar (reflecting the fact that more students are now studying full time).[15] Furthermore, there was a 5.9 per cent reduction in the number of students entering Scottish higher education institutions between 2010/11 and 2011/12.[16]

Perhaps of greater importance than summary levels of participation is consideration of whether or not participation is socially progressive – ie, are students from disadvantaged backgrounds as, more or less likely than those from non-disadvantaged backgrounds to study in further education or higher education? Table 6.2 reports the number of people (per 1,000) from the 20 per cent most deprived areas in Scotland that are in further education and higher education (upper part of table) and then directly compares this level of participation to that in non-deprived areas in Scotland.

Those from the (20 per cent) most deprived areas in Scotland are over-represented in further education (ratio of 1.63 in 2010/11), under-represented in higher education (ratio of 0.72 in 2010/11) and, since

Table 6.2:

Participation index and headcount participation in further and higher education, 2006/07 to 2010/11

	2006/07	2007/08	2008/09	2009/10	2010/11
Headcount per 1,000 people, multiply deprived areas					
Further and higher education	115.9	117.6	117.5	112.9	111.9
Higher education	37.2	36.4	37.4	38.4	41.0
Further education	80.9	83.4	82.2	76.4	72.5
Participation index for multiply deprived areas					
Further and higher education, ratio	0.97	1.01	1.03	1.04	1.12
Higher education, ratio	0.62	0.63	0.65	0.66	0.72
Further education, ratio	1.32	1.39	1.43	1.48	1.63

Source: Scottish Funding Council, *Scottish Participation in Further and Higher Education, 2006/07 to 2010/11*, 2012, Tables 2.4.1, 3.6.1 and 4.6.1

2007/08, have been over-represented in further/higher education combined (ratio of 1.12 in 2010/11). The share of students from Scotland's most deprived areas in further and higher education has increased year on year for the last four years. Indeed, for further education alone, if the same number 100 was given to represent the proportionate share of young people from Scotland's most deprived areas going to college, then the number 163 represents their actual share – ie, young people from deprived areas are significantly over-represented in Scotland's colleges.

However, although overall trends are 'progressive', these are unlikely to impact on income inequality by 2017 to any significant degree. First and foremost, as noted above, participation rates of students from Scotland's (20 per cent) most deprived areas remain much lower in higher education, rising to only 72 per cent of their proportionate share in 2010/11. Given that graduating from higher education is likely to bring greater lifetime financial rewards than graduating from further education, current participation levels may merely serve to perpetuate existing patterns of income inequality.

Second, there are significant variations across Scotland (Table 6.3 for 2010/11). For example, while in Angus 99 students from the district's (20 per cent) most deprived areas participate in higher education for every 100 students that should have attended (if the participation of children from deprived areas were typical of the district's participation), in Stirling there are only 44 students from the district's (20 per cent) most deprived

Table 6.3:

Headcount participation in further and higher education, by deprivation area status, local authorities in Scotland, 2010/11

Local authority	Further education			Higher education			Further education/ higher education
	Rate per 1,000		Ratio of	*Rate per 1,000*		Ratio of	Ratio of
	Less deprived	Most deprived	most to least deprived	Less deprived	Most deprived	most to least deprived	most to least deprived
Angus	66.0	110.3	1.67	53.6	53.1	0.99	1.28
Aberdeenshire	43.8	103.8	2.37	57.9	26.0	0.45	1.27
Scottish Borders	35.3	76.4	2.16	44.3	24.4	0.55	1.20
Aberdeen City	35.1	70.8	2.01	64.6	48.1	0.74	1.17
Dumfries and Galloway	45.1	68.3	1.52	42.0	31.3	0.75	1.13
Edinburgh City	36.7	67.3	1.84	61.5	41.3	0.67	1.09
North Ayrshire	41.8	64.4	1.54	53.7	38.9	0.72	1.06
South Ayrshire	37.3	58.3	1.56	54.6	42.6	0.78	1.06
Argyll and Bute	52.9	76.6	1.45	50.0	31.2	0.62	1.05
East Ayrshire	41.3	62.4	1.51	52.0	36.6	0.70	1.05
Perth and Kinross	41.9	58.8	1.40	50.0	37.3	0.75	1.05
Scotland	**44.9**	**69.2**	**1.54**	**57.1**	**39.8**	**0.70**	**1.05**
Dundee City	52.2	75.4	1.44	65.2	46.5	0.71	1.04
Fife	48.4	71.9	1.49	52.4	33.3	0.63	1.04
East Lothian	36.3	59.3	1.64	48.3	28.4	0.59	1.03
Renfrewshire	52.4	72.1	1.38	61.5	47.3	0.77	1.03
West Dunbartonshire	52.3	67.5	1.29	53.7	42.9	0.80	1.02
East Renfrewshire	36.0	67.0	1.86	80.1	51.9	0.65	0.99
East Dunbartonshire	39.6	70.4	1.78	76.8	45.5	0.59	0.97
Falkirk	41.0	54.8	1.34	44.7	32.2	0.72	0.96
Glasgow City	51.2	81.2	1.59	76.6	43.3	0.57	0.96
Highland	42.4	52.7	1.24	52.5	38.8	0.74	0.95
North Lanarkshire	45.1	58.4	1.29	52.3	36.4	0.70	0.95
Midlothian	38.8	46.9	1.21	46.2	31.5	0.68	0.90
Moray	47.9	–	–	50.9	24.8	0.49	0.90
Clackmannanshire	44.9	55.6	1.24	53.4	33.1	0.62	0.89
South Lanarkshire	39.0	52.8	1.35	57.6	33.9	0.59	0.89
West Lothian	46.9	55.7	1.19	48.2	30.2	0.63	0.89
Inverclyde	52.3	63.7	1.22	66.2	36.4	0.55	0.85

Stirling	37.2	51.8	1.40	58.6	25.8	0.44	0.79
Eilean Siar	74.3	–	–	57.1	–	–	–
Orkney Islands	118.1	–	–	56.9	–	–	–
Shetland Islands	185.0	–	–	59.9	–	–	–

Source: Scottish Funding Council, *Scottish Participation in Further and Higher Education, 2006/07 to 2010/11*, 2012, Tables 2.4.3, 3.6.3 and 4.6.2

areas for every 100 students that would have been expected to attend if children from deprived areas were represented in equal proportion. There are other interesting local patterns in these data. For example, participation in further education of people from the most deprived areas in rural Aberdeenshire and Scottish Borders far outstrips those from their district's less deprived areas, with participation being far less for higher education. On the whole, the likelihood of someone from a deprived area attending either further or higher education varies dramatically across Scotland (from 128 per cent of local participation norms in Angus to 79 per cent of local participation norms in Stirling).

Occupational pay gaps

Providing opportunities to work and enhancing the skills that will increase the chances of finding work (and finding better paid work) will only impact on income inequality if work is sufficiently well paid. At present, work does not pay well for everyone. Table 6.1 has already demonstrated that women in full-time employment are less well paid than men. This table also highlights the scale of the differences in typical pay across occupational groups. For example, men working in 'sales and customer service' in Scotland are typically paid £330.90 per week; men in 'professional occupations' are paid more than double this amount (£701.60 per week). Incidentally, the typical weekly pay for a man in 'sales and customer services' is well below the poverty threshold for a couple with two children aged five and 14 (Table 3.2). Such families would be reliant either on the state to lift them out of poverty (for example, through child benefit or tax credits) or on a second household income.

In recent years, public ire at variation in occupational pay has increasingly been directed at executive-level pay and the excessive financial packages that stretch pay inequality by increasing pay and other financial reward at the upper extreme. However, there has also been growing recognition among the anti-poverty sector that low pay is a significant problem in its own right. The Scottish Living Wage Campaign seeks to address this problem and in 2013 presented evidence that eight of the 32 local authorities in Scotland were not paying a living wage to their employees.[17]

A 'living wage' in November 2013 was defined as £7.65 per hour. In 2010, the Scottish government's own analysis on the impact of introducing a living wage for low-paid workers in the public sector suggests that it would 'not have a significant impact on the proportion of income accruing to households in the bottom three income deciles'.[18] However, tangible steps have been taken to tackle low pay in Scotland in recent years. The longstanding agreement to commit to gender pay equality (through single status) has been followed in Scottish local government by practical steps to revalue competencies previously undervalued through job evaluation, although there are concerns that this is too often done on the basis of 'levelling down' rather than 'levelling up'.[19] Announcements in recent Scottish budgets of government intention to freeze public sector pay were also tempered with some measures in place to protect the incomes of the lowest paid.[20]

Although far from welcome, the current financial climate has afforded an opportunity to make tentative steps toward greater equality in pay. Regrettably, to date this has been achieved by maintaining the income of the lowest paid, while allowing the income of middle-to-high earners (on aggregate) to fall.[21] Whether these adjustments will be sustained as the economy recovers is less clear. It is hoped that this is more of a temporary austerity measure, rather than the main driver to rebalance the value of under-paid work to ensure a future Scotland with less income inequality. In any case, some of the safeguards that had maintained the income of the poorest families in the UK have already been dismantled.[22]

Welfare benefit entitlement and take-up

The explicit goal of 'welfare reform' is to undermine the supposed comfort of 'living on benefits' and facilitate moves into employment.[23] These changes have not been well received by anti-poverty campaigners, many economists and, indeed, the Scottish government. Impact analysis has demonstrated that through welfare reform, those people who are dependent on benefits will be less well off in the years ahead.[24] The UK coalition government's own analysis demonstrates that the overall impact of recent tax and benefit policies are largely regressive – reducing the incomes of those in the lower half of the income distribution while increasing those in most of the top half.[25] Notwithstanding the difficulties these changes will present to the most financially vulnerable, the purported 'simplification' of the benefits system that is part of welfare reform could, in theory, offer the means to tackle one of the most persistent and perplexing problems that exacerbate income inequality – low take-up of welfare benefits.

The Department for Work and Pensions (DWP) estimates that, for the UK as a whole, there was between £750 million and £2,040 million worth of unclaimed income-related benefits in 2009/10, a pounds sterling take-up rate of between 82 per cent and 92 per cent. It is estimated that these entitled non-recipients number between 260,000 and 620,000 families, or between 77 per cent and 89 per cent of those who are entitled to claim.[26]

Scotland is not immune from this low take-up. The same DWP estimates suggest that Scotland's share of entitled non-recipients of income-related benefits in Great Britain is 11 per cent for income support/ income-related employment and support allowance, 8 per cent for both pension credit, council tax benefit and housing benefit and 7 per cent for job-seeker's allowance. On the whole, take-up is higher in Scotland than in other parts of Britain (for all but income support and income-related employment and support allowance). Scotland's share of entitled non-recipients of income-related benefits is lower than its share of entitled recipients. Even so, there is still a significant problem of non-take-up of welfare benefits in Scotland. This, along with the low financial value of benefits to which people are entitled, is undoubtedly exacerbating income inequality.

Conclusion

Income inequality has been a persistent problem in Scotland. There is no sign of this inequality lessening and no convincing evidence that, without significant shifts in policy, practice and strategy to address low pay, skills gaps, tax policy, welfare adequacy and benefit take-up, the key drivers of change will lead to a significant reduction in income inequality in the years ahead. However, even in a time of overall pay restraint and labour market 'restructuring', it may be possible to make progress against the solidarity purpose target if sufficient attention is paid to protecting and increasing the relative share of overall pay, and wider income distribution, of those in the bottom three deciles.

Notes

1 Office for National Statistics, *Regional Gross Disposable Household Income, Spring 2013, NUTS1 Regional GDHI, 1997-2011 datasheet*, Table 1, http://www.ons.gov.uk/ons/publications/re-reference-tables.html?edition=tcm%3A77-298694

2 See http://www.scotland.gov.uk/About/Performance/scotPerforms/purpose/solidarity

3 See note 2

4 See http://www.scotland.gov.uk/Topics/Statistics/Browse/Social-Welfare/Income Poverty/CoreAnalysis

5 Note that this comparison used Scottish government data and compares them with Eurostat data.

6 Caution is required with this statistic, given that it is based on a low number of women providing income data.

7 There is a need for cautious interpretation of these data, with low returns for all occupational groupings.

8 See http://www.scotland.gov.uk/Topics/People/Equality/18500/13411

9 See http://www.closethegap.org.uk/content/gap-statistics

10 Scottish government, *Equality Outcomes and Mainstreaming Report*, 2013, Annex J, http://www.scotland.gov.uk/Publications/2013/04/2397/0

11 Office for National Statistics, *Regional Labour Market Summary: seasonally adjusted*, 2013, Web table 18sa, http://www.ons.gov.uk/ons/rel/subnational-labour/regional-labour-market-statistics/november-2013/stb-regional-labour-market-november-2013.html

12 See http://www.skillsdevelopmentscotland.co.uk/our-services

13 See http://www.scotland.gov.uk/Topics/Statistics/Browse/Lifelong-learning/TrendFEStudents

14 See http://www.scotland.gov.uk/Topics/Statistics/Browse/Lifelong-learning/API0809/Students0910

15 See note 13

16 See note 14

17 Scottish Living Wage Campaign, *The Living Wage and the Public Sector in Scotland*, Briefing, 2013

18 Scottish government, *Low Pay and Income Inequality in Scotland: a living wage*, 2010

19 D Watson, C Judge and P Hunter, *Single Status and Equal Pay in Local Government*, MSP Briefing 124, Unison

20 See www.scotland.gov.uk/News/Releases/2010/11/17080954

21 M Whittaker, *Squeezed Britain 2013*, Resolution Foundation, 2013

22 As noted in 'Falling poverty in times of austerity?' in Chapter 5.

23 Department for Work and Pensions, *Universal Credit: welfare that works*, Cmnd 7957, 2010, https://www.gov.uk/government/publications/universal-credit-welfare-that-works

24 See http://www.scotland.gov.uk/Resource/0042/00426405.pdf

25 http://cdn.hm-treasury.gov.uk/budget2013_distributional_analysis.pdf, Chart 2F

26 Department for Work and Pensions, *Income-related Benefit Estimates of Take-up in 2009/10*, 2012

Seven

Who lives in poverty?

John H McKendrick

Summary

- Children are at greater risk of poverty than both working-age adults and pensioners, with one in five of Scotland's children growing up in poverty in 2011/12 (20 per cent), compared with 18 per cent of working-age adults and 12 per cent of pensioners.
- Since 1994/95, Scotland has experienced no change in the overall number of adults of working age who are living in poverty.
- Lone parents are more than twice as likely to be living in poverty compared with couples with children.
- Gender-based poverty is most marked among people of pensionable age – two-thirds of Scotland's poorest pensioners are women.
- It is important to consider both the risk of poverty and the composition of poverty if group differences are to be fully understood.
- Poverty is unevenly distributed across Scotland. The highest numbers of people living in poverty are found in Scotland's largest cities, particularly Glasgow, although material deprivation is also prevalent in rural Scotland, particularly for older people.

This chapter identifies the likelihood of living in poverty in Scotland for different groups (risk rate) and how much of Scotland's poverty is experienced by these groups (poverty composition).The risks of poverty are not spread evenly and, as was discussed in Chapter 4, there are many causes of poverty, some of which impact more strongly on particular groups.

Poverty varies across the lifecycle, by family and household type, by social status and according to where we live. The distribution of poverty across each is considered for different groups of the population. Children, youth, working-age adults and pensioners are considered for the *lifecycle*; lone parents, partnered parents and childless adults are considered for *families and households*; work status, gender, ethnicity and disability are considered for *social status*; and local authorities, urban/rural areas and data zones (very small areas) are considered for *place*.

It is important to remember that no group is homogenous and that real people share characteristics across these groupings that may increase or reduce the amount of poverty that they encounter. For example, although children in lone-parent households are, on the whole, at greater risk of experiencing poverty than children in two-parent households (43 per cent of children in lone-parent households are living in poverty, compared with 22 per cent of children in two-parent households – see Table 7.2),[1] the risk rate of a child experiencing poverty is far lower in a lone-parent household in which the lone parent works full time, than it is in a couple household in which both adults do not work (17 per cent, compared with 69 per cent – see Table 7.2). Similarly, it must also be understood that belonging to one of the groups with a higher at-risk rate of poverty does not in itself cause poverty. As Chapter 4 explained, poverty is caused by the interaction of political, social, economic and personal factors. Thus, lone parenthood, in itself, does not cause poverty. Rather, the way in which the labour market and the taxation and welfare system operate in Scotland (and the UK) means that lone parents are more likely to experience poverty. Poverty is not an inevitable outcome for lone-parent families.

Where possible, Scottish poverty data are used. Most importantly, this chapter uses the Scottish government's analysis of the *Households Below Average Income* (HBAI) data series; this provides a measure of income poverty for children, working-age adults and pensioners in Scotland.[2] Its additional analysis on the 2011/12 dataset, which has been published online, provides detail on poverty for a wider range of groups.[3] Where there is an absence of readily available data for Scotland, reference is made to the original HBAI data for the UK to describe variation within groups – for example, to identify groups of children that are at greatest risk of experiencing poverty in Scotland.[4] Although using UK data to understand poverty in Scotland is not unproblematic, commentary is limited to that data which is considered to provide insight into poverty in Scotland. Finally, reference is also made to more broadly based measures of area-based multiple deprivation in Scotland. Once again, this data is used carefully, as it does not strictly describe poverty, but rather communities with high levels of household deprivation.

Poverty across the lifecycle

Overview

Projections over the next 25 years suggest that the population of Scotland will rise from 5.222 million in 2010 to just over 5.76 million in 2035. Thereafter, the population is projected to continue rising, passing through the six million milestone in 2070 and reaching 6,158,000 in 2080.[5] This

Table 7.1:

Age-based variation in population living in households with below 60 per cent UK median income (after housing costs), including the self-employed, Scotland, 1994/95 to 2011/12

Year	Children	Working-age adults	Pensioners	All individuals
	%	%	%	%
1994/95	30	18	29	23
1995/96	32	18	31	23
1996/97	33	19	33	25
1997/98	31	18	28	22
1998/99	31	19	27	23
1999/00	32	20	28	24
2000/01	32	22	25	24
2001/02	31	19	24	22
2002/03	27	20	25	23
2003/04	27	18	21	21
2004/05	25	18	16	19
2005/06	24	19	16	20
2006/07	25	18	15	19
2007/08	24	19	16	19
2008/09	26	19	11	19
2009/10	25	20	12	19
2010/11	21	18	12	18
2011/12	20	18	12	17

Source: Scottish government, *Poverty and Income Inequality in Scotland, 2011/12*, 2013, Table A1

Notes:
1. Figures are derived from the Family Resources Survey.
2. The modified OECD equivalisation scales have been used in the calculations and the figures refer to income after housing costs.

projected growth will reflect an excess of births over deaths through until 2028/29 and a net in-migration flow, with more people migrating to Scotland than emigrating from it.

The number of people of working age is expected to increase to 2025 (from 3.27 million to 3.48 million), before falling back slightly to 2030, and returning to growth to reach a high of almost 3.5 million in 2035. There will be similar trends for children, with their number rising from 912,000 in 2010 to 968,000 in 2025, before falling steadily to 941,000 in 2035. As might be expected, there will be steady growth throughout in the number of people of pensionable age (from 1.04 million in 2010 to 1.32 million in 2035).

People's risk of poverty and the particular barriers to escaping that poverty vary considerably over the lifecycle (Table 7.1). Although children are at highest risk of poverty, there are particular problems associated with each age stage. Least progress has been made in reducing poverty among working-age adults, and the steady progress in tackling pensioner poverty from 1996/97 to 2004/05 has halted: there has been no reduction in pensioner poverty in Scotland in the last three years. However, we should avoid over-simplifying poverty to simple statements of particular challenges to be faced at a set of discrete life stages – experience of poverty at one stage in the lifecycle can also have a significant impact on an individual's risk of poverty later on. These figures also remind us that policy interventions can impact favourably on rates of poverty: while children and pensioners benefited from governments' anti-poverty targets and strategies that were characteristic of New Labour's early years in government, those of working age did not.

Children

Despite significant improvements over time that were discussed in the previous chapter, children are still at greater risk of poverty than either working-age adults or pensioners, with one in five of Scotland's children growing up in poverty in 2010/11 (20 per cent), compared with 18 per cent of working-age adults and 12 per cent of pensioners (Table 7.1).

However as Table 7.2 shows, the risk of children experiencing poverty in the UK varies hugely on account of family type, number of siblings, the work status of parents or carers, and the age of the mother. Risk rates are particularly high in lone-parent households (43 per cent), particularly when that lone parent is not working (65 per cent), in couple households with part-time (but not full-time) work (59 per cent in the UK), in couple households in which no one works (69 per cent) and in households with three or more children (36 per cent).

Higher risks of poverty need to be understood in the context of the

Table 7.2:

Variation among children living in households with less than 60 per cent contemporary median household income (after housing costs), UK, 2011/12

	Risk rate %	Children in low-income households %
Family type		
Lone parent	43	36
Couple	22	64
Family type and work status		
Lone parent, in full-time work	17	4
Lone parent, in part-time work	31	7
Lone parent, not working	65	25
Couple, one or more full-time self-employed	29	13
Couple, both in full-time work	5	3
Couple, one in full-time work, one in part-time work	10	8
Couple, one in full-time work, one not working	30	18
Couple, one or more in part-time work	59	11
Couple, both not in work	69	12
Number of children in household		
1	25	27
2	24	40
3 or more	36	33
Age of youngest child in household		
Under 5	31	51
5 to 10	24	25
11 to 15	24	18
16 to 19	24	6

Sources: Department for Work and Pensions, *Households Below Average Income 2011/12*, 2013, Tables 4.3-4.6

Notes:
1. UK figures are derived from the Family Resources Survey.
2. The modified OECD equivalisation scales have been used in the calculations and the figures refer to income after housing costs.

overall numbers of children experiencing poverty in the UK. Thus, it is also important to note that almost two-thirds of children in poverty live in households in which an adult is working (63 per cent of children experiencing poverty); most children experience poverty in households headed by a couple (64 per cent); and most child poverty is found in households with either one or two children (67 per cent) (Table 7.2). Indeed, it is only when households are classified according to the age of the youngest child that the risk rate and proportionate share of children experiencing poverty coincide – poverty is clearly more likely to be a characteristic feature of households with very young children (Table 7.2).

Young adults

As poverty data tends to be collected at the level of the household, as opposed to the individual, young adults' poverty is often concealed by household circumstances. Disentangling young adults' circumstances from household circumstances is intriguing. For example, while some young people must remain in the parental home because they cannot afford to live independently of their parents, others whose personal

Figure 7.1:

16–19-year-olds not in education, employment or training, Scotland, 2004 to 2012

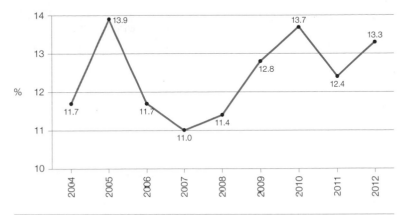

Source: Scottish government, drawn from *Annual Population Survey*,
http://www.scotland.gov.uk/Topics/Statistics/Browse/Labour-Market/MCMC-E1

Table 7.3:

Variation among working-age adults living in households with less than 60 per cent contemporary median household income (after housing costs), UK, 2011/12

	Risk rate	Working-age adults in low-income households
	%	%
Presence of children in household		
None	20	59
Some	23	41
Couple and child status		
Couple, no children	13	20
Lone man, no children	28	24
Lone woman, no children	28	15
Couple, with children	20	31
Lone parent	42	10
Work status		
Single/couple, one or more full-time self-employed	22	11
Single/couple, both in full-time work	6	10
Couple, one in full-time work, one in part-time work	8	5
Couple, one in full-time work, one not working	26	14
Single/couple, no full-time, one or more in part-time work	34	15
Workless, one or more aged over 60	32	4
Workless, one or more unemployed	71	15
Workless, other inactive	53	26

Age of head of family	No child	With child	No child	With child
16–19	35	53	6	5
20–24	26	53	12	5
25–29	15	33	6	5
30–34	17	26	4	6
35–39	19	23	3	7
40–44	24	20	5	8
45–49	19	17	5	5
50–54	17	17	6	3
55 and over	18	19	13	1

Source: Department for Work and Pensions, *Households Below Average Income 2011/12*, 2013, Tables 5.4, 5.5, 5.7 and 5.8

Notes:
1. Figures are derived from the Family Resources Survey.
2. The modified OECD equivalisation scales have been used in the calculations and the figures refer to income after housing costs.

income may be adequate may be classified as living in poverty on account of their parents' or carers' circumstances.

The primary focus of government concern about young people and poverty is to reduce the numbers who are described as being not in education, employment or training (NEET), or the 'more choices, more chances' (MC2) group as they are known in Scotland. Figure 7.1 shows that no overall progress has been made since 2004 in reducing the number of NEETs. Ominously, the proportion of Scotland's 16–19-year-olds who are not in education, training or employment is higher toward the end than the start of the period.

Working-age adults

Adults of working age in contemporary Scotland are no less likely to be living in poverty than their counterparts in the mid-1990s (Table 7.1). As for children, risk rates vary among adults of working age and, as was noted in the previous section, risk rates are higher in the UK among the youngest adults – 53 per cent of adults with children and aged under 25 years of age are living in poverty (Table 7.3).

Table 7.3 also shows that being a parent – and in particular, being a lone parent – and being in a household with less work, are associated with living in poverty for adults of working age in the UK (42 per cent of lone parents are living in poverty). These conclusions are predictable, but the poverty risk rate of working-age adults in workless households is notable – more than two-thirds living in households with unemployed adults are living in poverty (71 per cent).

Yet, once again, we must guard against reducing our understanding of poverty in the UK to the most at-risk groups. More than half of working-age adults living in poverty are from households without children (59 per cent), one-third of whom are living as a couple (20 per cent of all adults living in poverty). Over half of working-age adults living in poverty live in households in which at least one adult works (55 per cent).

Pensioners

In the years between 1996/97 and 2004/05, Scotland experienced a significant reduction in the number of pensioners living in poverty. There was another marked reduction in the number of pensioners living in poverty between 2007/08 and 2008/09. However, there has been no further reduction in the risk of pensioners living in poverty in the last three years (Table 7.1).

Families and households

Overview

In addition to demographic population change, social changes also alter the shape of the households in which we live. Among the most significant socio-population changes over the last few decades have been a decrease in family size; a decline in the number of couples who marry; more children being born outside marriage (the majority of whom are born to cohabiting couples); an increased divorce rate; and growth in the number of lone-parent households.

The number of adults living on their own in Scotland has been rising and is expected to increase by a further 50 per cent from 862,570 in 2010 (37 per cent of all households) to just under 1.29 million by 2035 (45 per cent of all households). The number of lone-parent households is also projected to rise dramatically from just over 165,760 households in 2010 to over 249,470 households in 2035, while households containing two or more adults with children is expected to fall from 420,190 (18 per cent of all households) in 2010 to 323,930 in 2035 (11 per cent).[6]

Lone parents

Lone parents are disproportionately represented among families experiencing poverty in the UK. They are more than twice as likely to live in poverty compared with couples with children (Table 7.3). The routes into lone parenthood are many and the characteristics of lone-parent families are varied. There are more than 165,000 lone parents with dependent children in Scotland, more than one-quarter of all family households (28.3 per cent).[7] However, lone parenthood is often not a permanent status, but is rather a stage in family life, lasting on average around five and a half years.[8] It has been estimated that one-third to one-half of all children in Scotland will spend some time in a lone-parent family.[9] The vast majority of lone parents are women (confirming common understanding), but often the reality of lone parenthood is at odds with some popular perceptions, with most lone parents having previously been married and the typical age of lone parents being 36 (contrasting the image of lone parents as single young mums).[10] At any point in time, less than 3 per cent of lone parents are teenagers and only 15 per cent have never lived with the father of their child.[11]

Partnered parents

Although lone-parent households are more likely to experience poverty (Table 7.3), the poverty experienced in two-parent households is equally important. For example, poverty is experienced in one in every five two-parent households in the UK (Table 7.3). Furthermore, almost one-third of the adults living in poverty in the UK are from two-parent households (31 per cent) – more than three times the number of adults living in poverty in lone-parent households (10 per cent) (Table 7.3). Thus, although the risk rate of poverty is higher for lone parenthood, there is more poverty in two-parent households in the UK.

Social status

Patterns of poverty are not only determined by the stage in life at which we are at, or our family status. Cross-cutting these factors are a range of social factors that are associated with the likelihood of living in poverty. Significant here is the impact of work status, gender, ethnicity and disability.

Workers/non-workers

Those in work in the UK are less likely to face poverty. Unsurprisingly, the risk of poverty is lower for households that are 'work-rich' (all adults working) than for households which are 'work-poor' (no-earner couples or for couples where part-time work is the only experience) (Table 7.3). Indeed, almost half of the adults of working age who are living in poverty are not in work (45 per cent), with the risk rate of poverty being even more marked (at 71 per cent) for workless households in which at least one adult is unemployed (Table 7.3).

However, these observations should not be taken to imply that poverty is absent from households with work. After all, more than half of adults of working age who are living in poverty in the UK are from households with work (55 per cent). This poverty is spread across a range of household types (defined by work status), with a significant proportion of 'all households in poverty made up of adults of working age' being self-employed (11 per cent); ones in which one is working full time and the other is not working (14 per cent); and ones in which no one is engaged in full time work, but one or more adults is engaged in part-time work (15 per cent). It is also significant to note that a number of adults experiencing poverty in the UK reside in households in which all adults are engaged in full-time work (10 per cent). Adult poverty is not solely a result of worklessness (entry into the labour market does not guarantee a route out of poverty).

Table 7.4:

Gender variation in living in households with less than 60 per cent contemporary median household income (after housing costs), UK, 2011/12

	Risk rate	Working-age adults in low-income households
	%	%
Adults by gender and children, individuals		
Men	19	35
Women	20	38
Children	27	27
Working-age adults, individuals		
Men	21	51
Women	22	49
Pensioners, individuals		
Men	13	36
Women	14	64

Source: Department for Work and Pensions, *Households Below Average Income 2011/12*, 2013, Tables 3.3, 3.4, 5.4, 5.7, 6.3 and 6.5.

Notes:
1. Figures are derived from the Family Resources Survey.
2. The modified OECD equivalisation scales have been used in the calculations and the figures refer to income after housing costs.

Gender

In the UK, more women live in poverty than men, although the risk of poverty is only marginally greater for women, relative to men (Table 7.4). The incongruence between risk and composition can be explained by the fact that women live to a longer age than men. For far too many women, later life is one that is characterised by poverty.

Scottish government analysis of the HBAI dataset adds to our understanding of gender and poverty in Scotland. Unreported in the figures for working-age adults in Table 7.4, is the higher risk of poverty for men among those working-age adults who live alone without children. Scottish government estimates, using a before housing costs measure, suggest that 21 per cent of such men live in poverty, compared with 17 per cent of women.[12] The reason that, as a whole, more working-age women live in poverty than working-age men is that there are nine times as many lone-parent households headed by women.

Disability

As Table 7.5 shows, in the UK, the risk rate of poverty is comparable between disabled pensioners and non-disabled pensioners (13 per cent, compared with 14 per cent) and disabled children and non-disabled children (27 per cent for each). In contrast, disability is associated with a higher risk of poverty for adults of working age (31 per cent for those living in a household in which someone is disabled, compared with 20 per cent of those who do not). However, there are far fewer disabled, than non-disabled people among the population living in poverty in the UK (21 per cent of people living in poverty are disabled in the UK). Scottish government analysis confirms the general finding, reporting that the risk of poverty has been significantly greater for families with a disabled adult, compared with those without disabled adults, since 2002/03.[13]

Ethnicity

Information about poverty and minority ethnic populations in Scotland is still scarce, hampered by the small number of respondents to the social surveys from which estimates are drawn, which in turn reflects the small size of minority ethnic populations in Scotland.

Table 7.5:

Variation by disability in living in households with less than 60 per cent contemporary median household income (after housing costs), 2011/12

	Risk rate %	Disability in low-income households %
Disability, whole population (by age stage)		
Disabled children	27	2
Disabled working-age adults	31	14
Disabled pensioners	13	5
Non-disabled children	27	26
Non-disabled working-age adults	20	47
Non-disabled pensioners	14	7
Disability, children (by family household composition)		
No disabled adult, no disabled child	25	70
No disabled adult, one or more disabled child	26	7
One or more disabled adult, no disabled child	35	18
One or more disabled adult, one or more disabled child	33	5
Disability, working-age adults (by family household composition)		
No disabled adult, no disabled child	19	69
No disabled adult, one or more disabled child	23	2
One or more disabled adult, no disabled child	29	28
One or more disabled adult, one or more disabled child	28	2
Disability, pensioners (household)		
No disabled pensioner	14	48
One or more disabled pensioner	13	52

Source: Department for Work and Pensions, *Households Below Average Income 2011/12*, 2013, Tables 3.3, 3.5, 4.3, 4.5, 5.6, 5.9, 6.3 and 6.5

Notes:
1. Figures are derived from the Family Resources Survey.
2. The modified OECD equivalisation scales have been used in the calculations and the figures refer to income after housing costs.

Data on the risk rate of poverty and composition of people experiencing poverty by ethnic background is available for the UK. Here, we find a higher risk rate of poverty among those of minority ethnic origin at each life stage (Table 7.6). For example, up to twice as many pensioners who are of minority ethnic origin are at risk of poverty, compared with those of

White ethnic origin (31 per cent for Asian British compared with 14 per cent for White British). However, it is important not to over-generalise the experience of poverty among minority ethnic groups. More than one-half of adult individuals (52 per cent) and children (55 per cent) of Pakistani ethnic origin are at risk of poverty, compared with around one-fifth of adult individuals (26 per cent) and one-third of children (33 per cent) of Indian ethnic origin.

However, given the very different histories and scale of minority ethnic immigration to Scotland, it cannot be assumed that these UK patterns pertain to Scotland. Scottish government analysis of available data confirms these conclusions. Using aggregated data from 2009/10 to 2011/12, it estimates that the risk of relative poverty in Scotland (using a before housing costs measure) is 15 per cent for White British, 24 per cent for Asian British and 32 per cent for other non-White minority ethnic groups (Mixed, Black, Chinese and other).[14] This analysis, while useful, also demonstrates the difficulties in using available data to understand ethnicity in Scotland; it is highly problematic to aggregate diverse ethnic groups in the manner necessary to attain a sufficient sample size for statistics on ethnicity and poverty in Scotland.

Place

Local authorities

Glasgow has far more than its fair share of Scotland's poverty, whatever estimate we use (Table 7.7). According to the UK government's estimate of local child poverty, one-third of Glasgow's children are living in a low-income family (32.2 per cent). According to the Improvement Service's modelling exercise, one in four of Glasgow's households are living in relative poverty (26 per cent). And, according to the Scottish government's Scottish Index of Multiple Deprivation, one in five households in Glasgow is judged to be income deprived (21.5 per cent) – this amounts to 127,260 people. Not surprisingly therefore, Glasgow has far more than its fair share of the 'most deprived areas' in Scotland – almost one in three of Scotland's most deprived areas are found in Glasgow alone (29.6 per cent). Although there has been a significant reduction in Glasgow's share of Scotland's 'most deprived areas' since 2004, Glasgow still has a disproportionately high share.

Table 7.6:

Variation by ethnicity in living in households with less than 60 per cent contemporary median household income (after housing costs), 2011/12

	Risk rate	Ethnic groups in low-income households
	%	%
Whole population (ethnicity based on adult head of household)		
White	19	80
Mixed	39	2
Asian or Asian British	40	11
Of which, Indian	28	*(3)*
Of which, Pakistani	53	*(4)*
Of which, Bangladeshi	52	*(1)*
Of which, Chinese	40	*(1)*
Of which, other Asian background	42	*(2)*
Black or Black British	38	5
Other ethnic group	42	2
Children (ethnicity based on adult head of household)		
White	25	76
Mixed	49	2
Asian or Asian British	46	13
Of which, Indian	33	*(4)*
Of which, Pakistani	55	*(5)*
Of which, Bangladeshi	55	*(2)*
Of which, Chinese	43	*(1)*
Of which, other Asian background	49	*(2)*
Black or Black British	44	6
Other ethnic group	48	2
Adult individuals (ethnicity based on adult head of household)		
White	19	80
Mixed	36	2
Asian or Asian British	38	12
Of which, Indian	26	*(4)*
Of which, Pakistani	52	*(4)*
Of which, Bangladeshi	50	*(1)*
Of which, Chinese	40	*(1)*
Of which, other Asian background	40	*(2)*

Black or Black British	37	4
Other ethnic group	42	2
Pensioners		
White	14	93
Asian or Asian British	31	4
Of which, Indian	27	*(2)*
Of which, Pakistani	37	*(1)*
Black or Black British	20	1
Other ethnic group	23	1

Source: Department for Work and Pensions, *Households Below Average Income 2011/12*, 2013, Tables 3.3, 3.5, 4.3, 4.5, 5.5, 5.8, 6.3 and 6.5

Notes:
1. Figures are derived from the Family Resources Survey.
2. The modified OECD equivalisation scales have been used in the calculations and the figures refer to income after housing costs.
3. The data are based on three-year averages.

Although poverty and deprivation is most prevalent in the City of Glasgow, Glasgow's neighbouring authorities of West Dunbartonshire, Inverclyde, North Lanarkshire and Renfrewshire are among those in Scotland with the highest rates of poverty. Further exacerbating west coast poverty are the high rates of poverty evident in North and East Ayrshire. Clackmannanshire, Fife and the City of Dundee are the only local authorities from the east coast of Scotland to feature prominently in the 'league table' of the local authorities with more of Scotland's poverty.

It is important to identify the parts of Scotland in which rates of poverty are most prevalent. And it is particularly important to identify which local authorities have high rates of poverty, given the growing significance being attached to local strategies to tackle poverty (see Chapter 14). It is also important not to ignore which local authorities have better than average rates of poverty, but in which reside sizeable numbers of people living in poverty.[15] For example, more people are income deprived in Edinburgh (50,730) than in every other authority in Scotland except for Glasgow and North Lanarkshire. The City of Aberdeen and Highland are also authorities with relatively favourable rates of poverty and income deprivation, but high numbers of people experiencing these conditions – for example, 19,570 and 23,510, respectively, of income-deprived people are living in these areas.

On the whole, the different ways of measuring local authority poverty in Scotland tend to describe local authorities in a similar way. Although Bramley and Watkins, quite rightly, urge caution in the findings

Table 7.7:

Six estimates of poverty in Scottish local authorities

Local authority	Population				Area measures	
	Children in low-income families	Income deprived	Households in relative poverty	Older people who are materially deprived	National share of 15% most deprived areas in Scotland	Local share of 15% most deprived areas in Scotland
	%	%	%	%	%	%
Aberdeen City	14.7	9.0	20	6	2.3	8.2
Aberdeenshire	8.5	6.8	16	5	0.5	1.7
Angus	14.5	11.0	18	6	0.3	2.1
Argyll and Bute	13.2	10.7	17	8	1.0	8.2
Clackmannanshire	22.7	15.6	20	7	1.4	21.9
Dumfries and Galloway	16.3	12.5	20	7	1.3	6.7
Dundee City	25.6	17.8	27	8	5.6	30.7
East Ayrshire	22.0	16.7	20	7	3.3	20.8
East Dunbartonshire	9.5	7.9	16	4	0.3	2.4
East Lothian	13.6	10.6	19	6	0.3	2.5
East Renfrewshire	9.4	7.8	14	4	0.7	5.8
Edinburgh City	17.9	10.4	22	7	5.5	9.8
Eilean Siar	10.3	12.6	20	10	0	0
Falkirk	17.1	13.1	18	6	1.8	9.1
Fife	19.7	13.3	20	6	5.9	12.8
Glasgow City	32.2	21.5	26	11	29.6	41.6
Highland	13.9	10.6	18	10	1.7	5.8
Inverclyde	23.6	17.9	24	8	4.5	40.0
Midlothian	17.9	12.3	18	7	0.3	2.7
Moray	12.3	9.6	17	6	0	0
North Ayrshire	25.0	17.9	23	7	4.7	25.7
North Lanarkshire	20.9	16.8	20	8	10.2	23.9
Orkney Islands	8.1	7.7	19	5	0	0
Perth and Kinross	11.2	8.7	16	5	0.6	3.4
Renfrewshire	18.6	14.7	18	7	4.9	22.4
Scotland	**18.5**	**13.4**	**20**	**7**	–	–
Scottish Borders	12.6	10.1	19	6	0.5	3.8
Shetland Islands	6.7	6.6	16	6	0	0
South Ayrshire	18.0	13.2	21	6	1.7	11.6
South Lanarkshire	17.4	14.0	19	7	5.4	13.3

Stirling	13.5	10.1	18	6	0.7	6.4
West Dunbartonshire	25.0	19.1	21	10	3.2	26.3
West Lothian	17.1	13.0	18	6	1.3	6.2

Sources: *Children in Low-Income Families Local Measure* (as at August 2011), http://hmrc.gov.uk/statistics/child-poverty-stats.htm#2; Scottish government, *Scottish Index of Multiple Deprivation 2012*, 2012, Tables 2.1c, 2.2c and 2.12; G Bramley and D Watkins, *Local Incomes and Poverty in Scotland: developing local and small area estimates and exploring patterns of income distribution, poverty and deprivation*, Improvement Service, 2013

from their modelling exercise for the Improvement Service, their work is very interesting in that it presents fresh perspectives of the geography of poverty in Scotland.[16] Distributions are much flatter for relative poverty and, in particular, for multiple deprivation in older households. Although Eilean Siar has one of the lowest rates of children living in low-income households, it has among the very highest levels of older people living with multiple deprivation. The proportion of households living in relative poverty may be higher in Dundee than Glasgow. Finally, the Scottish Index of Multiple Deprivation focus on 'small area clustering of deprivation' is wholly inadequate if used alone as an indicator of the incidence of disadvantage in island Scotland (and rural Scotland, more generally); there are no small areas of multiple deprivation in Shetland, Orkney, Eilean Siar and Moray, but rates of relative household poverty in these areas are 16, 19, 20 and 17 per cent, respectively.

The geography of local authority poverty should also focus on the wider region. Although a disproportionate share of Scotland's poverty is found in the City of Glasgow and neighbouring authorities, these swathes of poverty sit alongside East Dunbartonshire and East Renfrewshire, two of the authorities in Scotland in which poverty is least prevalent – less than one in 13 working-age adults are income deprived in these authorities, compared with one in five for the City of Glasgow.

Small area poverty

As was noted earlier, small area poverty in Scotland is of growing significance and presents challenges in interpretation. The broadly based idea of multiple deprivation demonstrates that Glasgow's problems are highly concentrated – approaching one-half of small areas in Glasgow are found to be among the 15 per cent 'most deprived areas in Scotland' (41.6 per cent), with almost one-quarter of small areas in Glasgow being among the 15 per cent 'most deprived areas in Scotland' (29.6 per cent).

The over-concentration of Scotland's most deprived areas in the City of Glasgow (referred to previously) also results in the virtual absence of 'deprived areas' in more rural authorities. For example, while 6.8 per cent of Aberdeenshire's households are 'income deprived', only 1.7 per cent of Aberdeenshire's small areas are among Scotland's 15 per cent most deprived areas (Table 7.7). The dispersion of deprivation and poverty is most striking for Eilean Siar. Although the proportion of income deprived in Eilean Siar is almost at the average for Scotland (12.6 per cent, compared with 13.4 per cent), none of Scotland's 15 per cent most deprived areas are found in this authority.

Table 7.8 lists the data zones with the highest levels of poverty and deprivation for four different measures. Office for National Statistics descriptors are used to lend character to the type of areas these represent. On the whole, large city data zones tend to feature as the very most impoverished. However, the actual data zones that are identified differ across indicators. Examples from outside the largest cities are evident (Renfrewshire and Inverclyde) and, most significantly of all, the micro-geography of multiple deprivation for older people suggests that the most intensive problems are to be found in Highland Scotland.

Urban and rural

As the discussion of poverty across Scotland's local authorities emphasises, poverty is most prevalent in urban settings, although there are rural dimensions of poverty that must be acknowledged. The Scottish government's own analysis of the HBAI data suggests that, although relative poverty is higher in urban than rural Scotland (using a before housing costs measure, 14 and 12 per cent, respectively), the difference is not so stark as to suggest that Scotland should only be concerned with poverty in urban areas. Sight must also not be lost of the fact that one-quarter of Scotland's poor live between the extremes of city and country – poverty is also experienced in Scotland's small towns, accessible and remote to larger centres of population.

Table 7.8:

Small areas with most poverty in Scotland, four measures for data zones

Rank	Area of data zone	% in poverty	Type of data zone
Children in low-income families			
1	Sighthill, Glasgow City	76.9	Multicultural inner city
2	Dalmarnock, Glasgow City	75.6	Struggling urban families
3	North Barlanark and Easterhouse South, Glasgow City	74.2	Struggling urban families
4	Maryhill East, Glasgow City	69.7	Struggling urban families
5	Greenock Town Centre and East Central, Renfrewshire	69.6	Educational centres
Income-deprived households			
1	Parkhead West and Barrowfield, Glasgow City	65	Struggling urban families
2	Drumchapel North, Glasgow City	58	Struggling urban families
3	Drumry East, Glasgow City	56	Struggling urban families
4	Paisley Ferguslie, Renfrewshire	53	Struggling urban families
5=	Keppochhill, Glasgow City	52	Struggling urban families
	Possil Park, Glasgow City	52	Struggling urban families
Households in relative poverty			
1	Sighthill, Glasgow City	46	Multicultural inner city
2=	Barmulloch, Glasgow City	45	Multicultural inner city
	Clovenstone and Drumbryden, City of Edinburgh	45	Multicultural inner city
4=	City Centre, Dundee City	44	Educational centres
	Muirhouse, City of Edinburgh	44	Struggling urban families
Older people who are materially deprived			
1	Ross and Cromarty Central, Highland	89	Countryside communities
2	Sutherland North and West, Highland	69	Countryside communities
3	Sutherland South, Highland	63	Countryside communities
4	Sutherland North and West, Highland	52	Countryside communities
5	Badenoch and Strathspey South, Highland	51	Farming and forestry

Sources: *Children in Low Income Families Local Measure* (as at August 2011), http://hmrc.gov.uk/statistics/child-poverty-stats.htm#2; Scottish government, *Scottish Index of Multiple Deprivation 2012*, 2012, Tables 2.1c, 2.2c and 2.12; G Bramley and D Watkins, *Local Incomes and Poverty in Scotland: developing local and small area estimates and exploring patterns of income distribution, poverty and deprivation*, Improvement Service, 2013

Conclusion

This chapter has highlighted how the risk of poverty for people in Scotland is related to their age, the kinds of households in which they live, their social status and the places where they live. Marked and important variations are apparent across these factors. However, it is also clear that poverty impacts on people to a greater or lesser extent regardless of how old they are, who they live with, their gender, ethnicity, work status or geographical location. It is, therefore, important to examine risk of poverty alongside the overall proportion of the population who make up these different groups and places – the people and places with the highest risk of poverty do not necessarily account for the greatest numbers of people living in poverty.

Notes

1 This poverty gap has reduced significantly in recent years, as lone parents' risk of poverty has fallen significantly. In *Poverty in Scotland 2007*, the respective risk rates of poverty that were reported were 48% compared with 20% and in *Poverty in Scotland 2011*, the risk rates were reported as 50% and 24%.

2 Scottish government, *Poverty and Income Inequality in Scotland, 2011/12*, 2013

3 http://www.scotland.gov.uk/Topics/Statistics/Browse/Social-Welfare/Income Poverty/CoreAnalysis

4 Department for Work and Pensions, *Households Below Average Income, 2011/12*, 2013

5 Registrar General for Scotland, Projected Population of Scotland: 2010 based, 2011, http://www.gro-scotland.gov.uk/statistics/theme/population/projections/scotland/2010-based/index.html

6 See note 5

7 http://www.gro-scotland.gov.uk/statistics/theme/households/projections/2010-based/tables.html

8 One Parent Families Scotland, *One Parent Families: a profile*, 2009

9 See note 8

10 See note 8

11 See note 8

12 See note 3

13 See note 3

14 See note 3

15 Scottish government, *Scottish Index of Multiple Deprivation 2012*, 2012, Table 2.12

16 G Bramley and D Watkins, *Local Incomes and Poverty in Scotland: developing local and small area estimates and exploring patterns of income distribution, poverty and deprivation*, Improvement Service, 2013

Eight
What is life like for people experiencing poverty?
John H McKendrick

Summary

- The financial wellbeing of low-income households has worsened in recent years, and the gap between low-income and high-income households remains marked.
- Exposure to the risk of fuel poverty is highly skewed by household income, with virtually all households with the lowest income experiencing fuel poverty, in contrast to virtually none of the highest earning households.
- For both adults and children, low-income living is associated with a range of poorer health outcomes.
- It is problematic to 'blame the poor' for adverse health outcomes, with low-income living sometimes being associated with more positive health behaviours – for example, there are lower levels of alcohol consumption among low-income households.
- Living in a deprived area is generally associated with less neighbourhood satisfaction.
- Children from deprived areas are consistently reported to have poorer access to local opportunities for safe play and to participate in fewer activities, compared with children living beyond these areas.

Introduction

This chapter considers the experience of living in poverty in contemporary Scotland, one of the wealthiest countries in the world. It focuses on the here and now. It does not speculate on the long-term consequences of living in poverty, or claim that people currently experiencing poverty will be forevermore condemned to a life of adversity. The experience of poverty and deprivation in Scotland is described in terms of financial wellbeing, health, community life and children's leisure lives. It draws on household income data and data comparing people living in and beyond multiply deprived areas. Without identification of the point at which low income reflects poverty for different household types, caution is required when using distribution of household income data to represent poverty. Similarly, living in a multiply deprived area does not imply living in poverty (nor does living outside a multiply deprived area imply an absence of poverty). Care is taken in interpreting these data when discussing poverty in Scotland. The chapter is based on quantitative data, only using qualitative data to introduce each theme. However, we begin by describing the importance of testimony and introducing the array of qualitative insights that enable us to better understand the reality of 'living with poverty in contemporary Scotland'.

More than numbers

There are many studies that have used the words of people experiencing poverty to convey to others what it is like to live in poverty in Scotland. Some of these have been written by academics,[1] others by anti-poverty activists,[2] still others by collectives of which people experiencing poverty are part.[3] It has been less common, although not unknown, for accounts to be written about poverty by those currently living with it.[4]

Just as it is important for those concerned to tackle poverty to update and refresh poverty statistics, it is also important that they engage with contemporary experiences, as conveyed by those currently living in poverty. In recent years, there have been a number of significant additions in Scotland to the canon of knowledge of what it is like to live in poverty. In partnership with community researchers, Fiona McHardy of the Poverty Alliance has published two substantial reports that have explored what living with poverty is like for young people in Stirling[5] and lone parents in Fife.[6] The Scottish Refugee Council has built on earlier work and reports the contemporary poverty experiences of refugees living in Scotland.[7] Perhaps most importantly of all, the drawing to a close of Scotland's first Poverty Truth Commission in 2011 has not implied the loss of a rich source of first-hand testimony that conveys the harsh reality and multi-faceted problems of living with poverty.[8] On the contrary, the insights that can be gleaned from those commissioners who are living in poverty are available in print,[9] in video[10] (including song[11]) and the commissioners have continued their work, having a strong presence at, and making powerful contributions to, a whole range of anti-poverty debates, initiatives and seminars in recent years.

'Nothing about us, without us, is for us', is the mantra of Scotland's Poverty Truth Commission, and is a reminder that all anti-poverty activity should seek to empower individuals and communities as they seek change to improve both their lives and Scottish society. To try to account for the experience of poverty in numbers might appear to fall far short of this goal. Numbers cannot fully capture the reality of what life is like for people living in poverty. In particular, the numbers that are available to us are unable to tell us what people think or how people experiencing poverty make sense of this condition. However, numbers are not without value. The numbers that are reported in this chapter summarise the collective experiences of people experiencing poverty. They provide insight into the scale of the problem that persists in Scotland and the injustice that nega-tive life experiences are more likely to be encountered by those living in poverty. It should always be acknowledged that behind every number is a real life.

Financial wellbeing

> 'It was very difficult. I did not eat during these times [to ensure that children can be provided for at Christmas, birthdays, school holidays or religious holidays].'[12]

For people living on a low income, a lack of money leads to a fragile exis-tence that involves the ever-present threat of falling into debt, being forced to choose between one necessity and another, going without, being trapped in 'dead-end' jobs, and being unable to save money.

National survey data reinforce these observations. Although slightly more people from low-income households report that they 'manage finan-cially well' than 'do not manage well' (30 per cent, compared with 27 per cent, for those households with an annual net income of less than £10,000), it is much more likely that those in Scotland who report that they are not managing their finances well are from low-income households (the 27 per cent compares with only 4 per cent from those in households with more than £30,000 annual net income).[13] It is more difficult to manage money well when working with a very low income. Similarly, while only

Table 8.1:

Savings and debt by net annual household income, Scotland, 2012

	£0–£10,000 %	£10,001–£20,000 %	£20,001–£30,000 %	Over £30,000 %	Scotland %
Savings: respondent or partner has any savings or investments					
Yes	49	60	69	82	66
No	40	33	24	10	26
Refused to say	10	7	6	7	7
Don't know	1	1	1	1	1
Debt: respondent or partner owes any money on credit, store or charge card					
Yes	12	20	35	42	66
No	84	77	65	58	69
Refused to say	4	3	3	4	5
Base	*500*	*1,150*	*800*	*890*	*3,330*

Source: Scottish government, *Scotland's People Annual Report: results from 2012 Scottish Household Survey*, 2013, Figure 6.4 and Table 6.8

Note: Without identification of the point at which low income reflects poverty, distribution of household income data does not measure poverty. Furthermore, the income data presented in this table are not equivalised. Care has to be taken in interpreting this data when discussing poverty in Scotland.

one-quarter of those from Scotland's (15 per cent) most deprived areas report that they are 'managing well', more than half of those living outside these areas report likewise (27 per cent, compared with 51 per cent, respectively).[14]

A more complex pattern of response is found for debt and 'savings or investments' – low-income households are less likely than high-income households to have both 'savings or investments' (a negative finding for low-income households) and credit, store or charge card debt (a positive finding for low-income households). As Table 8.1 shows, households with the lowest annual net income are four times as likely not to have savings or investments (40 per cent of those with an annual income of less than £10,000, compared with 10 per cent of those with an annual income of £30,000 or above). Thus, an unacceptable and disproportionate share of low-income households in Scotland does not have the financial means which lend themselves towards stability and enable those households to

Table 8.2:

Aspects of consumption by annual household income, Scotland, 2012

	£0–£6,000 %	£6,001–£10,000 %	£10,001–£15,000 %	£15,001–£20,000 %	£20,001–£25,000 %	£25,001–£30,000 %	£30,001–£40,000 %	Over £40,000 %	Scotland %
Cars available for private use									
Yes	39	36	49	63	79	87	93	98	70
No	61	64	51	37	21	13	7	2	30
Base	*310*	*1,150*	*1,960*	*1,620*	*1,350*	*990*	*1,320*	*1,560*	*10,260*
Home internet access									
Yes	58	47	53	69	86	94	95	98	76
No	42	53	47	31	14	6	5	2	24
Base	*100*	*370*	*630*	*550*	*420*	*320*	*400*	*520*	*3,300*

Source: Scottish government, *Scotland's People Annual Report: results from 2012 Scottish Household Survey*, 2013, Tables 8.2 and 9.1

Note: Without identification of the point at which low income reflects poverty, distribution of household income data does not measure poverty. Furthermore, the income data presented in this table are not equivalised. Care has to be taken in interpreting this data when discussing poverty in Scotland.

fend off unforeseen financial crises. On the other hand, low-income households are more than three times as likely as the most affluent households not to have any credit card, store card or charge card debt. Of course, this may not necessarily mean that debt is not a problem for low-income households.[15] Indeed, an exclusive focus on card-based debt masks an underlying credit problem with a reliance on high-interest modes of credit, such as payday loans.

Living on a low income is also associated with less ready access to those resources that are important to participate fully in contemporary Scotland, including those helpful in accessing the world of work. As Table 8.2 shows, households in Scotland with lower net incomes are most likely not to have home internet access, and not to have access to a car for private use. Thus, the majority of households with an annual net income of less than £6,000 do not have access to a car for private use (61 per cent) compared with a tiny minority of households with an annual income of over £40,000 (2 per cent). Many also do not have access to the internet at home (in this instance, 42 per cent, compared with 2 per cent, respec-

Table 8.3:

Household fuel poverty and extreme fuel poverty by weekly household income, Scotland, 2011

Weekly net household income	Number of households			
	Not 'fuel poor'	Fuel poor	Extreme fuel poor	Sample size
Less than £100	0	52,000	42,000	65
£100 – £199.99	41,000	291,000	96,000	444
£200 – £299.99	285,000	207,000	30,000	652
£300 – £399.99	304,000	70,000	11,000	483
£400 – £499.99	246,000	28,000	4,000	366
£500 – £699.99	366,000	22,000	3,000	541
£700 or more	443,000	14,000	0	595
All Scotland	1,684,000	684,000	185,000	3,146

Source: J Robertson and others, *Scottish House Condition Survey: key findings 2011*, Scottish government, 2012, Table 28

Notes:
1. The definition of fuel poverty that is used was specified by the Scottish Executive in the Fuel Poverty Statement, 2002. Households are defined as 'fuel poor' if they would be required to spend more than 10 per cent of household income on fuel. Households in extreme fuel poverty would be required to spend more than 20 per cent of their household income on fuel. See T Wilson and others, *Fuel Poverty Evidence Review: defining, measuring and analysing fuel poverty in Scotland*, Scottish government, 2012 for more detailed discussion. The 'not 'fuel poor' category includes a sub-category of 'marginal fuel poor' (who spend over 8% to 10% of their household income on fuel costs.
2. Without identification of the point at which low income reflects poverty, distribution of household income data does not measure poverty. Furthermore, the income data presented in this table are not equivalised. Care has to be taken in interpreting this data when discussing poverty in Scotland.

tively). Consumption that is pertinent to accessing the world of work does throw a consistent 'glitch' at the lower end of the household income scale in that those on the very lowest income (£0–£6,000 per annum) have higher consumption than those with a 'slightly higher' low income (£6,001 to £10,000).[16]

Trend data cautions against a presumption of progress. In recent years, rates of access to a car have fallen for many income groups, including those with the very lowest household incomes (from 43 per cent in 2009 to 39 per cent in 2012, for those with less than £6,000 per annum, reversing the trend in the years preceding that). Indeed, there is now a minority of car owners among households with an annual household income of less than £15,000 (49 per cent in 2011 for those receiving between £10,001 and £15,000 per annum, compared with 55 per cent in 2007).

If we step back to consider the basic necessities of existence, we

Table 8.4:

Benefit units receiving different types of benefits by national region in the UK, 2011/12

	Scotland	England	Wales	Northern Ireland	UK
	%	%	%	%	%
Working tax credit	5	6	8	7	6
Child tax credit	12	13	15	16	13
Income support	5	4	4	7	4
Pension credit	5	5	6	5	5
Housing benefit	14	13	13	13	13
Council tax benefit*	18	16	17	1	16
Retirement pension	25	25	29	23	26
Jobseeker's allowance	4	4	5	6	4
Incapacity benefit	4	2	4	4	3
Severe disablement allowance	–	–	–	1	–
Attendance allowance	2	3	3	2	3
Carer's allowance	1	1	2	2	1
Disability living allowance (care component)	7	6	9	9	7
Disability living allowance (mobility component)	7	6	9	10	6
Industrial injuries disablement benefit	–	1	1	–	1
Child benefit	20	23	23	26	23
Any income-related benefit	22	20	22	25	20
Any non-income-related benefit	55	57	62	60	57
All in receipt of benefit	60	61	66	65	61
All in receipt of tax credits	13	14	17	17	14
All not in receipt of state support	40	39	33	34	38
Sample size	3,816	17,289	1,055	2,274	24,434

Source: S Clay and others, *Family Resources Survey 2011/12*, Department for Work and Pensions, 2013,Table 2.9

Note: *This is support for rates, payable to those receiving housing benefit in Northern Ireland.

find unacceptable deprivations among Scotland's poorest people, despite some significant progress being made in recent years. For example, the Scottish government estimates that, until the sharp fuel price hikes of Autumn 2011, fuel poverty in Scotland had fallen from its peak of 2009. Furthermore, as Table 8.3 shows, although fuel poverty is almost absent among households in Scotland with a net weekly income of over £700, in sharp contrast, it seems to be a universal experience for all with a net weekly income of less than £100 and for the vast majority of those house-holds with a net weekly income of between £100 and £199 and between £200 and £299.

Although not markedly different from other national regions in the UK, Scotland will be vulnerable to the UK government's welfare reforms, given that the majority of households in Scotland are in receipt of some form of benefit (60 per cent) and a significant minority are in receipt of tax credits (13 per cent) (see Table 8.4).

Health

'What is poverty? Worry, worry worry. Everything is going up in price, everything apart from my wages. I feel physically sick with worry and I'm so cold… My hair is falling out with the stress. I don't see how things can change for me.'[17]

The problems caused by low-income living extend far beyond the ability to consume, with people living in poverty sensing that their worth is often rated on account of living in poverty. Being seen to be poor is to be seen to be less worthy, and leads to low self-esteem. People living on a low income experience stigmatisation on account of their poverty, a lack of emotional and practical support that could be provided by those in more powerful positions, and a feeling of being unable to participate fully in one's community.

Mental wellbeing is, not surprisingly, less than satisfactory among low-income households in Scotland. Table 8.5 presents evidence of the three indicators that are used in Scotland to gauge the psychological health of adults using standard measurement tools from the Scottish Health Survey. Although men and women report comparable overall levels of life satisfaction, for both of the other measures of mental distress among adults, and at each income level except middle income, women report more mental distress and less mental wellbeing than men. For example, signs of psychological disorder are shown by 29 per cent of women and 25 per cent of men in the households with the lowest income (Table 8.5). More than this, differences become more marked at the lower end of the income spectrum – for example, for men, there is a sharp dif-ference between quintile four (11 per cent showing signs of a psychologi-cal disorder) and those living in households with the very lowest household income levels (25 per cent).

Table 8.5:

Mental and physical health by household income groups (quintiles), across age and sex, Scotland, 2011/12

	20% lowest income household	Quintile 2	Quintile 3	Quintile 4	20% highest income household
Adults, self-assessed general health as 'bad or very bad', % in quintile					
Men	24	8	8	3	3
Women	18	14	9	4	3
Adults, mean life satisfaction					
Men	6.8	7.5	7.7	7.9	8.0
Women	7.0	7.3	7.8	8.0	8.1
Adults, Warwick Edinburgh Mental Wellbeing Scale					
Men	47.1	50.0	50.1	51.7	52.1
Women	45.9	47.5	50.5	51.3	51.4
Adults, 'possible presence of psychological disorder' from General Health Questionnaire, % in quintile					
Men	25	11	14	9	7
Women	29	21	11	12	15
Children, wellbeing, % in quintile					
Boys, SDQ of 14 or more	31	21	17	9	9
Girls, SDQ of 14 or more	16	12	8	7	2
Adults, longstanding illness, % in quintile					
Men	57	50	40	41	33
Women	60	52	47	47	44
Children, longstanding illness, % in quintile					
Boys	31	16	23	13	15
Girls	11	9	17	10	10

Source: L Rutherford and others, *Scottish Health Survey 2012*, Scottish government, 2013, Supplementary web tables, W3, W11, W15, W43, W47 and W731, http://www.scotland.gov.uk/Topics/Statistics/Browse/Health/scottish-health-survey/Publications/webtables

Notes:

1. Without identification of the point at which low income reflects poverty, distribution of household income data does not measure poverty. Furthermore, the income data presented in this table are not equivalised. Care has to be taken in interpreting this data when discussing poverty in Scotland.
2. Adults aged 16 and over were asked to rate their general health on a five-point scale ranging from 'very bad' through a mid-point of 'fair' to 'very good'.
3. Adults aged 16 and over were asked to rate their life satisfaction on a scale of 0 to 10, where zero represented 'very dissatisfied' and 10 represented 'very satisfied' (intervening points were not labelled). The *Scottish Health Survey* defines 8 as 'average satisfaction.'
4. The Warwick Edinburgh Mental Wellbeing Scale is used in Scotland as the national indicator to measure mental wellbeing. Fourteen items are assessed, with each rated from 1 (none of the time) to 5 (all of the time). Lower scores represent lower mental wellbeing, with scores ranging from 14 through 70 in total.
5. The General Health Questionnaire consists of 12 questions on mental distress and psychological ill health.

A point is allocated for every time an experience is described as occurring 'more than usual' or 'much more than usual' over the last few weeks. A score of four or more is taken as sign of a possible psychiatric disorder.
6. The Strengths and Difficulties Questionnaire (SDQ) was answered by parents on behalf of children aged 4-12 years. The SDQ comprises 25 questions covering aspects such as consideration, hyperactivity, malaise, mood, sociability, obedience, anxiety and unhappiness. These can be condensed into five component symptom scores corresponding to emotional symptoms, conduct problems, hyperactivity, peer problems and pro-social behaviour, ranging in value from 0 to 10. A total SDQ score (referred to here as a total deviance score) was calculated by summing the scores from each domain, with the exception of pro-social behaviour, ranging from 0 to 40. An SDQ of 14 or more reflects borderline or abnormal total difficulties.
7. Respondents reporting that they (or their child) had a physical or mental health condition that had lasted, or was likely to last, for 12 months or more were considered to have a long-term condition.

Physical health is also affected by living life on a low income. For both adults and children, there is a clear gender divide between those living with and without a limiting long-term illness (Table 8.5). Interestingly, for adults, at every income level, more women than men report having a limiting long-term illness. In contrast, for children, more boys than girls are reported to have a limiting long-term illness at every income level. In addition to the gender differences, physical ill health is also much more prevalent in low-income, compared to high-income, households.

Men and women from less deprived areas live longer and enjoy more years in good health (see Figure 8.1). The harsh realities of life expectancy statistics and healthy life expectancy statistics make for unpalatable reading. Men in the most deprived places in Scotland can expect to spend 20 of their 70 years being 'not healthy', compared with men in the most affluent places who can expect to spend 13 of their 81 years being 'not healthy'. Although women live longer, they can also expect to spend more years than men in ill health. Thus, women in the poorest places in Scotland can expect to spend over 24 of their 77 years being 'not healthy', compared with women in the most affluent places who can expect to spend just 14 of their 84 years being 'not healthy'. Indeed, expressed as area statistics, these figures most probably underestimate the different life experiences and expectancies of Scotland's rich, comfortable and poor.

Clearly, deprivation and low income prevent men and women from enjoying healthy lives. There is a train of thought that would apportion blame to 'the poor' for living an unhealthy life. Indeed, there is some evidence that men and women living in households with the lowest income are living less healthy lifestyles than those in the most affluent households.[18] However, it is too simplistic to reduce health behaviours to lifestyle choice and 'blame the poor', for three reasons. First, a culture of 'poor bashing' tends to marginalise the structural barriers and opportunity con-

Figure 8.1:

Life expectancy and healthy life expectancy by sex and deprivation area status, Scotland, 2009/10

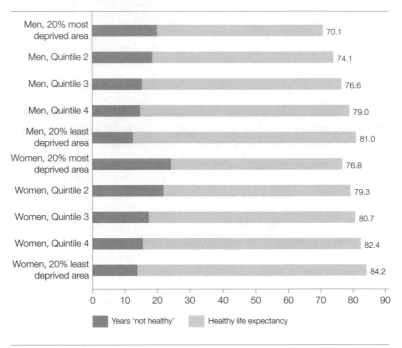

Source: Scottish Public Health Observatory, Healthy Life Expectancy Deprivation Quintiles, 2012, Tables 1 and 2, available at http://www.scotpho.org.uk/population-dynamics/healthy-life-expectancy/data/deprivation-quintiles

Notes:
1. Uses 'self-reported health' as a measure of ill health. The calculation of a healthy life expectancy was amended for 2009/10 and is explained in a technical paper that can be accessed at http://www.scotpho.org.uk/downloads/hle/HLE-technical-paper-2013-v5.pdf.
2. Living in a multiply deprived area does not imply living in poverty (nor does living outside a multiply deprived area imply an absence of poverty). Care has to be taken in interpreting this data when discussing poverty in Scotland.

straints that make it more difficult to live a healthy lifestyle. Second, 'blaming the poor' is a wholly inadequate response to the health of children. Whether or not adult guardians are to 'blame' for children's health conditions should not be used as a reason to absolve from responsibility local service providers for improving health among children in low-income households. For example, although evidence suggests that children in low-income households have a poorer quality diet (Table 8.6), it must be acknowledged that not all of their food consumption is within the household and that breakfast clubs, school lunches and after-school clubs each have a role to play in enhancing the quality of children's diet. Finally, not all of the evidence suggests that people in low-income households lead a less healthy life. For example, and in sharp contrast to the public persona of people experiencing poverty, alcohol is consumed more regularly and consumption of alcohol above recommended levels is greater for both men and women from high-income, as opposed to low-income, households (and also for women not from multiply deprived areas, compared to those living within) (Table 8.6). On the other hand, although affluent Scots consume more alcohol, there is a greater likelihood in lower income households for alcohol consumption leading to alcohol use disorders and social problems.

The complexities of understanding the relationship between low income and health outcomes is further demonstrated in Table 8.7, which considers healthy weight issues. Boys from low-income households are more likely than girls from low-income households to be overweight (43 per cent, compared with 36 per cent for those from the 20 per cent lowest income households); men are no more likely than women to be overweight from this same household income group (62 per cent for both women and men). For both boys and girls, there is a marked increase in the incidence of being overweight between those from the lowest income households and highest income households (43 per cent for girls, compared with 24 per cent for boys, and 36 per cent, compared with 25 per cent for girls, respectively). Being underweight is far less prevalent, particularly for boys from the lowest income households. Taken together, whereas boys, girls and women from low-income households are less likely than their counterparts in higher income households to have a healthy weight, the opposite is true for men.

Community life and environment

'Contrary to the images often portrayed in the media, [people living in poverty] are decent, honest, inventive and determined to change their communities and their personal situations.'[19]

People experiencing poverty are more likely to be living in deprived areas with inadequate services and facilities. Their physical environments are

Table 8.6:

Selected health behaviours by household income groups (quintiles), across sex and age, Scotland, 2012

	20% highest income household %	Quintile 2 %	Quintile 3 %	Quintile 4 %	20% lowest income household %
Drinking, men					
Never drunk alcohol	10	2	5	6	2
Ex-drinker	14	5	8	9	2
Drinks within government guidelines	36	43	44	41	41
Drinks in excess of government guidelines	40	51	44	44	54
Drinking, women					
Never drunk alcohol	9	6	8	7	5
Ex-drinker	15	7	9	12	4
Drinks within government guidelines	47	53	48	47	43
Drinks in excess of government guidelines	29	34	35	34	48
Drinking, men					
Low-risk drinking or abstinence	71	79	73	77	72
Hazardous drinking	18	19	22	20	25
Harmful drinking	7	2	2	1	2
Possible alcohol dependence	4	0	3	2	0
Drinking, women					
Low-risk drinking or abstinence	83	92	90	87	84
Hazardous drinking	13	7	8	11	15
Harmful drinking	2	0	2	1	1
Possible alcohol dependence	2	1	1	1	0
Likelihood of boys aged 2–15 consuming selected foodstuffs					
Oily fish, at least weekly	8	24	24	12	31
Drink skimmed/semi-skimmed milk	43	70	49	53	69
Drink non-diet soft drinks, daily	54	32	37	48	28
Chips, at least twice weekly	60	33	34	50	24
Potatoes, pasta or rice, at least five times week	33	61	53	44	69

Source: L Rutherford and others, *Scottish Health Survey 2012*, Scottish government, 2013, Supplementary web tables W651, W663 and W483

Notes:
1. Without identification of the point at which low income reflects poverty, distribution of household income data does not measure poverty. Furthermore, the income data presented in this table are not equivalised. Care has to be taken in interpreting this data when discussing poverty in Scotland.
2. The Scottish Health Survey uses the UK government's recommendations that women should not drink more than 2 to 3 units of alcohol per day and men should not exceed 3 to 4 units per day.
3. The Scottish Health Survey uses the AUDIT questionnaire to determine alcohol risks. Ten questions are asked with respondents answering on a five-point scale ranging from 0 (never) through to 4 (four or more times per week). A score of 0–7 is low risk, 8–15 is defined as hazardous, 16–19 as harmful and 20 or more as 'warrants further investigation for possible alcohol dependence'.

Table 8.7:

Weight problems, by household income groups (quintiles), across sex and age, Scotland, 2012

	20% lowest income household %	Quintile 2 %	Quintile 3 %	Quintile 4 %	20% highest income household %
Underweight					
Boys	1	1	2	–	4
Girls	2	2	3	3	1
Men	4	2	1	1	1
Women	2	2	2	2	3
Overweight or obese					
Boys	43	35	31	29	24
Girls	36	23	30	21	25
Men	62	70	67	71	70
Women	62	65	63	61	49

Source: L Rutherford and others, *Scottish Health Survey 2012*, Scottish government, 2013, Supplementary web tables W847 and W875

Notes:
1. Without identification of the point at which low income reflects poverty, distribution of household income data does not measure poverty. Furthermore, the income data presented in this table are not equivalised. Care has to be taken in interpreting this data when discussing poverty in Scotland.
2. Children are aged 2–15. Men are aged 16 or over.
3. BMI is used to define underweight and overweight (either side of the healthy BMI range of 18.5 to 25). See L Rutherford and others, *Scottish Health Survey 2012*, Scottish government, 2013, section 7.2.3 of the source report for details.

Table 8.8:

Perceptions of personal safety by deprivation area status, Scotland, 2012

	15% most deprived areas %	Rest of Scotland %	Scotland %
How safe respondent feels walking alone at night			
Safe (very, fairly)	66	85	82
Unsafe (bit, very)	33	14	17
Don't know	1	1	1
Base	*1,320*	*8,160*	*9,480*
How safe respondent feels at home at night			
Safe (very, fairly)	95	98	98
Unsafe (bit, very)	5	2	2
Don't know	0	0	0
Base	*1,400*	*8,490*	*9,890*

Source: Scottish government, *Scotland's People Annual Report: results from 2012 Scottish Household Survey*, 2013, Table 4.13

Note: Living in a multiply deprived area does not imply living in poverty (nor does living outside a multiply deprived area imply an absence of poverty). Care has to be taken in interpreting this data when discussing poverty in Scotland.

often badly cared for and 'depressing', and they are more likely to feel unsafe in their neighbourhood.

Table 8.8 uses information from the Scottish Household Survey to compare perceptions of night-time safety at home and in the wider neighbourhood. On the whole, the majority of people in Scotland perceive themselves to be safe in their own homes at night, and there is little significant difference between those living in the most deprived areas and the rest of Scotland in the proportion who feel unsafe in their own home. However, there is a marked difference in perceived safety in the wider neighbourhood at night. Twice as many people from the most deprived areas in Scotland do not feel safe walking alone at night in their neighbourhood (33 per cent, compared with 14 per cent of those living outside the most deprived areas).

Local area differences extend beyond perceptions of safety. As Table 8.9 shows, people living in the most deprived areas of Scotland (also the areas with a disproportionate share of people experiencing poverty in Scotland) are more likely to express displeasure over anti-social behaviour

Table 8.9:

Experience of neighbourhood problems, by deprivation area status, Scotland, 2012

	15% most deprived areas %	Rest of Scotland %	Scotland %
General anti-social behaviour			
Vandalism, graffiti, damage to property	13	5	7
Groups or individual harassing others	8	3	3
Drug misuse or dealing	13	4	6
Rowdy behaviour	18	10	11
Neighbour problems			
Noisy neighbours/loud parties	18	9	10
Neighbour disputes	9	4	5
Rubbish or litter lying around	28	20	21
Animal nuisance, such as noise or dog fouling	34	27	28

Source: Scottish government, *Scotland's People Annual Report: results from 2012 Scottish Household Survey*, 2013, Table 4.9

Note: Living in a multiply deprived area does not imply living in poverty (nor does living outside a multiply deprived area imply an absence of poverty). Care has to be taken in interpreting this data when discussing poverty in Scotland.

in their neighbourhood (13 per cent have experienced vandalism, graffiti or damage to property, compared with 'only' 5 per cent expressing such concern outside areas of deprivation). Similarly, residents of multiply deprived areas are more likely to acknowledge problems with their neighbours (34 per cent reported animal nuisance, compared with only 27 per cent of those living outside deprived areas).

Life on a low income means one is less able to participate fully in society. Whether such participation is manifest in education or leisure, political participation or having a voice in local/national decision making, it is a fundamental right to which many people experiencing poverty have less experience and access. As Table 8.10 shows, those living in households with lower incomes are also less likely to give up time to assist as a volunteer or organiser – for example, 19 per cent of those in households with an annual income of less than £6,000, compared with the Scottish average of 29 per cent.

Table 8.10:

Whether gave up time to help as a volunteer/organiser in the last 12 months by annual household income, Scotland, 2012

	£3,000–£6,000 %	£6,001–£10,000 %	£10,001–£15,000 %	£15,001–£20,000 %	£20,001–£25,000 %	£25,001–£30,000 %	£30,001–£40,000 %	Over £40,000 %	Scotland %
Yes	19	22	22	24	28	32	34	40	29
No	81	78	78	76	72	68	66	60	71
Base	*290*	*1,100*	*1,870*	*1,540*	*1,260*	*900*	*1,190*	*1,380*	*9,530*

Source: Scottish government, *Scotland's People Annual Report: results from 2012 Scottish Household Survey*, 2013, Tables 8.2 and 9.1

Note: Without identification of the point at which low income reflects poverty, distribution of household income data does not measure poverty. Furthermore, the income data presented in this table are not equivalised. Care has to be taken in interpreting this data when discussing poverty in Scotland.

Growing up in poverty and in deprived areas

'I don't mind my choices being limited, but my sons are and that's frustrating.' (Lone parent, Fife)[20]

It is widely recognised that having adequate opportunities to play and participating in a range of activities is beneficial for children.[21] The Growing Up in Scotland research provides the means for exploring the impact of poverty on the lives of Scotland's youngest children. A series of reports, published in 2010 and 2011, have demonstrated how Scotland's youngest children fare if they are living in poverty: developmental differences are evident for physical wellbeing, social skills, emotional health, cognitive ability and communication skills;[22] significant events, such as a household migration or a parental separation, are both more likely to be experienced by children living in low-income families and to lead to children subsequently living in a low-income family;[23] and persistent poverty is experienced by many young children, with analysis suggesting that persistently poor children are more likely to face disadvantages than temporarily poor children.[24]

Table 8.11:

Opportunities for children's play, by deprived area status, 2012

	Playground %	Park %	Games pitch (including football) %	Field/open space %	School playground %	Natural/wooded area %	Access to at least one play area/street play %	Base %
Availability of play area								
Deprived area	42	51	36	34	21	20	81	*220*
Rest of Scotland	54	59	45	52	36	47	89	*1,330*
Safe for children to walk or cycle to play area on their own								
Deprived area	51	43	48	44	–	–	43	*50*
Rest of Scotland	70	62	62	66	66	47	59	*400*
Safe to visit play area with two or three friends								
Deprived area	60	53	61	54	–	–	48	*50*
Rest of Scotland	75	70	70	72	71	53	61	*400*
Concerns of bullying by children in play area								
Deprived area	68	60	56	60	–	–	42	*50*
Rest of Scotland	37	40	37	33	32	37	24	*400*
Concerns of children being harmed by adults in play area								
Deprived area	51	55	48	53	–	–	38	*50*
Rest of Scotland	36	36	34	33	28	43	24	*400*
Youngest age at which it would be safe for child to visit play area without supervision								
Deprived area	9.8	10.3	10.2	10.6	–	–	9.1	*40*
Rest of Scotland	9.2	9.4	9.4	9.2	9.3	10.3	8.5	*380*

Source: Scottish government, *Scotland's People Annual Report: results from 2012 Scottish Household Survey*, 2013, Tables 7.6–7.8

Note:
1. Data in these tables report findings from households containing a child aged between 6 and 12 years old.
2. Living in a multiply deprived area does not imply living in poverty (nor does living outside a multiply deprived area imply an absence of poverty). Care has to be taken in interpreting this data when discussing poverty in Scotland.
3. Column heading 'Access to at least one play area' pertains to the rows on 'Availability of play area'.
4. 'Deprived area' in this instance means one that is included in Scotland's 15% most deprived areas.

Data from the Scottish Household Survey also provides some insight into the impact on play and activity participation of children living in multiply deprived areas. Although the most recent round of data draws on a small sample, it reaffirms earlier findings, which were based on a larger sample.

Compared with other children, those from deprived areas in Scotland are reported to have less ready access to different types of play space in their local area; there are greater parental concerns for children's safety travelling to these play spaces; there is more concern for children's safety in these play areas; and children must reach an older age before parents consider it to be safe for them to visit these areas without supervision (Table 8.11). Clearly, there are more concerns over children's play in Scotland's most deprived areas.

Children from deprived areas are reported to be disadvantaged at every turn. Of particular note is the dearth of access to natural and wooded areas for play (47 per cent have no local access to such space, compared with 20 per cent of those from non-deprived areas). This may be disconcerting to play professionals, given the value of natural play environments. There is a broad consensus that it becomes safe for children to

---

Table 8.12:

Activities of young people aged 8 to 21, by deprivation area status, Scotland, 2012

	15% most deprived areas %	Rest of Scotland %	Scotland %
Music or drama	22	27	26
Other arts	4	7	7
Sports or sporting	42	56	53
Other outdoor activity	16	21	20
Other groups or clubs	20	25	24
Representing young people's views	2	3	3
Mentoring or peer education	2	5	4
Base	*350*	*2,040*	*2,390*

Source: Scottish government, *Scotland's People Annual Report: results from 2012 Scottish Household Survey*, 2013, Table 7.9

Note: Living in a multiply deprived area does not imply living in poverty (nor does living outside a multiply deprived area imply an absence of poverty). Care has to be taken in interpreting this data when discussing poverty in Scotland.

independently visit local playspaces in the later years of primary school, although, once again, it is perceived that children from deprived areas must wait a little longer before their parents/guardians perceive that it is safe. For example, 10.3 is judged to be the age at which it is safe for them to visit their local park without supervision, compared with 9.4 for children outside these deprived areas. This is not to be underestimated; almost one year in the life of a primary-school child is a significant length of time.

Disadvantage is not only associated with play space. Parents also report that children and young adults from deprived areas participate less frequently in a whole range of leisure activities (Table 8.12). Some of the differences in rates of participation are quite striking: 56 per cent of those living outside deprived areas participate in sports, compared with only 42 per cent from deprived areas. Together, while one-quarter outside deprived areas do not participate in any activity (26 per cent), as many as one-third within deprived areas experience no activities (34 per cent).

Conclusion

This chapter has demonstrated that low income and living in deprived areas have far-ranging impacts on Scotland's adults and children. A lack of money leads directly to insecurity, and an inability to meet life's basic necessities. Poverty also strips people of their dignity and is associated with poorer mental health. Physical ill health is also more prevalent among the men, women, boys and girls of Scotland's lower income households. Lower life expectancies (and lower healthy life expectancies) look set to continue as Scotland's more deprived communities are more likely to be less pleasant places to live and in which concerns for personal safety are heightened. Finally, children from the more deprived areas in Scotland are consistently disadvantaged in terms of access to safe play and participation in activities.

We have also drawn attention to the ways in which experience of poverty is gendered. Far from making progress in tackling such gender inequity, recent Scottish government analysis suggests that women's poverty might be increasing (more than men's poverty) as a result of policy decisions undertaken by the UK government. Although cynics may consider this conclusion to be politically motivated (particularly in the lead-in to the referendum and in the context of the Scottish government's flagship commitment to improve childcare provision), there can be no doubting the evidence, or the reality, of gendered poverty from which these conclusions are drawn.

Although a bleak picture has been portrayed of life on a low income and in deprived places in contemporary Scotland, we should not lose sight of the continuing resilience of people living in some of Scotland's poorest communities. As well as highlighting the difficulties people face, we must also recognise the quality in many people's lives, and their desire to get on, get heard and overcome. The present conditions that many experience need not determine their futures, if we can find effective means to support and enable Scotland's most disadvantaged communities and tackle the underlying poverty that too often undermines their resilience.

Notes

1   J H McKendrick, *Life in Low income Families in Scotland: a review of the literature*, Scottish Executive, http://www.scotland.gov.uk/Publications/2003/09/18064/25739

2   L Burnett, *Dignity Shouldn't Have to be Earned*, Poverty Alliance, 2006

3   Poverty Truth Commission, *Findings of the Poverty Truth Commission*, 2012, http://www.povertytruthcommission.org

4   Among the exceptions are: B Holman with Carol, Bill, Erica, Anita, Denise, Penny and Cynthia, *Faith in the Poor*, Lion Publishing, 1998

5   F McHardy, *'Lost Sheep Looking for Somewhere to Go': a study into young people in the transition from school to employment, education or training*, Poverty Alliance, 2011

6   F McHardy, *Surviving Poverty: the impact of lone parenthood. Research into the experiences of lone parents in rural Fife*, Poverty Alliance, 2012

7   See http://www.scottishrefugeecouncil.org.uk/about/refugee_stories

8   See note 3

9   Nine poverty 'stories' can be downloaded from the 'Stories' section of the Poverty Truth Commission at http://www.povertytruthcommission.org.

10 See 'Videos and Photos' section of http://www.povertytruthcommission.org.

11 See 'A Dickensian Tale' section of http://www.povertytruthcommission.org

12 See note 6, p29

13 Scottish government, *Scotland's People Annual Report: results from the 2012 Scottish Household Survey*, 2013, Figure 6.2

14 See note 13, Table 6.4

15 K Dryburgh, *Debt Advice in Scotland: the role of the Scottish CAB service in the debt advice landscape*, Citizens Advice Scotland, 2012, http://www.cas.org.uk/system/files/publications/Debt-advice-in-Scotland.pdf

16 The glitch may reflect difficulties in obtaining accurate data for the most severely

income deprived households. More generally, the problem of obtaining accurate household income estimates is acknowledged in the technical report that accompanies the substantive research findings report (S Hope and I Nava-Ledezma, 'Limitations of the Data', *Scottish Household Survey: methodology and fieldwork outcomes 2011*, 2012, section 6). Thus, it is possible that the glitch is an anomaly and that there is generally lower consumption at the lower end of the household income spectrum.

17 Extract from Marie McCormack, Commissioner – see note 3, p7
18 L Rutherford and others (eds), *Scottish Health Survey 2012*, Scottish government, 2013
19 Extract from Anne Marie Peffer, Commissioner – see note 3, p5
20 See note 6, p21
21 B Manwaring and C Taylor, *The Benefits of Play and Playwork*, SkillsActive, 2007
22 Save the Children, *Thrive at Five: comparative child development at school-entry age*, 2012, http://www.savethechildren.org.uk/sites/default/files/images/Thrive-at-Five-report.pdf
23 J Chanfreau, M Barnes, W Tomaszewski, D Philo, J Hall and S Tipping, *Growing Up in Scotland: change in early childhood and the impact of significant events*, Scottish government, 2011
24 M Barnes, J Chanfreau, and W Tomaszewski, *The Circumstances of Persistently Poor Children*, Scottish government, 2010

Section Four
Poverty, welfare and the constitutional question

Nine

The constitutional question: welfare unionism versus welfare nationalism?

Gerry Mooney

Introduction: context, themes and issues

Welfare reform and the future of the welfare state – both at a UK and a Scottish level – have become increasingly understood as central to the debate around the constitutional future of Scotland and, a point which is all too frequently overlooked, of the UK too. In this introduction to Section Four, some of the key aspects of this are explored, as a way of providing the context for the chapters in this section, from the two main sides of the constitutional debate: the case for Scotland remaining within the union and the argument for independence. While referring here to two 'main sides' to the argument, it is important to acknowledge that this is more complex and nuanced, with different arguments being advanced and different positions being adopted.

The political and policy landscape of contemporary Scotland is shaped by the particular policy objectives of the UK coalition government that were highlighted in Chapter 1. The 'bedroom tax' has come to prominence not only as a mark of the continuing challenges of policy interdependence which exist in the context of devolution (housing being devolved and housing benefit being a reserved power), but also as symbolic of a growing political difference between the UK and Scottish governments. In this respect, it is also deployed by supporters of independence as a way of advocating the distinctiveness of Scottish values and approaches.

That welfare issues have become entangled with the constitutional debate should not come as a surprise. Social welfare has long been central to discussions in the post-1945 era of Britishness and of the UK itself. UK-wide institutions, such as the NHS, the education system and social security, have long been held as pivotal elements in the union, a union which in many respects has been a 'welfare union'. There is a powerful narrative that the historical development of the welfare state in post-1945 Britain played an important role in binding the UK together. Yet it is all too easy to overlook the fact that, even in the classic period of the Beveridgean welfare state during the 1950s to 1970s, there were huge differences in the quality of social citizenship and welfare provision, and that the welfare state in Scotland was, in some ways, different from other parts of the UK. The UK welfare state was, simultaneously, a Scottish welfare state. Administrative and organisational differences in the delivery of health and social services in Scotland (and education and criminal justice) were always distinctively and uniquely Scottish, and remind us that there was considerable divergence before devolution. Nonetheless, this aside, the narrative of a UK social union built around the welfare state has remained a powerful one – one that even Scottish nationalists such as Alex Salmond have taken as so symbolic to argue that independence for Scotland is also about 'preserving' the philosophy and assumptions of the post-1945 UK welfare state in Scotland for the benefit of the rest of the UK – particularly of England, where the UK government is diverging more and more from Beveridgean principles and the idea of all-encompassing state provision.

We are further reminded here that, in debates about policy divergence in the UK after devolution in 1999, it is policy in England that appears to be diverging much more significantly, as governments in the devolved administrations, particularly in Wales and Scotland, continue to hold that the principles of the post-World War Two welfare state remain key to the provision of public and social services and the maintenance of social wellbeing.

This also throws up some key points of difference in the pro-union camp – and, in particular, between the two main unionist parties. There is little sign from the Conservatives that welfare and social solidarity on a UK-wide basis have any role to play in defending that union. Indeed, as the Conservatives seek to reform welfare and fundamentally reshape the relationship between state and individual, what remains of a UK welfare state is being diminished and eroded, a process which has given enormous political capital to the supporters of Scottish independence. Against this, however, the Labour Party argues that the welfare state is important in binding the UK together – and that Scottish independence would diminish such a welfare state. This is argued despite New Labour's having pursued an agenda of welfare reform when in government, which spoke of increasing conditionality and could be seen in other ways as harsh and punitive, and which worked in some respects to distance the party from its heartlands – heartlands that included core votes in Scotland. The UK welfare state has been under continuous 'reform' – but from 1979 until today the pace of reform has been immense, and has contributed in both intended and unintended ways to a growing sense that welfare and social citizenship is different across different parts of the UK.

In this respect, it is not devolution in itself that fragmented the post-1945 welfare state, but it could be seen as both consolidating and enhancing processes already taking place, processes that were driven by long-term economic change, deindustrialisation and successive waves of UK government 'reform'. However, the current period of welfare reform by the UK government, a government that commanded very little support in Scotland at the 2010 UK general election, together with devolution and the fact that there is an SNP-run Scottish government in Edinburgh, has opened up new discursive, political and policy-making spaces for debates around a distinctively 'Scottish' approach to welfare and the possibilities of a Scottish welfare state, both of which would reject the approach of the current UK government. The 'bedroom tax' is symbolic of such discussions, but these extend across the full gamut of welfare provision and public services.

The question of what kind of welfare state we wish to see in Scotland is now more than ever linked with questions about the future direction of Scottish society, and that crucially means also its constitutional future. Perhaps it would be more appropriate to rethink this and argue that the constitutional question has become a question of the kind of welfare state we wish to see in Scotland, a question that invokes important issues around citizenship and solidarity. Further, this is also a question of how we imagine communities of social solidarity today. Are these to be UK-wide, allowing resources to be pooled across different territories and a much larger taxpaying population? Or a preferred community of social solidarity among Scots? Nationalism and notions of community are interwoven in many different ways. The idea of a welfare community built around progressive understandings of welfare has become a potent element in this mix.

'Welfare unionism', central to the post-1945 UK story, is now bumping into a reinvigorated 'welfare nationalism' of a uniquely Scottish form, in which welfare unionism is increasingly judged as having failed. Yet welfare unionism was itself always also a form of welfare nationalism – but a *British* nationalism. It is only now in the context of the Scottish independence debate that such welfare unionism has come to the fore – primarily as a result of Labour Party politicians seizing on this to defend the union. Their partners in the pro-union campaign, the Conservatives, by contrast, have distanced themselves from such.

Welfare unionism and welfare nationalism, together with British nationalism and Scottish nationalism, represent polar points of influence in this debate: contrasting, conflicting but also overlapping stories of a welfare past – and of a welfare future.

Scotland's political landscape and social welfare

If the 2007 Scottish election result produced a totally unexpected outcome in the shape of an SNP government, albeit a minority one, the May 2011 Scottish elections were widely represented as marking a watershed in Scottish politics. The SNP romped to victory with 69 seats, thereby producing the Scottish Parliament's first ever single-party majority government. For the designers of the Scottish Parliament, this was a complete reversal of fortunes – the Scottish government now had a strong mandate to pursue an independence agenda and its goal of a referendum on independence.

The Edinburgh Agreement, signed in October 2012, was the result of protracted discussions between the Scottish and UK governments about the how and when of the referendum. It was agreed that the vote would be held in 2014 and administered by the Scottish government under a special provision of the Scotland Act 2012, passed by Westminster. This allows the Scottish government to set the question. Furthermore, and as is now well known, there will be a single question on independence – with no fall-back option for 'more' devolution. However, leaving aside the referendum question itself, there are four possibilities for Scotland's constitutional future:[1]

- The status quo: but this is not promoted as an option, even by the pro-union parties.
- Devolution plus: some additional powers for the Scottish Parliament (favoured by Labour, Liberal Democrats and Conservatives).
- Devolution max (referred to by some commentators as 'independence lite'): maximum available powers to the Scottish Parliament while remaining within the UK, which appears to be the favoured position of the majority of voters in Scotland, including among SNP and Labour supporters.
- Full independence: supported by the SNP, the Greens, the Scottish Socialist Party and Solidarity.

The constitutional debate

The debate goes further than that discussed by the Calman Commission in 2009. This recognised growing demands for greater political and fiscal independence, leading to the Scotland Act 2012, and which will be introduced in 2016, irrespective of the outcome of the independence referendum.[2] This debate has been structured around two main campaign groups, both of which are umbrella organisations that encompass various political parties, voluntary and charitable organisations, business and trade union interests, as well as celebrities and other individuals.

The pro-UK campaign is organised around the slogan 'Better Together'.[3] Also launched in spring 2012, it is supported by the three main pro-UK parties (Conservative, Labour and Liberal Democrat) and is headed by ex-Chancellor of the Exchequer and Scottish Labour MP, Alistair Darling.

The pro-independence campaign, organised around the slogan 'Yes Scotland', was launched in May 2012.[4] One of the key organisations behind 'Yes Scotland' is the Scottish Independence Convention, which was established in 2005 by four pro-independence political parties (the SNP, Scottish Greens, the Scottish Socialist Party and Solidarity).[5]

This then provides the context for the following two chapters. In Chapter 10, Jim Gallagher presents the case on behalf of the pro-UK 'Better Together' campaign, arguing that the UK welfare state offers the best platform for social solidarity to be maintained, with 'the common risks of everyday life' ameliorated by UK-wide taxation, benefits and public spending. Jim Gallagher also argues that independence would break the long-held assumption that disadvantaged areas can be supported by less disadvantaged ones. Fiscal risks would, therefore, in the event of independence, fall largely on an independent Scotland.

Chapter 11 advocates the case for independence. Here, Cailean Gallagher argues that Scotland has the economic and fiscal capacity to eradicate poverty and to ensure that prosperity is shared equally across the population. A better welfare state can be created on the back of independence, allowing a system that is more in tune with Scottish needs – and Scottish aspirations.

Notes
1 See I McLean, J Gallagher and G Lodge, *Scotland's Choices*, Edinburgh University Press, 2013

2   Commission on Scottish Devolution, *Serving Scotland Better: Scotland and the United Kingdom in the 21st century*, Commission on Scottish Devolution, 2009, http://www.commissiononscottishdevolution.org.uk/uploads/2009-06-12-csd-final-report-2009fbookmarked.pdf

3   http://www.bettertogether.net

4   http://www.yesscotland.net

5   http://www.scottishindependenceconvention.org

Ten
Poverty and the case for the union

Professor Jim Gallagher

Introduction

Conventional arguments for Scotland's union with the other countries of the UK focus on the political and the economic union. Political union allows for common defence, shared security and setting Scotland's place in the world as part of the UK. Economic union means a single market, freedom of movement of goods and labour with resultant economic benefit.

Both arguments are valid. Indeed, they are largely the arguments of 1707 – union bringing peace, security and trade – and were sustained through the eighteenth and nineteenth centuries. But a dimension of social justice became part of the union in the twentieth century – in essence, that resources were pooled to provide pensions, benefits and public services on an equitable basis across the whole of the UK. To political and economic union has been added the dimension of social union.

Allocating spending according to need

Ever since the abolition of the poor laws, a principle of British fiscal policy has been that expenditure is determined by need and not by local taxable capacity. Pensions, unemployment assistance, health and welfare services are to be supported by general taxation, levied across the country according to the ability to pay and not found out of local resources like poor law ratepayers. This was very much a campaign of the left: trade unions argued for national unemployment assistance and the Labour government of 1945 created the National Health Service, not local authority hospitals funded by ratepayers and patient fees.

The geographical distribution of resources for spending on public services is highly contentious – whether by the Barnett formula or the local authority grant system. But how much is spent in different parts of the country on pensions and benefits is determined solely by the circumstances of individuals and their entitlements. Benefits are the largest single government programme. As a result, not only are benefits the big automatic stabiliser of economic activity across cycles, they are also the major redistributor of resources across regions of the UK. Money follows need, even if it is not enough to meet it. This can be seen in Table 10.1, showing regional expenditure on social protection per head.

Table 10.1:
Social protection spend per head, by region/nation, 2011/12

Region/nation	Spend per head £	Indexed to UK = 100
North East	4,223	112
North West	4,048	107
Yorkshire and the Humber	3,769	100
East Midlands	3,597	95
West Midlands	3,814	101
East England	3,475	92
London	3,631	96
South East	3,354	89
South West	3,762	100
England	*3,696*	*98*
Scotland	*4,063*	*108*
Wales	*4,236*	*112*
Northern Ireland	*4,210*	*112*
UK	**3,768**	**100**

Source: HM Treasury, *Public Expenditure Statistical Analyses 2013*, Tables 9.15 and 9.16, 2013, www.gov.uk/government/organisations/hm-treasury/series/public-expenditure-statistical-analyses-pesa

Good-quality data on regional tax receipts were not available at the time of writing, but other economic data confirm that spending implies substantial fiscal transfers from richer to poorer regions. In Scotland, tax receipts are slightly below the UK average (ignoring oil for the moment[1]), so these figures imply a transfer to meet need. Closer examination shows that spending on individual benefits varies markedly between regions by need – for example, high housing benefit costs in London.

Patterns of public expenditure on services are similar, demonstrating clearly that social solidarity operates within the UK. This contrasts markedly with the European Union (EU). Despite EU citizenship and a common Eurozone currency, social solidarity is much more limited. German taxpayers do not pay for Greek pensions, nor do northern European economies support public services in poorer southern countries.

From Scotland's perspective, two arguments justify social solidarity within the UK. The first is pragmatic. The full resources of the UK economy support public services and benefit payments, irrespective of economic performance in Scotland. This argument was made on Scotland's behalf in the decades following the 1970s, when industrial decline resulted in the need for social protection and other public spending and investment.

The second is more principled. Throughout the history of Scottish social reform, the left has consistently argued for UK solutions on essentially moral grounds: people in need should benefit equally in Scotland and elsewhere in the UK, essentially because they belong to the same community. Scottish reformers argued for a single system of unemployment assistance to replace the local poor law, a single old age pension across the UK, a uniform national health service and, more recently, a national minimum wage and tax credits supporting those in work. We share with those with whom we belong.

You can make a contrary argument: the only relevant community is Scotland, and social solidarity should be confined to that level. Crudely, poor people in Scotland matter more than those elsewhere in the UK, and only they have a claim on Scottish resources for support. Obviously, this argument fails on moral grounds. It is completely contrary to every approach of progressives in Britain for the last century or more.

But it fails also on pragmatic grounds. Nationalists will argue that, when the UK is indulging in substantial fiscal retrenchment and cutting many benefits, poor people in Scotland would be better off with a Scottish welfare system. They argue that Scotland would wish for, and be able to afford, at least as generous welfare as now and a reversal of policies such as the unjust 'bedroom tax', impacting cruelly on vulnerable claimants. This superficially attractive argument is not sustainable, once we have a clear understanding of an independent Scotland's potential fiscal position.

The recent literature is clear about Scotland's overall fiscal position.[2] Scottish onshore tax revenues are roughly equivalent, per capita, to the UK average; Scottish public spending, however, is markedly higher, by about 10 per cent per head. If that was all there was to it, an independent Scotland would be in a very difficult fiscal position. The difference, however, can almost be made up if all North Sea oil revenues are used to maintain present levels of public expenditure. If Scotland were to spend, rather than save, North Sea oil, it could initially maintain present levels of public expenditure, borrowing slightly less than the UK to make up its deficit.

There are obvious problems with this. First, oil is a significant, but dwindling and volatile, resource. It should really be put into an oil fund, so that the benefits can be spread over a longer period. No one knows how long it will last, but it will not go on forever. Forecasts differ, but all agree that future revenues will be less than at present. If it were spent to maintain present levels of benefits, then we will eventually fall over a financial cliff.

It is an unfortunate aspect of the present referendum debate that supporters of independence simply assert that oil revenues are the answer to all fiscal challenges. For example, a recent Scottish government paper on pensions compares annual Scottish pension and benefit spending with annual tax take, including an estimate of the proportion of oil revenues that would fall to an independent Scotland.[3] Of course, this is a smaller proportion than for the UK as a whole. But the comparison is a misleading one: pension liabilities continue and get bigger; oil gets smaller and eventually stops. Welfare issues should not be misused in the debate in this way

Pooling risks as well as resources

This is not an argument for Scottish dependency, but for the benefits of pooling resources across a wider community so that risks can be managed and benefits secured in the long term, by reliance on a wider and more diverse economy than Scotland's alone. Scotland has been at least as much a contributor to the common pool of resources as it has benefited from them, once oil revenues are taken into account. In recent decades, Scotland has contributed substantial oil revenues to the common pool, and drawn from that pool to support benefits and other public services. As oil revenues decline, within the UK Scotland will continue to rely on common resources, just as it contributed to them.

A social union is a pooling of risks as well as resources. Paying benefits to the elderly, those unable to work and so on is an example of the community managing risks through social insurance. The welfare state was built initially around schemes of mutual insurance. This still has a real presence today in national insurance contributions, which entitle individuals to certain benefits, notably old age pensions. It is an obvious principle of insurance that the wider the pooling of risks, the more secure the payment of benefits. National insurance, at the UK level, is the biggest insurance scheme of all, and guarantees pensions and benefits for Scots in a way that would be more difficult to do were Scotland a small independent state.

An obvious example is old age pensions. The good news that we are all likely to live longer creates fiscal pressures on the payment of pensions (and other age-related services). It turns out that Scotland is getting older quicker than the rest of the UK: the age structure of the population means the pressure will be even greater than in the UK as a whole. This is well established in Office for National Statistics, General Register Office for Scotland and, indeed, in Scottish government publications. As the Institute for Fiscal Studies puts it, 'funding the benefits system in the decades ahead may prove somewhat more burdensome for an independent Scotland'.[4] Within a shared UK social security system, where resources are pooled, risks like this are pooled also.

A further worrying aspect of the Scottish government approach is to deny or obfuscate the demographic realities. In the same pensions paper, Scottish ministers seek to argue that Scotland is better able to sustain the demographic challenges on pensions by referring to a 'dependency ratio' for Scotland compared to the UK, which looks less difficult. Unfortunately, this ratio includes the under-16s as well as pensioners. The facts are the opposite of the picture painted. This does no one any good, and debates about the constitution and poverty deserve better than such behaviour.

Scotland's social conscience

If Scotland is indeed more willing to deal with poverty than a Conservative England, does it need independence to do so? Not necessarily. Many of the tools for dealing with the long-term roots of poverty are already in the hands of the Scottish Parliament. For adults, work is the best route out of poverty: training people to give them the skills they need is devolved. Education and social care are the services best placed to help children. The devolved NHS can address health inequalities, and housing policies deal with squalor. Indeed, the Scottish government could today reverse the effects of the 'bedroom tax' by using its housing powers to support social landlords. Why won't it? Soon the Scottish Parliament will have increased tax powers, enabling it to increase public spending if it wants to. What is needed is not independence, but the capacity to imagine things can be better and the political will to make them happen. Sadly, politicians

– perhaps reflecting Scottish public opinion – have preferred populist policies, like making services free, consciously redistributing resources to the better off.

Conclusion

Despite current challenges, the UK remains a welfare state and operates a system of social solidarity in which the common risks of everyday life – old age, illness and unemployment – are pooled, together with the taxable resources to pay for pensions, benefits and other public spending. Independence could only break this deep form of social solidarity. That would have a moral dimension, contrary to the whole approach of progressive politics in Britain for the last century, and would link the capacity to deal with poverty to the resources of a particular area. From Scotland's perspective it would also be imprudent, as it would import fiscal risks that are better managed at a UK level. If Scotland truly wants to deal with poverty, many of the tools are already in Holyrood's hands: but we have to tell the politicians to use them.

Notes

1 Scottish government, *Government Expenditure and Revenues in Scotland 2011/12*, 2013, http://www.scotland.gov.uk/Topics/Statistics/Browse/Economy/GERS

2 For example, see Institute for Fiscal Studies, Fiscal Sustainability of an Independent Scotland, 2013, http://www.ifs.org.uk/comms/r88.pdf

3 Scottish government, *Pensions in an Independent Scotland*, 2013, http://www.scotland.gov.uk/Publications/2013/09/3492

4 Institute for Fiscal Studies, *Government Spending on Benefits and State Pensions in Scotland: current patterns and future issues*, 2013, http://www.ifs.org.uk/bns/bn139.pdf

Eleven
Poverty and the prospects of independence

Cailean Gallagher

No life or childhood can occur more than once. Society betrays each of the 200,000 children in Scotland who still live in poverty.[1] In the face of rising deprivation, our political and civil society must act, and if it lacks the powers to do so it must gain those powers. A positive vote in this year's referendum will bring to Scotland the political powers needed to fight poverty, to ensure labour and social contribution is rewarded with prosperity not penury, and to make the country's wealth work for all.

The 'No' path: austerity and the growing divide

Policies of successive Scottish governments were recognised in the last edition of *Poverty in Scotland* as having improved the lives of those in poverty.[2] But people's income, welfare and economic conditions are the main determinants of poverty, and the powers and policy options relevant to these are currently reserved to Westminster. The present UK government is not using these powers for good, and has forsaken the statutory commitment of the Child Poverty Act 2010 to eradicate child poverty by 2020. Progress made under New Labour is backsliding, and trends predict that 65,000 more children will be living in poverty in Scotland by 2020.[3]

Since the early 2000s, the gap between living costs and incomes has continued to widen,[4] leaving more people living below minimum income standards.[5] The recession exacerbated this trend, and people in the UK have experienced some of the deepest wage cuts in Europe.[6] Four out of five jobs created in Britain since 2009 are low paid and those at the bottom are not feeling any economic recovery.[7]

In these conditions, the coalition government continues to tighten the screw on low-income families, keeping benefits well below inflation and even further below the real cost of living. Its Welfare Benefits Up-rating Act[8] further reduced benefits and was described by CPAG as 'a poverty producing measure', meaning that the 'progress on child poverty in the last 15 years – with 1.1 million children taken out of relative low-income poverty – will be lost.'[9] The Act repeats Thatcher's detachment of income supplements from living costs, which has been described as the critical reason for enduring poverty throughout the 1980s and 1990s.[10] For over a generation, the drill has been one step forward and two steps back and, even with a changing of the guard in the 2015 general election, this will be the routine.

The UK government's current consensus is to cut social security and reduce the budget. To fuel its campaign, London politicians and media have stirred enmity between those on low wages and those on welfare. Meanwhile, its austerity programme, suppressing wages and benefits for the poorest, widens the real divide between the majority and the super-rich.[11] Pro-union campaigners insist that pooling the resources of Britain is the greatest benefit of the union, but this is fantasy: the Westminster system allows an elite to pull the wealth from the people who produce it, leaving ever more people in poverty. The UK is on track to being the most unequal country in the developed world.[12]

We can afford a better way

The direction of Westminster is a crucial consideration, but the question of independence is fundamentally about decisions being taken in Scotland. After more than a decade of devolution, people trust Scottish governments to make better decisions than Westminster,[13] and generally believe that crucial powers over tax and welfare should be located in Scotland.[14] Independent of Westminster's regressive decisions, Holyrood could use its full economic and social powers to align employment, health and education policies with the ambition of social solidarity and security for all. Rather than being undermined by benefit cuts, health policy would reflect and complement the benefits system. Early years policy could address deep-rooted material inequalities that determine children's educational and social success.

The confidence and ability of Scotland to govern itself is not in doubt; nor should people doubt Scotland's financial ability to implement progressive policies and fight poverty. Economic evidence shows a newly independent Scotland could afford to increase spending on social security and investment. The economic case is strong: in the words of the Treasury, 'Scotland's economic performance is superior to the rest of the UK when London is excluded.'[15] Scotland's current spending on welfare is marginally higher per head of the population than the overall welfare spending in the UK, but it accounts for a smaller share of our national wealth and tax revenues.[16] Scotland's public finances have been healthier than the UK's to the tune of £12.6 billion over the past five years.[17] Indeed, Scotland has generated more taxes per head for every one of the last 30 years.[18] The evidence is clear: we cannot afford the traumas of Westminster – and we are wealthy enough to be a fairer society.

'Yes' for a Scotland that works

What will be the aspirations of independent governments after a 'Yes' vote? This will, of course, depend on the people's choices in the 2016 election and beyond. But our future democracy will hold the same assets and virtues as the current political sphere where the fight against poverty is at the heart of our politics.

Both Scottish Labour and the SNP remain committed to eradicating poverty and fighting for social justice. Activists and campaigners are already investigating how full political independence could be used to make Scotland a fairer country, where poverty and exclusion are challenged. Projects like the Common Weal[19] and Oxfam's *Our Economy*[20] aim not just to fight but also to prevent poverty – with emphasis on common ownership of the economy, jobs that value people's skills, real power for communities to harness local resources, and clear rights for those both in and out of work.

The contributory principle, the universalist principle, the living wage, a guaranteed citizens' income, flexible work, free quality childcare – all these ideas are already in our political vocabulary, despite lacking the powers to implement them in Scotland, and each can be part of the political agenda after independence.

Collective knowledge, experience and expertise will shape Scotland's anti-poverty strategy. Organisations such as the Poverty Alliance and CPAG will bring the reality of living in poverty to the forefront of politics, with research and testimony projects like EPIC[21] and People Like Us.[22] Charities and researchers will help shape a new system of collecting data to measure wellbeing and economic success, developing the Scottish Index of Multiple Deprivation with work like Oxfam's Humankind Index.[23]

A better welfare state

As for welfare, the Scottish government's expert working group on welfare is investigating principles that might form the foundation of a new social state, including income support and adequate social insurance, while the Fiscal Commission is examining the scope for universal access to childcare. The SNP is likely to remain committed to universalism as the foundation of its welfare policies, while Scottish Labour may approach welfare based on the principle of first providing for those in most need, and emphasising the importance of the contributory principle in social insurance. It is clear that both parties would abolish the 'bedroom tax', reverse regressive Westminster changes, and set new and better priorities for welfare.

Any government's welfare programme would be influenced by groups like the Scottish Campaign on Welfare Reform, which represent the strength and joint will of charity, trade union, civil society and political organisations in Scotland. In its *Manifesto for Change*, the Scottish Campaign on Welfare Reform coalition demands that 'benefits should be set at a level where no one is left in poverty and all have sufficient to lead a dignified life.'[24] This principle is expanded in the Scottish Council for Voluntary Organisations' *Welfare in Working Order*, which highlights the fact that non-retired households, including many working households, cannot reach the publicly recognised minimum income standard by relying on current Westminster benefits, a fact which:[25]

> ... should focus the debate in Scotland on achieving income adequacy via an appropriate balance between earnings (including between minimum wage and living wage), contributory benefits (based on social insurance principles) and means-tested support.

Wages, work and wealth

Welfare is only a starting point, because Scotland's increasingly low-wage economy undercuts a welfare society, and most poverty is still rooted in working households. According to the UK government's own Social Mobility Commission, two-thirds of children living in poverty have one working parent and three-quarters of them are working full time.[26] One in five employees earning below the living wage threshold are denied access to the means to live a decent life.[27]

So low wages and insufficient incomes are the basic cause of poverty – and the most important changes that independence can bring relate to the economy and to the structure of work and pay. The STUC and the 'Better Way' campaign have called for a living wage in the private, as well as the public, sector[28] – an aspiration echoed by the First Minister in a recent speech.[29] Trade unionists have also highlighted opportunities for changing the work environment in Scotland, so that low wages, instability of jobs and poor working contracts and conditions are replaced with a fair and dynamic jobs market, where work is accessible, rewarding and secure.

Life is particularly tough for many women, especially lone parents. Past gains under previous governments have gone into reverse: lone-parent unemployment is rising and underemployment is at a record high. With independence, we could prioritise the real problem of poverty among one-parent households. Measures suggested by Women in Scotland's Economy,[30] Engender[31] and Close the Gap[32] include promoting economic development in Scotland that is attentive to women's needs, including childcare needs, and providing rewarding employment regardless of gender.

Developing a better economy will take more than a few years, but with the co-ordination of unions, campaigners, government, communities and progressive enterprise, the balance of the economy can be tipped in favour of women and men at the middle and lower end of the jobs market and class structure – ensuring flexible work, decent childcare, and fair reward for work and participation in society.

Conclusion: two futures

Scotland is a prosperous country and will continue to be post independence. The question for those fighting poverty is how we can ensure that this prosperity is shared and that poverty is eradicated. This is fundamentally a question of the way the economy develops in the long term, combined with the way we secure rights and wages for people's work, and how we develop a social welfare system that provides from each according to their ability to each according to their need.

In this light, there are two futures on offer this year.

With a 'No' vote, alternating Westminster governments will continue to take us one step forward only to force us back to mitigation and containment. This is not a future that will change the foundations of society into one in which wealth is shared, lives are freed from poverty and social decency becomes the norm.

The 'Yes' path brings the prospect of transition to a better, fairer society. It will not be straightforward, but the great opportunity to reform our society and economy makes this path rise before us as an inspiration and a responsibility, not a burden. For in every instance of poverty, we find another reason to work for change, and with skill and determination the powers of independence can be used to make Scotland a just society, where no one lives in poverty and everyone can attain the life they deserve.

Notes

1   J Dickie, *Poverty in Scotland Summary Briefing*, CPAG, August 2013, p1
2   J H McKendrick and others, *Poverty in Scotland 2011*, CPAG, 2011, pp156, 168, 181, 216 and 219
3   End Child Poverty, *Child Poverty Map of the UK*, 2013, p40
4   'Squeezing the hourglass', *The Economist*, 10 August 2013
5   D Hirsch, *A Minimum Income Standard for the UK 2013*, Joseph Rowntree Foundation, 2013, p5
6   http://www.bbc.co.uk/news/business-23655605
7   Trades Union Congress, *The UK's Low Pay Recovery*, 2013
8   HM Government, *Welfare Benefts Up-rating Act 2013*, The Stationery Office, 2013
9   CPAG, *The Double Lockout: how low-income families will be locked out of fair living standards*, 2013, p39
10 See note 9, p10
11 H Stewart, 'Shocking figures reveal the growth in UK's wealth gap', *The Observer*, 10 February 2013
12 D Dorling, *Injustice: why social inequality persists*, Policy Press, 2011, p327
13 R Ormston and S Reid, *Scottish Social Attitudes Survey 2011: attitudes to government, the economy and public services in Scotland*, Scottish government Social Research, 2012, pp5–7
14 YouGov/*Sunday Times*, Survey Results, 13 to 16 September 2013, p3
15 HM Government, *Scotland Analysis: macro-economic and fiscal performance*, The Stationery Office, September 2013, p16
16 Scottish government, *Public Spending for Scotland*, April 2013, p2
17 Scottish government, *Scotland's Balance Sheet*, p3

18 Scottish government, *Scottish Historical Tax Receipts*, April 2013

19 http://scottishcommonweal.org

20 K Trebeck and F Stuart, *Our Economy: towards a new prosperity*, Oxfam, 2013

21 http://povertyalliance.org/epic

22 http://www.cpag.org.uk/scotland/people-like-us

23 Oxfam, *Oxfam Humankind Index: the new measure of Scotland's prosperity, second results*, 2013

24 Scottish Campaign on Welfare Reform, *A Manifesto for Change*, April 2010

25 J McCormick, *Welfare in Working Order: points and principles for the Scottish debate*, Scottish Council for Voluntary Organisations, 2013

26 Social Mobility and Child Poverty Commission, *State of the Nation 2013: social mobility and child poverty in Great Britain 2013*, 2013

27 M Whittaker and A Hurrell, *Low Pay Britain 2013*, Resolution Foundation, 2013

28 http://www.stuc.org.uk/rebuilding-collective-prosperity/equality-justice/living-wage

29 A Salmond, SNP conference speech, 19 October 2013

30 http://www.gcu.ac.uk/wise

31 http://www.engender.org.uk

32 http://www.closethegap.org.uk

Section Five
Principles for a more equitable Scotland

Twelve
Identifying the themes
Gill Scott

In 2014 Scotland experiences a historic debate which has, at the very least, opened up discussion about the potential for change in the country and the sort of society that could be achieved. Like many, the editors and contributors to this book hope that the way forward is for a progressive, inclusive society that ensures Scotland moves away from being one of the most unequal societies in Europe. Chapter 9 has outlined how many of the debates about the potential of independence have focused on welfare, social cohesion and social redistribution. The ways to address poverty, insecurity and inequality must be an important part of that debate. In this, we agree with the Jimmy Reid Foundation, which argues:[1]

> Scotland – independent or not – must make a decision. If we continue on the current path, the inevitable destination is greater inequality and ever fewer public services on which to rely. If we want something different, we have to choose it.

The early chapters of this book have highlighted two things. First, poverty has not disappeared: Scotland remains one of the most unequal societies in Europe. Second, without clearer policies to address the issues, poverty and insecurity will continue to blight the lives of those living in poverty and will also affect the potential for a more cohesive, vibrant society where the wellbeing of all is improved.

It has become increasingly clear that a number of factors are contributing to the problem. There is a rise in low-paid, insecure jobs; the tax system fails to reduce inequalities; public services are under threat and those using them are experiencing greater stigmatisation; the most vulnerable have little power to change policy in a way that meets their needs; and, while Scotland prides itself on rich local traditions, there is a democratic deficit at local authority level. These are not merely issues for constitutional change, but demand clearer ideas for social and economic change.

In the chapters that follow, some of these issues are addressed and solutions offered. They are not the only solutions under discussion – the range of debate is wide in the run-up to the referendum.[2] However, the essays here reflect a range of approaches that have been identified as significant principles for a strong, cohesive and more equal Scotland.

While, at present, powers to adjust the rate of income tax are largely reserved to Westminster and therefore difficult to adjust without independence, the use of existing powers and more fiscal autonomy in Scotland has been looked at by a number of writers as a means to shape the nation's social and economic landscape. Research by David Bell and colleagues, for example, has shown that council tax could be a very effective means of reducing income inequality, by reducing tax for those currently on lower council tax bands and increasing it for those on higher bands.[3] Mike Danson and others have examined how more devolved tax-raising powers would allow a more integrated combination of wealth, land and resource taxes that could produce more socially just outcomes.[4] Others have examined how a more federated system of taxation would better suit Scotland.[5] In the chapter included here (Chapter 17), Carlo Morelli and Paul Seaman focus on income tax. They provide a strong and detailed case for changes to income tax that could reduce the levels of inequality in the country. They argue that there is scope for policy measures to address income inequalities and, based on an analysis of government household income statistics, they show how progressive forms of income taxes that focus on the highest earners can have a marked impact on income inequality.

Stephen Boyd's contribution reminds us very powerfully that the structure of the economy plays a large part in the generation of poverty and how deficiencies in policy are failing to address that. He identifies the growing insecurity of jobs and reductions in median pay that have occurred in recent years. Like the recent Joseph Rowntree Foundation review of devolved approaches to child poverty that shows, among other things, how devolution has allowed some variation in economic development but could do more,[6] Boyd argues that the Scottish government has still to fully address the issues even within existing powers. He also argues that there is a pressing need to identify which workers are suffering the most, to boost wages through greater use of a higher minimum wage, and to support collective bargaining in a way that mirrors the Nordic experience of sectoral bargaining forums.

As Chapter 9 reminds us, the welfare state, not only in Britain but also throughout western Europe, has proved extremely resilient and the concept of universalism has, until recently, been central to its development. Although many would argue that universalism is essential to social solidarity within the welfare state, the concept of universalism has been increasingly challenged. Means-tested benefits and services are increasingly popular among politicians but, as Walker and others remind us, this makes the defence of universalism more important than ever.[7] Mike Danson's essay does just this by drawing on comparative material to argue powerfully that universalism in public services in Scotland should not be abandoned. Universal services achieve better outcomes for all: the poor are less stigmatised; gender equality is greater; government and wider economic efficiencies parallel universalist provision of public services; and the economic impact is greater than selective services. His argument also reminds us that, on virtually all measures of economic success, league tables are topped with strong universal welfare states. It is a possible and valid direction for the future, where social investment and social justice are taken seriously.

The two chapters that follow are more concerned with power and resources at different levels of government and political participation. They reflect increased concerns about a democratic deficit in relationships between poorer communities and government at local and national level and about a relative failure of local authorities to deliver effective strategies to reduce poverty.

The chapter from Stephen Sinclair and John H McKendrick identifies the very real risk that decentralisation of anti-poverty policy within Scotland poses for those living in local authority areas where resources or political will prevent effective anti-policy strategies from working. This is despite the existence of priorities for poverty reduction for all local authorities being drawn up at Scottish government level. However it is also important to note that they provide evidence of innovation and impact where local level anti-poverty strategies are well developed.

Fiona McHardy and Robin Tennant's contribution, based as it is on recent action attempting to increase the democratic inclusion of the least powerful, shows how the political landscape can be changed. It highlights how people with the experience of poverty can play an active role in anti-poverty policy development in Scotland, but demands ring-fenced resources and greater legislative support for participative anti-poverty policy making to ensure the democratic deficit at local or national level is addressed. It is a valuable argument at a time when Scotland's first Commission on Strengthening Local Democracy meets to consider how to build local democracy into Scotland's future.[8]

The final two chapters remind us of the importance of addressing issues of equality in any future Scotland. Equality of opportunity was heralded as one of the key principles at the heart of the establishment of the Scottish Parliament in 1999. The use made of equal opportunities powers granted to the Scottish government at the time has been positive. However, there has been at best a variable political commitment and there has, moreover, been a lack of clear leadership that would have an impact on at the least public sector employers. Angela O'Hagan's essay underlines how approaches to policy making could advance equality by making better use of existing domestic and international legislative and institutional levers, and highlights the need for equality to be a central political goal, whatever the constitutional status.

Gareth Mulvey's contribution serves to remind us that, while poverty at the moment has become virtually an automatic outcome of the asylum process in Scotland, it does not have to be the norm. He argues that the removal of policies and practices that produce negative outcomes should be one of the guiding principles of policy, and that ensuring that asylum seekers have the right to work and furthering work on skill recognition would be a positive step forward.

Taken together, the contributions provide us with some key principles that we think are important for the reduction of poverty and insecurity of the most vulnerable: using tax redistribution to reduce income inequality; ensuring access to decent jobs that can lift people out of poverty; developing and maintaining universal public services that work for all; ensuring equality of opportunity is incorporated into policies; and, in recognising the disempowerment that affects the most vulnerable, making sure that the needs and voices of the poor are recognised in the labour market and at all levels of the political arena.

Notes

1 Jimmy Reid Foundation, *The Common Weal: a model for economic and social development*, 2013

2 See P Bryan and T Kane, *Class, Nation and Socialism: the red paper on Scotland 2014*, Glasgow Caledonian University Archives, 2013; Scottish Council for Voluntary Organisations, *Third Sector Visions for a Scotland of the Future. A better state: inclusive principles for Scottish welfare*, 2013; David Hume Institute and Scottish Futures Forum, Constitutional Change 'Conversations', 2013, http://www.scotlandfutureforum.org/david-hume-institute.html; Devolution Plus Group, *Improving Social Outcomes in Scotland*, 2012, www.devoplus.com

3 D Bell, D Comerford and D Eiser, 'Constitutional Change and Inequality in Scotland', in *The Economics of Constitutional Change*, Economic and Social Research Council, 2013, http://esrcscotecon.com/2013/09/15/constitutional-

change-and-inequality-in-scotland-david-bell-david-comerford-and-david-eiser

4   M Danson, L Macfarlane and W Sullivan, *Investing in the Good Society: five questions on tax and the Common Weal*, Jimmy Reid Foundation, 2013

5   A Trench, *Funding Devo More: fiscal options for strengthening the union*, Institute for Public Policy Research, 2013

6   J McCormick, *A Review of Devolved Approaches to Child Poverty*, Joseph Rowntree Foundation, 2013

7   A Walker, A Sinfield and C Walker, *Fighting Poverty, Inequality and Injustice: a Manifesto inspired by Peter Townsend*, Policy Press, 2011

8   Commission on Strengthening Local Democracy, http://www.localdemocracy. info

Thirteen
The benefits of universalism

Mike Danson

On virtually every possible measure of social and economic success, all league tables are topped by societies with strong universal welfare states.[1] Because they have these universal social contracts, they are high performers; it is not because they can afford them that they are able to have generous systems, but it is the reverse that is critical – inclusion and cohesion are the fundamentals for success.[2]

Introduction

In recent times, successful economies and societies have demonstrated high levels of coherence and equity, and an essential component in this performance has been the commitment to universalism. The Nordic countries, in particular, lead the world in terms of standards of living, innovation and creativity,[3] equality and fairness;[4] their levels of benefits for those out of work or living with disabilities are close to average salaries, and quality of life for all is prioritised.[5] This is consistent with the academic research which stresses partnership working and networking as the basis for economic competitiveness in the twenty-first century, rather than Fordist production models.[6] This emphasis on inclusion and the involvement of workers, citizens and entrepreneurs with business and the state underpins the sustained high performance of these small nations as well as city regions in the *Länder* of Germany.[7] And key to their economic foundations are social contracts which promote identity with each other, the community and the nation through universalist principles.

In stark contrast are the so-called Anglo-Saxon welfare models of the US and UK. With their neoliberal principles of competitiveness driving wages and benefits lower in real terms to achieve a market share in low value-added sectors of retailing and many services, they offer a vision of a society based on individualism and consumerism. The drivers invoked here promise rich rewards for a few and stagnation for the many, as so cogently argued by commentators across the spectrum.[8] Universalism and the very concept of certain universal benefits being available to all have come under extreme attack in the last two decades as the post-war Keynesian consensus has been destroyed.

To try to understand why the support and inclusion of all is a principle worth defending, promoting and expanding, particularly at a time when Scotland has the potential to pursue that principle, this chapter explores the rationale for universal benefits, and universalism more generally, and presents some arguments on how such a welfare and social contract might look in a Scotland where these are appreciated. This draws on previous research with the Poverty Programme at Oxfam[9] and the Jimmy Reid Foundation,[10] where further details and evidence can be found.

Universal efficiencies

Including the poor in society is not only an elementary priority for many but also considered necessary on grounds of efficiency and to ensure that we all benefit from all our talents. There are fundamentally three strategic approaches to achieving this: first, selectivity, where services are targeted at and delivered to particular groups of people directly. This requires the means to identify who is poor, sick or disabled and who is not, and these processes are often difficult and socially divisive. Stigmatisation and hierarchies become embedded into lives, and societies which pursue such approaches undermine the inclusion and realisation of the skills and experiences of the people affected.[11] Second is solidarity, building social cohesion through overlapping, intertwined networks of mutual responsibility and support. However, these can be exclusive where mutual support moves incrementally outwards to include others, but haphazardly and inconsistently. The third approach is universalism, where services are provided to everyone as a right. Universalism does not distinguish between people on the basis of income or wealth when benefits are directed at broad categories, such as older people or children. In the UK, education and health services have tended to be universally provided for the last half century, until recently when privatisation and fees, for instance, were introduced (in England especially).

However, universal benefits are criticised in terms of cost and affordability, despite their popular support and their advantages over alternative means of delivering services. Among the counter arguments to these voices, the economic and social advantages are to the fore, with societies that offer equal rights proving to be better for everyone while, in contradistinction, those that are less equal are worse for everyone.[12] In *The Spirit Level*, Wilkinson and Pickett argue that unequal societies:[13]

> ... have more violence, they have higher teenage birth rates, they have more obesity, they have lower levels of trust, they have lower levels of child well-being, community life is weaker and more people are in prison.

There is also the broader argument of self-interest: when everyone has rights, all have a stake in the services, and all are better off as all ensure that services are well delivered, benefits spill over, and the concept of insurance is clear.

While the Scottish Parliament has retained or extended almost all the areas of universalism established since 1945, elsewhere in the UK (but especially in Westminster policies for England), there have been significant and accelerating moves away from universalism to selectivity in university fees and in many elements of support for older people. In the Jimmy Reid Foundation report, we argue why, *by definition*, this tendency, under the guise of efficiency and targeting, increases social and economic inequality and diminishes, rather than enhances, the status of the poor and other disadvantaged groups.[14] So, the targeting in these strategies frequently fails to deliver its own objectives of supporting those most in need and controlling overall expenditure because of stigmatisation, adverse publicity about those who are entitled to claim and costs of identifying claimants. It is self-defeating, therefore, because selectivity requires processes and procedures that separate benefit recipients from the rest of society, increasing stigmatisation and reducing take-up.[15] Further, although superficially criticised as suffering from too much deadweight, universalism is incredibly efficient – for example, the selective element of pension entitlement is more than fifty times more inefficient than the universal element measured in terms of fraud and error alone, and without even taking into account the cost of administration.[16]

Ironically, given the suggestion that cuts are required to reduce overall spending, in economic terms universalism is clearly shown to deliver 'merit goods' (assets and skills that benefit all as well as the individual) and 'public goods' (things that could not be delivered without collective provision), which selectivity simply cannot deliver.[17] These sorts of goods and services are subject to market failures. The benefits of universalism are most apparent in education (accepted by practically all societies in the world) and health (such as immunisation and the eradication of diseases). The economic impact of universalism is much greater than the economic impact of selectivity because of the multiplier profile of expenditure; the poor spend a much higher proportion of their incomes locally, so supporting the national economy, while the incomes taxed to pay for these would have been disproportionately devoted to imports and other expenditures overseas. It also creates positive economic stability by mitigating the swings in the business cycle and creating much more economic independence among the population: universal benefits empower 'mothers, carers, the long-term sick and disabled, giving them greater confidence and self-esteem – both essentials for wellbeing and, where appropriate, engagement with the labour market – and diminishes their dependency on others.'[18] Such social security generates confidence and self-esteem which encourages enterprise and job seeking among those who can work – the opposite argument from the neoliberal threats and coercion used by conservative governments to attack universalism and decent levels of welfare support.[19]

Universalism creates a higher and more progressive economy – directly, through raising the incomes of the poorest closer to the median (levels of inequality are significantly lower in countries with strong welfare systems and extensive universal benefits), and indirectly by contributing to a high tax base through the creation of higher value-added jobs. This latter dynamic impact is explained by the generation of pre-distribution progressivity as those moving into the labour market gain more secure, higher paid and higher skilled employment.[20] This in turn establishes positive and reinforcing cycles of increasing confidence, enterprise and skills utilisation, which also improves economic stability, reduces price bubbles and creates more efficient, flatter income distribution. It is impossible to disentangle redistributive tax and universalism – if universalism is reduced, redistributive taxation is reduced and visa versa; they interact and raise the quality of life and living standards for all but the mega rich.

Social democratic systems perform much better in terms of gender equality, and universal benefits have an important and complementary role in promoting this.[21] They do not suffer from the inherent bias built into a system designed within a framework of assuming a male breadwinner model of welfare.

More generally, there is a 'paradox of redistribution': when benefits are not targeted exclusively towards low-income groups there is a higher take-up among the poor as they suffer less from stigmatisation, adverse publicity by a biased media and political class. Social security systems based on universalism most benefit low-income groups in the aggregate.[22] Solidarity and inclusion are significant factors behind the success of universal systems – where social services are 'rationed' for those on the lowest incomes, the quality of the services declines in the absence of 'majority buy-in' for those services. When 'we are all in this together' genuinely, rather than competing for the nation's resources, we all benefit; that is what 'society' should mean. As Townsend argued:[23]

> What is at stake is not just the most technically efficient or cheapest means of reaching an agreed end. It is the kind and quality of the society we wish to achieve in Britain.

Reflections

Selectivity is not a form of universalism, but the rejection of universalism. As is clear from the pronouncements from Westminster politicians, from a right-wing, neoliberal media and commentators who refuse to identify with their neighbours and fellow citizens, selectivity is a cost-driven judgement, even though it often fails to deliver many 'savings' that they claim. By contrast, universalism is a function-driven judgement, achieving efficient and effective outcomes to the benefit of all. Selectivity and universalism are elements of two entirely different political philosophies – universalism, inextricably linked to the European social model; selectivity, a spawn of US neoliberalism. Both are based on political principles and value judgements. As has been apparent in the accelerating attacks on the post-war consensus of a strong welfare state offering protection 'from the cradle to the grave', wherever we find moves from universalism to selectivity, we find privatisation and corporate profiteering, often at the expense of those least able to bear the impact.

The international, historical and contemporary evidence strongly suggests that the appropriate response to austerity is to increase universal provision and so stimulate economic activity, equalise damaging wealth disparity, and improve both government and wider economic efficiency. The simplistic models and strategies of cuts, tax cuts for the rich and increasing inequity have condemned us to the longest sustained recession in history.

A divisive, economically inefficient system, which increases inequality, reduces the quality of social services, stigmatises and damages the wellbeing of the poor but benefits owners of large corporations, is being advocated without any coherent evidence-based case being made.

Universalism is progressive: it complements and underpins an economy based on good jobs, with high levels of skill utilisation and pay;[24] it is supported by redistributive taxation and offers a seamless provision of social welfare for all in a linked social system. It has produced the most effective society civilisation has yet achieved. We undermine that system at our peril.

Notes

1 M Danson, 'Whose Economy? Scotland in Northern Europe: balancing dynamic economies with greater social equality', presentation to The Economy, Energy and Tourism Committee 4th annual joint seminar with the Scottish Trades Union Congress on 'Growth versus the Scottish Government's 'Golden Rules' and Economic Strategy', 21 February 2012, http://www.scottish.parliament.uk/parliamentarybusiness/CurrentCommittees/47772.aspx

2 J Stiglitz, *The Price of Inequality: how today's divided society endangers our future*, WW Norton, 2012; R Wilkinson and K Pickett, *The Spirit Level: why more equal societies almost always do better*, Allen Lane, 2010

3 Commission of the European Communities, *Industrial Innovation: innovation union scoreboard*, 2012, http://ec.europa.eu/enterprise/policies/innovation/facts-figures-analysis/innovation-scoreboard/index_en.htm

4 A Sinfield, 'Whose Welfare State Now?', in *Whose Economy?*, 2011, http://policy-practice.oxfam.org.uk/publications/whose-welfare-state-now-146174

5 See note 1

6 See note 2

7 See note 1

8 See L Elliott and D Atkinson, *Going South: why Britain will have a third world economy by 2014*, Palgrave Macmillan, 2012 for their forecasts of how the UK's long-term decline will continue unabated into the future.

9 K Trebeck, *Our Economy: towards a new prosperity*, Oxfam, 2013, http://policypractice.oxfam.org.uk/publications/our-economy-towards-a-new-prosperity-294239; M Danson and K Trebeck, *No More Excuses: how a Common Weal approach can end poverty in Scotland*, the Jimmy Reid Foundation, 2013, http://reidfoundation.org/wp-content/uploads/2013/08/Poverty1.pdf

10 M Danson, R McAlpine, P Spicker and W Sullivan, *The Case for Universalism: an assessment of the evidence on the effectiveness and efficiency of the universal welfare state*, the Jimmy Reid Foundation, 2012, http://reidfoundation.org/portfolio/the-case-for-universalism-an-assessment-of-the-evidence-on-the-effectiveness-and-efficiency-of-the-universal-welfare-state

11 The argument here is not that individual processes and means cannot be introduced to address specific negative instances of stigmatisation – for example, using pre-paid cards in schools has been found to lessen the stigma that is associated with free school meals. Rather, the overall thrust of a system which stresses and relies on selectivity is to create an environment and atmosphere that seeks to divide, to stigmatise and to exclude.

12 R Wilkinson and K Pickett, *The Spirit Level: why more equal societies almost always do better*, Allen Lane, 2010

13 R Wilkinson quoted in BBC, *The Spirit Level: Britain's new theory of everything?*, 2012, http://www.bbc.co.uk/news/uk-politics-11518509

14 See note 10

15 Commission on Social Justice, *Social Justice: strategies for national renewal: report of the Commission on Social Justice*, Vintage, 1994, p10; P Townsend, *Poverty in the United Kingdom*, Penguin Books and Allen Lane, 1979

16 See note 15; F Field, M Meacher and C Pond, *To Him Who Hath: a study of poverty and taxation*, Penguin Books, 1977; C Walker, 'For Universalism and Against the Means Test', in A Walker, A Sinfield, and C Walker, *Fighting Poverty, Inequality and Injustice: a Manifesto inspired by Peter Townsend*, Policy Press, 2011, pp133–52

17 B Rothstein, *Is the Universal Welfare State a Cause or an Effect of Social Capital?*, QoG Working Paper Series, 2008, pp3–4, http://www.qog.pol.gu.se/digitalAssets/1350/1350669_2008_16_rothstein.pdf

18 See note 10, p7

19 Commission on Social Justice, *Social Justice: strategies for national renewal: report of the Commission on Social Justice*, Vintage, 1994, p8

20 See note 10

21 See note 17; Norden, *Gender Equality in the Nordic Countries*, 2013, http://www.norden.org/en/about-nordic-co-operation/areas-of-co-operation/gender-equality/gender-equality-in-the-nordic-countries; M Anderson, *Nordic Countries Top Gender Equalities List: what are they doing right?*, 2010, http://www.theglasshammer.com/news/2010/10/14/nordic-countries-top-gender-equality-list-what-are-they-doing-right

22 See note 10, p4; P Spicker, *The Idea of Poverty*, Policy Press, 2007; W Korpi and J Palme, 'The Paradox of Redistribution and Strategies of Equality: welfare state institutions, inequality, and poverty in the western countries', *American Sociological Review*, 63 (5), 1998, pp661–87

23 P Townsend, 'Selectivity: a nation divided', in *Social Services for All?*, Fabian Society, 1968, p121

24 As argued by K Trebeck, *Our Economy: towards a new prosperity*, Oxfam, 2013, http://policypractice.oxfam.org.uk/publications/our-economy-towards-a-

new-prosperity-294239 and M Danson and K Trebeck, *No More Excuses: how a Common Weal approach can end poverty in Scotland*, the Jimmy Reid Foundation, 2013, http://reidfoundation.org/wp-content/uploads/2013/08/ Poverty1.pdf, based on analyses of J Stiglitz, *The Price of Inequality: how today's divided society endangers our future*, WW Norton, 2012, R Wilkinson and K Pickett, *The Spirit Level: why more equal societies almost always do better*, Allen Lane, 2010, and others.

Fourteen
Going local? Anti-poverty activity in contemporary Scotland

Stephen Sinclair and John H McKendrick

Local anti-poverty activity in Scotland

For more than fifty years, Scotland's anti-poverty activity has had, at least in part, a local dimension.[1] The Urban Programme of the late 1960s was the forerunner of schemes designed to tackle the inter-related problems of regeneration, deprivation and poverty. It was followed by a mix of large-scale area transformations in the 1970s, such as the Glasgow Eastern Area Renewal (GEAR) scheme and targeted interventions at smaller areas, such as Strathclyde Regional Council's Areas of Priority Treatment programme. Local enterprise companies followed in the 1980s, social inclusion partnerships were introduced in the late 1990s, and the targeted thematic local interventions that were part of the Closing the Opportunity Gap strategy came after 2004.

In addition to local anti-poverty work in Scotland initiated by government, there has been an array of grassroots activity led by such groups as the Dundee Anti-poverty Forum, Moray Against Poverty, Easthall Residents Association (Easterhouse, Glasgow) and others.

The Child Poverty Act 2010

The 2010 Child Poverty Act introduced a statutory duty on local authorities in England and Wales to tackle child poverty, but this did not apply to local government in Scotland. Nevertheless, the Scottish government's Child Poverty Strategy for Scotland[2] made it clear that tackling child poverty was a responsibility shared between national and local government, and the Scottish government depends on local authorities and their community planning partners to help it meet national objectives and targets. Indeed, the second annual review of the Strategy identifies 'places' as one of its three focal themes (alongside 'pockets' and 'prospects').[3]

Chapter outline

This chapter addresses three issues:

* Powers. What *can* local government in Scotland do to reduce poverty?
* Actions. What *has* local government done to tackle poverty?
* Recommendations. What *should* local government do?

Support for a wide range of local actions to tackle poverty in Scotland comes from think tanks,[4] anti-poverty practitioners,[5] people experiencing poverty[6] and organisations representing people experiencing poverty.[7] Although acknowledging this wider agenda, this chapter focuses on the role of local government (and its partners) in tackling child poverty locally.

Local government and tackling poverty in Scotland

Powers: what can government in Scotland do about poverty?

It is widely accepted that the policy levers that can make the most signif-icant contribution to reducing poverty (including child poverty) in the UK are not devolved to central and local government in Scotland – control of economic management, taxation and social security remain with the UK government. In particular, much of the decline in child poverty since 1998/99 was due to investment in child benefit and child tax credit and to increases in employment, especially among lone parents (initially assisted by the various New Deals).[8] About one-quarter of the fall in child poverty over that period was linked to higher rates of employment for lone parents, and this was a particularly marked development in Scotland.

An additional limitation to tackling poverty in Scotland at the current time is the UK government's fiscal austerity measures: these imposed a 12 per cent real-terms cut between 2010/11 and 2013/14, to be followed by a further 4 per cent cut in 2016, if the UK government meets its budget targets.[9] Low-income families with children have been, and are likely to be, disproportionately affected by these cuts.[10]

Nevertheless, devolution granted Scotland 'one of the widest ranges of competences of any devolved or federated government in Europe',[11] and substantial powers and scope to influence household poverty are available to Scottish national and local government. These powers were extended in the Scotland Act 2012, and the introduction of the local housing allowance with the reform of housing benefit added to the responsibilities of government in Scotland.

The range of options to tackle child poverty available to local government in Scotland is greatly increased if anti-poverty activity is considered to involve more than reducing the numbers of children living in low-income households. Material deprivation is one of four measures of poverty in the Child Poverty Act 2010 (see Chapter 3), and to reduce children's material deprivation is an explicit target for the Scottish government.[12] While local government in Scotland might have restricted capacity to increase household incomes directly, it can mitigate the effects of poverty through providing services that enhance the quality of life for lower income households. In this sense, local government (and its partners) has a critical role to play through providing services and opportunities for enrichment that redress the disadvantage of living in poverty.

Actions: what has government in Scotland done about poverty?

In this wider sense, local government in Scotland already delivers a wide range of services to tackle child poverty. However, effective anti-poverty activity requires more than routine delivery of statutory services. As Chapter 1 considers aspects of the Scottish government's anti-poverty programme, the discussion below focuses on distinctive local measures.

The Concordat between the Scottish government and local authorities signed in 2007 afforded local government the opportunity to specify local priorities in line with a National Performance Framework. This relationship has not been conflict free, particularly in a period of cuts – for example, there was disagreement over the funding of free school meals. Analysis of single-outcome agreements (the tools through which local priorities are articulated) undertaken in 2009 concluded that, while child poverty was on the agenda of community planning partners, it was questionable how high a priority it was. At that time, no single-outcome agreement had clearly articulated the full range of policy levers nor actions that could be taken to tackle child poverty. For example, out of 32 single-outcome agreements, only four stated that tackling child poverty was a priority; only two had set a local outcome to reduce child poverty; and only one referred to developing a local child poverty strategy.[13]

Subsequent analysis in 2012 found that there has been some progress in the actions taken by community planning partners on child poverty, but their local child poverty actions are rather routine, and there remains scope to develop more strategic approaches.[14] Two-fifths of single-outcome agreements have a specific local poverty outcome. Less common are the more intensive approaches that could be used to tackle child poverty: local action plans (16 per cent), working with a child poverty development group (5 per cent) and undertaking child poverty impact assessments (5 per cent) are the exception, rather than the norm, among Scottish local authorities and community planning partnerships.

Analysis of responses to the Scottish government's consultation on developing the Child Poverty Strategy for Scotland suggested that strong leadership was required for an effective local strategy.[15] It is therefore somewhat worrying that, although three-quarters of local authority officers responsible for child poverty policy within community planning partnerships felt in 2012 that this issue was a local policy priority, less than half thought that it was a local *political* priority.[16]

New single-outcome agreements were submitted by community planning partnerships to the Scottish government in summer 2013. These were intended to sharpen the focus of their activity by prioritising key areas, including increasing employment, improving early years development and achieving better outcomes for older people. Community planning partnerships are required to 'include clear performance commitments that will lead to demonstrable improvements in people's lives' and to reduce inequalities between groups rather than merely improve average outcomes.'[17] It will be interesting to appraise whether this new iteration of single outcome agreements has embraced the tackling child poverty locally agenda.

More generally, it must be acknowledged that both the Scottish government and local government in Scotland have been broadly united in their hostility to the agenda and many of the policies of the UK government. In current circumstances, local actions to ameliorate the negative effects of welfare reform and cuts to public services are just as important as introducing new strategies under the guise of the Child Poverty Strategy for Scotland.

Recommendations: what should government in Scotland do about poverty?

Action is required in five strategic areas to address poverty in Scotland.

Tackling poverty should be core business. There is merit in devising anti-poverty strategies and 'poverty proofing' – evaluating the extent to which each and every resource allocation is tackling poverty.[18] However, beyond this, central and local government in Scotland need to embrace the principles that such processes imply: local public servants must internalise the belief that tackling poverty is core business, and service managers and frontline staff alike must routinely consider how mainstream services and standard operations impact on poverty. Formal impact assessments and toolkits are more likely to be effective if based on this foundation.

Effective provision of core services and opportunities. Redressing the gap between groups involves redistributing resources and services to favour those most in need, and ending the continuing 'inverse care law' in public service access and provision.[19] Local government should be able to specify its direct contribution to ensuring that the 'necessities of life' are available to all of its children who are living in poverty. This is greatly aided if they reflect on the full package of local services and opportunities that they provide to children living in poverty, and consider how these could be improved. This requires greater transparency concerning how resources and funding streams are directed to address poverty.

Localism. The Christie Commission[20] advocated localisation and also proposed a new, proactive approach to public service provision, with a focus on: prevention; capitalising on community assets rather than responding to deficits; empowerment of, and co-production with, service users; designing services around people's needs; changing the working practices of public organisations and service deliverers; and improving local partnership and collaboration between agencies. Several of these factors inter-relate: empowering communities requires their involvement in policy, thereby developing and cultivating their strengths. In addition, the most severe, concentrated and compounded forms of deprivation exist in small neighbourhoods and require very localised action, which makes community engagement and co-production more feasible.[21] 'Localism' has also been a prominent theme in UK government policy, but the shared terminology perhaps disguises contrasting approaches.[22]

Employment support services. Much of the fall in child and household poverty achieved in Scotland up to 2006 was associated with increased parental employment.[23] International evidence testifies to the importance of high-quality and affordable childcare in enabling employment and reducing household poverty. In this respect, the Children and Young People (Scotland) Bill, which proposes to increase early learning and child-care to a minimum of 600 hours for three- and four-year-olds, is a step in the right direction, but not the end of the road that must be taken.

The private sector. If poverty really is '*everybody's* business'[24] rather than merely that of the public and charitable sectors, then what are the respon-sibilities of the private sector? International comparisons show that lone parents in the UK and Scotland are more likely to leave employment than they are in countries with lower rates of household poverty. Furthermore, employment only reduces poverty if it is well paid and relatively secure. Addressing these issues requires dealing not only with childcare but also the attitudes and practices of employers.

It is evident that current policies do not move those furthest from the labour market into jobs that actually lift them out of poverty. This is, in part, due to the fact that, compared to other developed nations, the UK is a low-wage economy: 20 per cent of all workers are in low-paid jobs and many households need two earners, or to have their wages supplemented by tax credits, to avoid poverty.[25] Wages at the lower end of the labour market have fallen in recent years and are not expected to reach their 2008 level until 2020. As John Veit-Wilson dryly observed, when two-thirds of children living in poverty are members of employed households, it could be argued that employment is as much (if not more) a 'cause' of poverty than unemployment.[26] Employers paying such low wages benefit significantly from tax credits, as they are, in effect, subsidised by taxpay-ers. It is therefore reasonable to demand more in return for this support, such as the requirement that subsidised employers provide in-work train-ing, which will enhance employees' ability to retain and progress in employment. In addition, more could done to encourage employers to pay a living wage, and the public sector should be an exemplar in this.

Conclusions

Although progress has stalled in recent years and is likely to be reversed if recent policies continue, it is apparent from the analysis of trends in poverty in the UK and Scotland since 1999 that it is possible to reduce poverty, although concerted action is required to achieve even relatively modest improvements. However, it is also clear that 'more of the same' is not sufficient to significantly reduce poverty, let alone eradicate it: both the scale and nature of activity must change. To mitigate the effects of austerity and cutbacks on lower income households, local and national government in Scotland will have to show a level of commitment and determination which matches that shown by the UK government in imposing these penalties on the most vulnerable in society.

Notes

1 V Higgins and R Ball, 'Local Authority Anti-poverty Strategies in Scotland', *Public Policy and Administration*, 1999, 14.1, pp60–75

2 Scottish government, *Child Poverty Strategy for Scotland*, 2012, http://www.scotland.gov.uk/Resource/Doc/344949/0114783.pdf

3 Scottish government, *Annual Report of the Child Poverty Strategy for Scotland*, 2013, http://www.scotland.gov.uk/Publications/2013/09/2212/0

4 C Wood and others, *Poverty in Perspective*, Demos, 2012, section 2, http://www.demos.co.uk/publications/povertyinperspective

5 http://www.employabilityinscotland.com/learning-network/about-us

6 http://povertytruthcommission.org/index.php?id=4

7 http://povertyalliance.org/what_we_do

8 A Garnham, 'Foreword', in *Ending Child Poverty by 2020: progress made and lessons learned*, Child Poverty Action Group, 2012, p3

9 M McAteer, 'Years of Challenge: securing the future for public services: continuous improvement in difficult times', Institute of Revenues, Rating and Valuation Scottish Conference, Crieff, 1 September 2010

10 K Stewart, 'Child Poverty: what have we really achieved?', in *Ending Child Poverty by 2020: progress made and lessons learned*, Child Poverty Action Group, 2012

11 M Keating, *Policy Making and Policy Divergence in Scotland after Devolution*, Devolution Briefing No.21, Economic and Social Research Council, 2005

12 http://www.scotland.gov.uk/About/Performance/scotPerforms/TechNotes/child deprivation

13 C Telfer and others, *Single Outcome Agreements 2009: an analysis by mem-*

bers of the Campaign to End Child Poverty in Scotland, Campaign to End Child Poverty in Scotland, 2009

14 J H McKendrick and S Sinclair, *Local Action to Tackle Child Poverty in Scotland*, Save the Children, 2012

15 Reid Howie Associates, *Tackling Child Poverty Strategy in Scotland: an analysis of written consultation responses*, Scottish government, 2011, http://www.scotland.gov.uk/Publications/2011/03/21120115/0

16 See note 14

17 Scottish government/Convention of Scottish Local Authorities, *Single Outcome Agreements: guidance to community planning partnership*, 2012, www.scotland.gov.uk/Resource/0040/00409273.doc

18 J H McKendrick, *Desperately Seeking Poverty (Alleviation): towards poverty sensitive budgeting in local government*, Whose Economy? seminar paper, June 2011, http://policy-practice.oxfam.org.uk/publications/desperately-seeking-poverty-alleviation-towards-poverty-sensitive-budgeting-in-146175

19 P Matthews and A Hastings, 'Middle-class Political Activism and Middle-class Advantage in Relation to Public Services: a realist synthesis of the evidence base', *Social Policy and Administration* 47(1), 2013

20 http://www.scotland.gov.uk/Publications/2011/06/27154527/0

21 C Mair and others, *Making Better Places: Making Places Better: the distribution of positive and negative outcomes in Scotland*, Improvement Service, 2011

22 J Raine and C Staite (eds), *The World Will Be Your Oyster? Perspectives on the Localism Bill*, Institute of Local Government Studies, 2012

23 M Brewer and others, *Child Poverty in the UK Since 1998/99: lessons from the past decade*, Working Paper 10/23, Institute for Fiscal Studies, 2012

24 HM Treasury, Department for Work and Pensions and Department for Children, Schools and Families, *Ending Child Poverty: everybody's business*, Office of Public Sector Information, 2008

25 V Alekesan, 'Employment and Child Poverty', in *Ending Child Poverty by 2020: progress made and lessons learned*, Child Poverty Action Group, 2012

26 J Veit-Wilson, review of Glennerster and others, 'One Hundred Years of Poverty and Policy' and Platt 'Discovering Child Poverty', *Journal of Social Policy* 34(4), 2005

Fifteen
Poverty, power and participation in the policy process

Fiona McHardy and Robin Tennant

Introduction

For more than twenty years the Poverty Alliance has worked across Scotland with people with direct experience of poverty to bring that knowledge and expertise to bear on anti-poverty policy making. A valuable body of evidence has now been developed on what works when seeking to put that experience at the heart of policy making. This chapter outlines how people experiencing poverty can be, and have been, meaningfully involved in developing, implementing and evaluating policies aimed at tackling poverty in Scotland. It considers the importance, the benefits and the challenges in the current policy context, and outlines the steps required to ensure the effective involvement of people experiencing poverty in the formation and implementation of anti-poverty policy making.

What is participation about and why is it important?

Participation in policy development can take many different forms.[1] These include forums, research, petitions and a variety of focused community activities – in short, a range of activities that engage people in reflecting on their situation and looking for solutions in a way that can have a real impact on themselves and those making policy decisions. The principles of participative processes are underpinned by concepts of active citizenship, and democracy and empowerment. Without it, according to Bort and others:[2]

> ... there is only central planning by professional administrators, a weak culture of debate and discussion about community issues and a declining interest in politics.

However, involvement and engagement are not easily achieved. They are significantly affected by existing power structures that exclude the voices of the poor and powerless, by the fact that people experiencing poverty have restricted access to decision-making processes, and by a lack of access by those in poverty to the resources (personal, organisational and material) that could shape and impact decision making.[3]

Addressing these difficulties means that the key benefits for policy making from involving people in poverty can be gained. What are these benefits? First, involving people in policy making can create public trust in government and thus increase civic capacity and raise the quality of democracy.[4] Second, it is believed to help to contribute to wider social cohesion and empowerment of communities.[5] Third, it provides benefits to individuals in terms of increased political efficacy and skills, such as communication.[6] Perhaps most importantly for people experiencing poverty, it provides the opportunity to engage with a perspective of 'lived experience' and to articulate to those in power the realities and challenges of their situation.

Despite this, many of the positive benefits of participation are context dependent. Context impacts on the 'success' of a participative process, and we need to remember that measurement of success must take into account the political and institutional context within which the participative process operates. If measurement of success does not take this into account, expectations can outrun success and people may give up on the process far too early. There are factors that constrain or enhance the participative processes. On policy issues that are termed as more complicated or politically sensitive, there may be particular challenges that need to be recognised at an early stage. Second, there is a need to recognise the existing baseline of participation and redress the barriers to effective participation. The dialogue must be set in a context of a shared baseline or starting point. This may often need to include resourcing and capacity building communities for effective engagement. This has to go beyond merely removing the financial barriers that prohibit people experiencing poverty from engaging. While financial barriers represent major factors in limiting participation, so too do things like confidence, awareness of process and location of engagement. Effective dialogue requires processes to support people with their engagement, and representation of more disadvantaged groups requires support in terms of articulating their needs and understanding and engaging in policy making.

Avenues for policy making

The institutional contexts and structures for involvement in anti-poverty policy making are not the same across the UK and Scotland. Across both devolved and reserved contexts there is a limit to the breadth of policy areas in which people have the opportunity to engage, as well as the sustainability of the policy mechanisms available to them. Indeed, Brodie and others argue that the UK and Scotland are actually the least democratic nations at the local level in Europe.[7]

Nevertheless, at a Scottish level, a number of policy avenues have widened the opportunities for participation within policy processes. Firstly, at a local authority level, the introduction of community planning through the Local Government Act 2003 widened opportunities for people to engage. Community planning partnerships were led by local authorities, and were designed to co-ordinate partnership working and initiatives at the regional, local and neighbourhood level.

Although this provides an opportunity for influencing policy making, community planning focuses predominately on service delivery and is limited to the local level.[8] Currently there remains no systematic structure for active involvement at national level.

Under development, which theoretically should enhance opportunities at a local level, is the Community Empowerment (Scotland) Bill. This is currently consulting on a number of areas, such as ownership of community assets, but, despite this, no area within the Bill focuses on directly influencing the national policy agenda.[9]

Within delivery of public services in Scotland, there had been an increased emphasis on participation and co-production through the Christie Commission report.[10] This recommended that services must be designed with service users and that service design should draw on understanding the needs and assets of communities. While this report provides a welcome focus on the importance of participation, this will have limited impact without supporting structures and resources to involve low-income communities.

In a UK context, the Westminster government has also introduced a number of policies affecting participation. In 2000, the government implemented the code of practice on consultation.[11] This was followed, in 2001, by a more significant move when a duty was placed on all NHS bodies to involve members of the public in service planning, operation and delivery. In 2009, this duty to involve was extended to require all local authorities and a number of public bodies to involve people in policy processes (which was then repealed in 2011, effectively losing, once again, an opportunity for communities to influence the local and national policy agenda[12]).

Influencing the national agenda in Scotland

While it would be easy to get depressed about the lack of progress on incorporating participative processes into policy making, there are positive stories about. One of the most recent examples, aimed at a national policy level and which promoted active involvement of people experiencing poverty, was the Poverty Alliance's Evidence, Participation and Change project (EPIC) in Scotland, which ran from 2009 to 2013. This project sought to fill a gap in structured dialogue at the national level. The aim of the project was to create processes whereby people with experience of poverty had the opportunity to play an active role in anti-poverty policy development in Scotland and to demonstrate how this could be done. The project drew influence from participative processes at the European level through the Lisbon strategy and the 'open method of co-ordination'. The project provides a demonstration of the model of participation for people experiencing poverty that did not previously exist in Scotland and a useful case study in involvement in national anti-poverty policy making.

The EPIC project set up a number of structured mechanisms for involving people in participatory processes, such as community research, policy forums and an annual assembly. Central to the success of the project was the support developed to allow engagement of those working with national policy making. The project developed a stakeholder forum that focused on specific processes and maintained a tight approach to issues. It brought together people with experience of poverty, officials with responsibility for addressing poverty in Scotland and key voluntary sector organisations. Many participative processes are unsuccessful due to the scope of the issues they try to tackle, and this stakeholder forum structured its focus specifically on targeted areas within the Scottish government's framework for tackling poverty, Achieving Our Potential.[13]

The project also built the capacity of all of those engaging within the processes. A key focus was on preparation work, including assisting policy makers in working in ways with which they may be unaccustomed. Key areas of EPIC saw, for example, the involvement of community activists in a way that helped emphasise the importance of the social fund to Scottish government officials, and their involvement in making Scottish government and the Convention of Scottish Local Authorities aware of the limits to the Community Empowerment Bill. Dialogue within the project was conducted in a respectful way with a clear emphasis placed upon a two-way exchange process, as opposed to simply a one-sided extraction.[14] Clarity within the process was critical to its success. Clear objectives were set to ensure participants had defined roles in terms of their contribution to policy areas such as the child poverty strategy. The project also focused on feedback mechanisms that were built into the process to allow for transparency to all involved. A significant amount of time and effort was also put into the engagement and support of people directly experiencing poverty.

Despite this, the project faced pressures as the wider economic context and the policy context changed. These were changes that impacted directly on those experiencing poverty and their capacity to be involved, but they also presented challenges in the delivery of anti-poverty strategies and policies across Scotland that all those engaged in policy development faced. UK changes in welfare, a reduction in employment, reductions in standards of living and organisational changes within departments – these all impacted on the work of EPIC. A realistic appraisal of what can be achieved has to recognise such changes.

Conclusions

To conclude, participative processes provide a way of conducting more inclusive policy making. To undertake such processes, and for them to be effective requires a number of factors to be at play, such as commitment from decision makers, focused aims, and clear and meaningful participation. Despite the success of projects such as EPIC, there is still a lack of opportunity for people experiencing poverty to influence policy at the national level within Scotland and the UK. Where opportunities do exist, they are still largely found within local level planning and service delivery, and even at that level there is still room for improvement. In order for participative processes and solutions to be effective, ring-fenced resources must be provided for disadvantaged demographics and there must be both wider commitment and wider legislative support to build and increase opportunities for participative anti-poverty policy making.

Strengthening participative processes is essential if the interests of the poorest are to have an impact on policy making, and if policy making is to be more effective in dealing with their concerns.

Notes

1 P Kelly, *Involving People in Poverty in Policy Development: lessons from the UK*, the Poverty Alliance, 2012

2 E Bort, R McAlpine and G Morgan, *The Silent Crisis: failure and revival in local democracy in Scotland*, the Jimmy Reid Foundation, 2013

3 See note 1

4 Organisation for Economic Development, *Engaging Citizens in Policy Making: information, consultation and public participation*, 2001

5 E Brodie, T Hughes, J Jochum, S Miller, N Ockenden and D Warbuton, *Pathways Through Participation: what creates and sustains active citizenship?*, National Council for Voluntary Organisations, Institute for Volunteering Research and Involve, 2011

6 See note 5

7 See note 2

8 See note 1

9 Scottish government, *Community Empowerment and Renewal Bill Consultation*, 2012

10 Christie Commission, *Commission on the Future Delivery of Public Services*, 2011

11 Cabinet Office, *Code of Practice on Consultation*, 2000

12 Involve, *Duty to Involve*, 2011

13 S Welford, 'The Poverty Alliance Evidence Participation and Change Project, Putting Participation into Practice in Scotland', in European Anti-poverty Network, *Breaking Barriers: Driving Change: case studies of building participation of people experiencing poverty*, 2011

14 See note 13

Sixteen
Wages, the labour market and low pay
Stephen Boyd

This chapter considers developments in the Scottish labour market over the past five years and what emerging trends mean for Scotland's citizens and for the prospects of effectively tackling poverty. It also examines deficiencies in policy responses at both UK and Scottish level and suggests how these can be improved. If progress towards fair pay, decent work and a more equal society is to be achieved, it is essential that the long-established policy consensus on labour market policy is challenged.

Few things unite UK and Scotland's political classes like the benefits of a flexible labour market policy. That the UK is one of the least stringently regulated labour markets in the developed world is, it is regularly argued, a source of competitive advantage and the reason unemployment has not reached the levels anticipated at the start of the 2008/09 recession. That lack of effectively designed, implemented and enforced regulation, which is one of the factors explaining the UK's high share of low-wage work, under-employment and falling wage share, is ignored or dismissed.[1]

Given the depth and length of the recession and subsequent prolonged period of economic stagnation, it is certainly true that headline unemployment has not reached the levels feared as the banks crashed in autumn 2008. However, too close a focus on headline rates risks obscuring what has actually happened in the intervening period. For the story of the last five years is primarily one of rapidly increasing insecurity of work, declining real wages and disguised unemployment.

The current state of the Scottish labour market

The Scottish labour market has certainly improved since summer 2010 when, in the wake of the banking crisis-precipitated recession, unemployment was at its highest and employment was at its lowest. Putting aside for a moment the quality of work created, Scotland's employment rate has improved and at a faster rate through 2013 than in the UK as a whole. However, the current employment rate of 71.8 per cent is still 4 per cent below its pre-recession peak and only 2.6 per cent above the trough of summer 2010.[2]

It is a similar story with unemployment. Again, the striking feature is that Scotland's unemployment rate remains 3.2 per cent higher than the low of summer 2008 and only 1.7 per cent below the peak of summer 2010.[3]

The salient point about the Scottish labour market between 2008 and 2013 is not the comparatively decent performance on headline unemployment, but rather the embedding of trends, some of which were already apparent prior to 2008. These include falling real wages, the decline in full-time employee jobs, rising part-time work, rapidly increasing under-employment and growing long-term unemployment.

Women, who make up two-thirds of the public sector workforce and three-quarters of the part-time workforce, are especially vulnerable to current trends. The problems facing young people, always at a disadvantage in the labour market even in good times, are reflected in stubbornly high unemployment figures: the International Labour Organization unemployment rate for 16–24-year-olds of 20.5 per cent fell by only 0.9 per cent in the year to March 2013.[4]

It is when the surface of the headline labour market is scratched away that the true picture is revealed. In Scotland, a full five years after the start of the recession:

- The claimant count sits at 119,000, 58 per cent above its pre-recession level.
- The latest credible (first quarter, 2013) estimate for the under-employment (those who want more hours in their current job, a new job with more hours or an additional job) rate in Scotland is 9.7 per cent, or 244,000 workers.[5]
- Very long-term unemployment (as measured by those claiming jobseeker's allowance for over two years) continues to rise at a rapid rate – by 42 per cent in the year to October 2013.[6]
- The latest official data show that there are now 127,000 fewer full-time jobs in Scotland than before the recession (a decline of 6.7 per cent) and 63,000 more part-time jobs (an increase of 10.1 per cent).[7]
- In the year to July–September 2013, male unemployment fell by 21 per cent; female employment increased by 3 per cent.[8]

Reflecting the paucity of quality labour market information available at Scottish level, it is difficult even to guess at the increase in insecure forms of working, such as zero-hour contracts. The Office for National Statistics estimates the number of zero-hour contracts in the UK at around 250,000.[9] This is widely regarded as a massive underestimate, with the Chartered Institute of Personnel and Development estimate around four times higher.[10] However, what is truly interesting about the Office for National Statistics work is the rate of growth over the past year: an increase of one-third in 2012.

The Scottish government's laudable cohesion target aims to reduce the gap in employment rates between Scotland's best and worst local authority areas. However, between 2011 and 2012, the gap increased by 2.8 percentage points from 16.3 to 19.1 per cent, thereby exacerbating longstanding regional inequalities.[11] The claimant count rate ranges from 5.4 per cent in North Ayrshire and West Dunbartonshire to 1.5 per cent in Aberdeen City and 0.8 per cent in Aberdeenshire.[12] Joint STUC/Scottish government analysis finds that 'generally, the areas with the highest claimant count rates have seen the highest increases since 2008.'[13]

In June 2013, the highest employment rates were in the Orkney Islands (82.8 per cent), Moray (79.6 per cent) and Aberdeenshire (79.5 per cent), and the lowest in Glasgow City (59.9 per cent), North Ayrshire (61.7 per cent) and Dundee City (64.3 per cent).[14]

The latest reliable figures show that, in Scotland, for the year to the first quarter of 2013, private sector job gains (over 60,000) comfortably outstripped public sector jobs losses (8,300).[15] However, this is the only recent period in which this was the case. It is more illuminating to consider the changes over a longer period:

- From its peak in 2009, public sector employment (excluding financial institutions) has fallen by 52,000 or 8.6 per cent. Full-time equivalent employment has fallen by 51,300 to 499,500.
- From its peak in 2008, private sector employment (including financial institutions) has fallen by 5,000 or 0.3 per cent.

Of course, if private sector job gains fully compensated for the loss of public sector jobs, then the new jobs created would be similar in terms of hours, wages, pensions and terms and conditions. All the indications are that this is simply not happening.

Wages

Median gross weekly pay in Scotland in 2007 was £360.20.[16] This had risen to £396.10 by 2012. However, if median pay had increased in line with inflation, it would have stood at £423.22 by 2012. A worker earning median pay (exactly halfway along the income distribution – half earning more, half earning less) is therefore 6.4 per cent, or £27.12 a week and £1,410.24 a year, worse off. However, given that median pay continued to rise until 2009 due to long-term pay deals, the drop since the end of 2009 has actually been greater – 8.1 per cent according to the Scottish government.[17]

Over this period, real median hourly earnings for males (£16.12) fell by 5 per cent and by 6.7 per cent for women (£13.78). Part-time earnings for both men and women fell by more than £1.00/hour for both men (to £11.50, a fall of 8.7 per cent) and women (to £10.29, a fall of 8.4 per cent).

The distribution of earnings growth across Scotland is also extremely uneven: five (UK) constituency areas have seen (residence-based) real wage declines of over 15 per cent, while 12 witnessed increases over this period.

Of the 18 per cent of employees (418,000 people) earning less than the living wage in Scotland, 93 per cent work in the private sector, 64 per cent are women and 40 per cent are women working part time.

Policy responses and how these can be improved

The problems afflicting the labour market since 2008 are mainly a reflection of the low demand for labour caused by the recession. Therefore, the UK coalition government's determination to pursue an agenda of rapid and immediate austerity has undoubtedly contributed to making things worse. This policy error has been compounded by ill-advised supply side 'reforms' aimed at further weakening the minimal protections afforded to workers in the UK. Thankfully, Scotland is insulated from the coalition's direct attack on national collective bargaining in the public sector, which risks removing an important tier of good jobs from fragile regional economies.

It is difficult to conceive of an agenda so damaging to the interests of workers and communities while being so irrelevant to the challenges facing the economy.

The Scottish government has very limited ability to address problems of low demand – there is no facility to increase borrowing to boost short-term activity. Through the course of the recession, the Scottish government has sought to bring forward as much capital spending as possible (some £300 million in 2010), switch spending from resource to capital budgets and to introduce micro-measures aimed at keeping young people in work, such as Safeguard an Apprentice. While generally a commendable programme, its impact on the labour market is limited.

The single biggest boost to the labour market would be for the UK government to postpone fiscal consolidation to such a time as the economy can bear it. When it comes, consolidation should be more weighted towards tax rises for those who can afford it, rather than spending cuts that hit the most vulnerable.

It is also essential that the attack on employment rights is dropped. This is a risible attempt to appease feral employer organisations and the right-wing commentariat. While this programme will reduce wages and job quality, it does nothing to address the many factors, such as lack of access to finance, which are actually preventing company and jobs growth.

The Scottish government has done a decent job since 2008, but more could be achieved by abolishing costly flagship policies, such as the council tax freeze and small business bonus, and use the considerable savings to invest in jobs, services and active labour market programmes of genuine quality. It is quite staggering that the UK continues to spend less on active labour market programmes than any other European Union nation. As a percentage of GDP, Denmark (1.166 per cent) spent over 28 times what the UK (0.041 per cent) spent on active labour market measures.[18] The Scottish government can help address this appalling situation.

The Scottish government has also done little to evaluate the impact on disadvantaged groups of its response to the weak labour market. For instance, no gendered analysis has been produced to quantify the impact of switching resources from departmental (sustains quality female employment) to capital budgets (generates additional male employment).

There is clearly much more to be done to convince government at all levels that falling real wages in the short term and a falling wage share in the longer term are problems that must be addressed. Government should be doing all it can do boost wages in the economy, particularly at the bottom end through increasing the minimum wage, and extending the living wage directly in the public sector and, where possible, in the private sector through procurement and other devices.

Of course, the best and most efficient way to increase wages would be for collective bargaining coverage in Scotland to grow to Nordic proportions. It is grimly comical how this vital component of the Nordic models is routinely ignored, even by commentators of the left. The Scottish government could lead by establishing sectoral bargaining forums, starting with low wage sectors.

Notes

1 For a discussion of these issues see STUC, *Wrong Plan for Growth: Budget 2011, the global competitiveness report and the dangers of formulating policy on a false premise*, 2011

2 All current labour market data are drawn from Office for National Statistics, *Regional Labour Market: Scotland*, November 2013

3 See note 2

4 See note 2

5 D Bell and D Blanchflower, *A New Underemployment Index for Scotland*, The Economics of Constitutional Change, 2013

6 See note 2

7 See note 2

8 See note 2

9 Office for National Statistics, *Estimating Zero Hour Contracts from the Labour Force Survey*, 2013

10 Chartered Institute of Personnel and Development, 'Zero hour contracts more widespread than thought', Press Release, 5 August 2013

11 Scottish government, *Local Area Labour Markets in Scotland 2012*, 2013

12 STUC analysis of NOMIS claimant count figures, November 2013

13 Scottish government/STUC, *Labour Market Trends*, Scottish government, December 2013

14 See note 13

15 Scottish government/Office for National Statistics, *Public Sector Employment in Scotland Q1 2013*, August 2013

16 Office for National Statistics, *Annual Survey of Hours and Earnings*

17 Scottish government/STUC, *Labour Market Trends*, Scottish government, June 2013

18 STUC, *Labour Market Report*, March 2013

Seventeen
Redistribution and income inequality

Dr Carlo Morelli and Dr Paul Seaman

A central tenet of the authors of each of the chapters in this book is the belief that policy makers have the ability to address the problems which limit the life chances of the most vulnerable sections of Scottish society. While other chapters deal with poverty in detail, in this chapter we place a focus on income inequality. Our reason for doing so is simply that any focus on poverty that ignores income inequality will itself be fundamentally lacking in its recognition that it is income inequalities that can first create, and then reinforce, poverty over time.

Poverty in Scotland has remained stubbornly resilient to change. This represents a major challenge to the Scottish government with its solidarity target aiming to 'increase overall income and the proportion of income earned by the three lowest income deciles as a group by 2017.'[1] In this chapter we examine the potential for income inequality to be addressed. The Scottish government currently has tax-varying powers limited to adjusting the standard rate of income tax by three pence in the pound.[2] The Scotland Act 2012 will enact further taxation powers by introducing the Scottish rate of taxation from 2016, but as it will remain a single tax rate, albeit covering higher incomes, it will remain a relatively unprogressive form of taxation.[3] The forthcoming referendum on Scottish independence, irrespective of the outcome, is also highly likely to lead to changes in this settlement. On both sides of the independence debate is to be found support for much wider and deeper devolution powers. Thus, irrespective of the outcome of the referendum in September 2014, the findings of this chapter will retain their relevance on the extent to which current taxation thinking can be utilised to address income inequality.

Devolution and inequality

Devolution as a means of decentralising state functions continues to be understood within the framework of encouraging more localised decision making.[4] Moves to increasing equality within this framework are often limited to examining participation in government by minority or discriminated-against groups or changes in the culture and language of decision making. While these approaches, in general, suggest a broadly favourable interpretation of the first decade of UK devolution, assessments of the impact outside of parliamentary structures are less favourable. Measures of income inequality in Scotland indicate no impact of devolved government,[5] or worse still, that political devolution can become a means by which inequalities increase[6] and neoliberalism can become embedded within sub-state ideologies.[7]

It is against this background of competing interpretations of devolution that this chapter examines the scope for policy measures to address income inequalities. We ask the simple question: if the Scottish government were to use the current tax-varying powers at its disposal, how redistributive would this be? In order to examine this question, our analysis is performed on the Scottish household data from the second wave (2010/11) of the Understanding Society dataset. Understanding Society is a new UK survey of households containing details of income and other characteristics for each and every household member in the surveyed household. We take as our starting point the most recent gross monthly income that households are in receipt of and then apply a series of tax increases and/or benefit increases in order to see their effect (in isolation and in combination) on income inequality in our sample of Scottish households.[8]

In the estimations that follow, we calculate the level of income the Scottish government would receive if the existing income tax-varying powers were implemented to their maximum, an increase of three pence in the pound on the standard rate of income tax. This would raise an average additional tax of £521.05 per household per annum. All of the other potential tax changes, and all of the potential expenditure changes, that we examine would be set to raise, or cost, £521.05 per household per annum. Thus, a combination of any one of the tax changes with one of the expenditure changes would be budget neutral.

We examine the effect on income inequality of a range of income- and consumption-based tax changes as indicative of the sensitivity of income inequality to different forms of taxation. The four tax changes are:[9]

- the Scottish variable rate (3p on the basic rate of income tax);
- an additional higher rate of income tax (16.2 per cent) on all taxable income over £35,000;
- an additional car tax of £455.37 per car;
- an additional alcohol tax of 90.62 per cent of the current, post-tax price of alcohol.

The additional income can then be spent on vulnerable groups in the form of additional universal expenditure changes – distributing the money equally:

- among those aged 65 or older;
- according to the number of dependent children under the age of 16;
- among those in receipt of disability living allowance;
- among full-time students aged 16 or older.

We report our findings as the ratio between the incomes of the richest 20 per cent of equivalised households compared to those of the bottom 20 per cent of equivalised households.[10] Thus, in Table 17.1 we see that the richest 20 per cent of households have 6.166 times household income compared with the poorest 20 per cent of households. The introduction of the Scottish variable tax reduces this inequality slightly (6.110). This decline is to be expected as only those who are receiving taxable income are affected, while the poorest households would be exempt from the additional taxation. However, the much more pronounced reduction for the higher rate tax change (5.979) demonstrates that progressive income tax is required to make a marked difference to income inequality.

An alternative to income-based taxation would be consumption-based taxation, though this would require additional powers to be given to the Scottish government. Nevertheless, in terms of a consumption-based form of taxation, our choices of an additional vehicle tax or alcohol tax result in an increase in inequality to 6.262 and 6.287 respectively. Our choices of vehicle- or alcohol-based taxes are chosen to examine the extent to which consumption-based forms of taxation may be focused on higher income households for goods for which consumption rises with income. That neither form of consumption-based taxation produces a reduction in income inequality suggests that the Scottish government has little opportunity to use consumption as a means to achieve greater income equality, at least not for widely consumed goods. The regressive nature of taxes on cars and alcohol reflects the fact that in an advanced economy neither can be seen as 'luxury goods'.

Table 17.1:

Equivalised Scottish household income inequality arising from additional taxation (required to raise £521.05 per household per annum)

	Ratio of household income of 20% of richest households compared with 20% of poorest households
No tax increase	6.166
3p Scottish variable rate	6.110
Taxable income above £35,000	5.979
Car tax	6.262
Alcohol tax	6.287

In Table 17.2 we examine the impact of redistributing the additional taxation to specific low-income households defined by their demographic characteristics. The table replicates, in column 2, the results presented in Table 17.1. Each subsequent column then demonstrates the extent to which the income ratio between the richest and poorest households shifts once the additional tax revenue derived from each form of taxation is allocated to the characteristic household type. Thus, for example, increasing the standard variable rate by three pence and distributing the proceeds evenly among all individuals aged 65 or over would reduce the ratio from 6.166 to 5.737. In all cases, the ratio in each row is lower than our original ratio (6.166). As expected, if income is removed from households through taxation and returned to low-income households, income inequality will be reduced.

However, the table tells us more than this. First, progressive taxation is the most redistributive, with the taxation of individuals above the higher income tax threshold (taxable income above £35,000) providing the lowest household income ratio in each column. Thus, for column three, focusing on households with members aged 65 and over, levying the tax on individuals with income over £35,000 and redistributing the income to households containing pensioners sees a reduction in the ratio from 6.166 to 5.616. Second, the higher number of children in our sample means that the additional expenditure is more thinly distributed, lowering the impact on income inequality for these households.

Table 17.2:

Ratio of richest 20 per cent of equivalised households to poorest 20 per cent of households from additional income by household type

	No spending change	Adults aged 65 and over	Dependent children	Adults with a disability	Full-time students
No tax change	6.166	5.791	6.007	5.940	5.928
3p Scottish variable rate	6.110	5.737	5.952	5.885	5.873
Taxable income above £35,000	5.979	5.616	5.826	5.760	5.748
Car tax	6.262	5.872	6.097	6.027	6.014
Alcohol tax	6.287	5.893	6.119	6.014	6.036
Number of individuals	–	1,110	1,435	313	306
£ given to each individual	–	£1,350.51	£1,044.65	£4,789.35	£4,898.91

The final important feature of Table 17.2 is that it is by allocating the resources to those aged over 65, full-time students or disabled adults that we generate the greatest reduction in income inequality. This feature of income inequality is in line with many of the stylised facts that we know about child poverty.[11] The high numbers of households with children and their higher incidence of poverty in Scotland means the change in income inequality is less than that with smaller numbers of households where non-working adults are to be found, such as those aged over 65, disabled people or full-time students where the additional income is much higher per individual than that per individual child.[12] To address child poverty means that a much greater degree of progressivity is required.

Conclusions

A number of points can be taken from our analysis. First, and most importantly, our analysis suggests that progressive forms of income taxes that focus on the highest earners can have a marked impact on income inequality. The extent of progressivity within the tax system is important and requires further modelling. Our results examined the higher rate tax threshold and not the highest rate tax threshold, due to limits on data for the highest earning individuals. Second, the extent to which income inequality can be addressed depends on the selectivity of the expenditure. Where higher numbers of households are recipients of additional expenditure, such as households with children, the impact will be lower compared with households with fewer recipients, such as disabled adults or full-time students. Forms of selectivity, including means testing, would also be expected to generate still greater reductions. Finally, limiting the tax-varying powers to only the standard variable rate, as is currently within the powers of the Scottish government, or the single Scottish rate, as will be the case under the Scotland Act 2012, will not be sufficiently redistributive to help redress Scotland's entrenched legacy of income inequality.

Notes

1 See http://www.scotland.gov.uk/About/Performance/scotPerforms/purposes/solidarity

2 Scotland Act 1998, http://www.legislation.gov.uk/ukpga/1998/46/part/IV

3 HM Revenue and Customs, *Clarifying the Scope of the Scottish Rate of Income Tax*, Technical Note, May 2012, http://www.hmrc.gov.uk/news/technote-scot-taxrate.pdf

4 See T Rees and P Chaney, 'Multilevel Governance, Equality and Human Rights: evaluating the first decade of devolution in Wales', *Social Policy and Society*, 2011, pp210–28; S Jones, N Charles and C Davies, 'Transforming Masculinist Political Cultures? Doing politics in new political institutions', *Sociological Research Online*, 14, 2/3, 2009, http://www.socresonline.org.uk /14/2/1.html

5 C Morelli and P Seaman, 'Devolution and Inequality: a failure to create a community of equals?', *Transactions of the Institute of British Geographers*, New Series 32, 2007, pp523–38

6 T Vassilis, A Rodríguez-Pose, A Pike, J Tomaney and G Torrisi, 'Income Inequality, Decentralisation and Regional Development in Western Europe', *Environment and Planning*, Vol 44, 2012, pp1278–1301

7 A Law, 'Between Autonomy and Dependency: state and nation in devolved Scotland', in G Mooney and G Scott (eds), *Social Justice and Social Policy in Scotland*, Policy Press, 2012, pp25–42

8 The Understanding Society household panel dataset has two waves of data in the public domain. It is the latest and largest longitudinal household panel dataset available. Space prevents a full description of our estimations, but full details are available from the authors on request.

9 To raise the equivalent additional income from a 3p increase in the standard variable rate requires an additional 16.275p increase in the higher rate tax level, and

additional £454.72 increase in car tax or an additional 90.13 per cent increase on tax on the current price of alcohol.

10 We equivalise household income to take into account housing and other costs, after the taxation and spending is applied.

11 J H McKendrick, 'Who Lives in Poverty?', in J H Mckendrick, G Mooney, J Dickie and J Kelly (eds), *Poverty in Scotland 2011: towards a more equal society*, CPAG, 2011, pp91–110

12 Focusing on means-tested benefits, such as child tax credit or working tax credit, would reduce income inequality further for households with children.

13 Understanding Society does not provide a measure of wealth that is compatible with our gross income data, making a study of unearned income beyond the scope of this study.

Eighteen
Asylum seekers and refugees: a litmus test for Scotland?

Gareth Mulvey

Introduction

As Scotland moves towards the 2014 referendum on independence, beneath the acrimony there is a debate trying to emerge about what sort of society Scotland could be, and how the referendum might impact upon that. Asylum seekers and refugees are a useful litmus test for where Scotland is and where Scotland could be. Much policy in relation to asylum is reserved to the UK government, but many immigrant policies are devolved. This chapter argues that reserved policy matters are both failing asylum seekers and refugees, and are simultaneously storing up problems for the devolved government. The negative effects of reserved policy are therefore important for Scotland in the present, but point to how to avoid such future affects.

Why does this matter?

While it is often said that the way the most vulnerable are treated in any society is a true test of that society, this is not the only reason why the position of asylum seekers and refugees should be of concern. There are also economic reasons. Much of what is known about the test of 'good' policy suggests the need for early intervention and preventative measures. Asylum policy at present fails that test. What is more, all levels of government, and society more generally, should have an interest in social justice and how to create more harmonious communities. The effects of reserved asylum policy create ongoing areas of concern for refugees, and therefore for policy makers, communities and Scotland more generally.

Critical review of policy

UK asylum policy has been characterised by legislative activism, with seven major pieces of legislation over the past nineteen years, and a raft of secondary legislation and rule changes. There is not the space here to outline all policy change that has an impact on the lives of asylum seekers and refugees.[1] Instead, this chapter will focus on a few aspects of policy that have had profound equalities effects. From 2000, the dispersal of asylum applicants around the UK to relieve pressure on south east England was, in many cases, housing driven. Asylum seekers were located in parts of cities that had 'spare' housing capacity, predominantly in deprived areas. Thus, in Glasgow almost all asylum seekers were located in deprived housing estates. In 2002, the Labour government also took the decision to remove asylum seekers' right to work on the false proposition that work acted as a 'pull factor' for economic migrants to claim asylum.[2] Finally, newly recognised refugees have 28 days to vacate Home Office-provided accommodation and support and access mainstream benefits. The effect is that almost all newly recognised refugees are made homeless. Added to employment difficulties, the result is that refugees are effectively being integrated into poverty.

The devolved context

Immigration policy (who is able to come to the UK) is a reserved policy area, but much of immigrant policy (what happens to people once they get here) is devolved. This means that, beyond restrictions imposed by the asylum process, the Scottish government has had some leeway in terms of policy around migration issues. Under all Scottish governments since the establishment of the Parliament in 1999, the Scottish perspective has differed somewhat from that of Westminster. While primary policy has been scarce, there have been differences. With regard to overall migration, the main development was the 'fresh talent' initiative, which began in 2004 to enable graduates from Scottish universities to work in Scotland. It was subsequently subsumed by the points-based migration system established by the UK government before being abolished.

The Scottish government's view of refugees and people seeking asylum has also been somewhat different, with a far more positive discourse from all parties in the Scottish Parliament. Added to that, all Scottish governments from the outset have taken a different view of integration to that of Westminster, whereby the Scottish view is that integration should begin the day an asylum seeker arrives in Scotland, in contrast to Westminster's approach that it should only begin on being recognised as a refugee. In practical terms, this has meant some financial support to community and voluntary organisations, but it has also allowed greater access to further education for those still in the asylum process, as well as continuing access to healthcare for those whose cases are refused. While the impact of this approach set against that of the UK has yet to be established, the symbolism remains important.

The right to work and employment

The absence of the right to look after themselves and their families during the asylum process has multiple impacts on asylum seekers and refugees. Many talk of the health effects of enforced idleness, in particular mental health, while parents often refer to being denied the right to be role models for their children.

However, one of the primary effects of not being allowed to work, one borne out by the UK Border Agency's own survey of new refugees, is the effect on those subsequently recognised as refugees who face a constant struggle to access the labour market.[3] In a Scottish survey of 262 asylum seekers and refugees, just over 20 per cent of those entitled to work were in paid employment. This finding is not related to the present economic downturn, as those recognised as refugees prior to the recession were no more likely to be in employment than newer arrivals. What is more, the struggle is across the board, with highly educated and highly skilled refugees also struggling to find work, and certainly struggling to find work commensurate with their skill levels.

Deskilling and the non-recognition of skills are two major issues in this regard, with the former resulting from the asylum process and the latter, despite progress by the Scottish government, still problematic. With regard to the asylum process, over half of all refugees in this Scottish study waited for over a year to be recognised as refugees, with over 40 per cent of respondents in each year of application waiting for over a year. While this, in itself, creates concerns about skill atrophy, the fact that many also wait for long periods to access language classes has a considerable effect in terms of employment outcomes.

Added to that, the gaps in employment histories also make access to the labour market difficult. Many research respondents indicated that they had been left behind in terms of technological developments and faced an uphill struggle to bridge these gaps. Others felt that employers were less likely to offer them work without recent activity in the labour market, but that they were unable to develop a work history because of labour market barriers.

Refugees who do find employment are concentrated in low-paid work, with restricted hours and evidence of zero-hour contracts. Lack of security pervades many aspects of refugees' lives. While sporadic employment has its own specific problems in terms of security, planning and childcare, there is also the concern that Jobcentre Plus is not flexible enough to adjust to non-standard forms of employment.

For those in employment, the benefits are multiple. While low pay rates make financial benefits less than clear, refugees feel that they should work, that they want to work, and that work helps them make friends, improve language skills and better understand the society in which they now live. This also has mental health benefits. Indeed, the feeling of being useful should not be an underestimated result of employment.

Integrating into poverty

As already alluded to, low pay means that even those in employment face financial hardship. When all respondents involved in this research project (whether in work, out of work or not allowed to work) were asked how they felt about their finances, the indication is widespread financial struggle, with over 68 per cent saying that they were finding it difficult or very difficult to cope.[4] Although the questions are somewhat different, the Scottish Household Survey results indicate that refugees and asylum seekers struggle financially even more than the 15 per cent most deprived in Scotland, 23 per cent of whom say they struggle to manage financially.

Not surprisingly, many of the financial problems that people identified are linked to either employment restrictions or the struggle to find jobs. The poverty trap, whereby available work pays little more than benefits, is evident. It is worth reiterating, however, that the vast majority of refugees simply want to work and, for them, no financial calculations are made.

Financial struggle for those in the asylum process, and especially for refused asylum seekers, many of whom subsequently go on to be recognised as refugees, is even more acute. For the former, financial support has been static. Those in receipt of asylum support are provided with about half the amount of income support for those over 25 and for lone parents, just £35 per week. It is worth reiterating that the purpose of income support is to prevent poverty and destitution, and yet half of this amount is deemed sufficient for those in the asylum system, some of whom are in that system for long periods of time. While the British government argues that the provision of all housing costs mitigates this hardship, such an argument is not sustainable, given the fact that housing support is also provided for many of those on income support, and so the comparison is a spurious one. In addition, low income is usually measured after housing costs, and £35 per week after housing cannot be seen as anything other than a poverty income.

Even more extreme is the absolute poverty experienced by refused asylum seekers, who receive no support at all. They are required to vacate their accommodation and live from a combination of charities and friends.[5]

There is therefore a concern that refugees and asylum seekers are integrating into poverty. The process itself, locating asylum seekers almost exclusively in the most deprived communities and denying them the ability to have their skills and experiences recognised and to access the employment market at an early stage, play a major role. Add to this the cost of securing and furnishing homes, the cost of upskilling, the lack of familial support for childcare and regarding remittances and that struggle becomes clearer. Being integrated into socially excluded communities with low income levels should not be the ultimate destiny of refugees as a homogenous mass. However, reserved policy is at present ensuring this.

Policy prescriptions for 2014 and beyond

There are a variety of means by which policy could be changed to prevent poverty being a natural or automatic outcome of the asylum process. While more in-depth work on policy options is beyond the remit of this book, they can be seen in a recent report by the Scottish Refugee Council.[6] Nevertheless, it is worth reiterating some of the potential solutions. First of all, the Christie Commission into the future of public services argued that public services should 'prevent negative outcomes'. Thus, the removal of policies and practices that produce negative outcomes should be one of the guiding principles of policy. In that regard, ensuring that asylum seekers have the right to work, and furthering work on skill recognition would be a positive step forward. Allied to this, early language support would help to prevent a delay in the ability to find employment. In terms of finances, asylum support is not enough on which to live a dignified existence. Not only should asylum seekers receive full income support, it should be provided by the Department for Work and Pensions rather than the Home Office, easing the transition from the asylum process into being a refugee. In addition, support should be paid in cash from the moment an individual claims asylum, until s/he is either recognised as a refugee or leaves the country. Attempting to 'starve them out' is both immoral and ineffective.

Notes

1   V Squire, *The Exclusionary Politics of Asylum*, Palgrave MacMillan UK, 2009; W Somerville, *Immigration under New Labour*, Policy Press, 2007; G Mulvey, 'When Policy Creates Politics: the problematising of immigration and the consequences for refugee integration', *Journal of Refugee Studies*, 23(4), 2010, pp437–62

2   V Robinson and J Segrott, *Understanding the Decision-Making of Asylum Seekers*, Home Office Research Series 243, 2002; H Crawley, *Chance or Choice? Understanding why asylum seekers come to the UK*, 2010, http://www.refugeecouncil.org.uk/policy_research/research

3   A Cebulla, M Daniel and A Zuruman, *Spotlight on Refugee Integration: findings from the survey of new refugees in the United Kingdom*, Home Office Research Report 37, 2010

4   G Mulvey, *In Search of Normality: refugee integration in Scotland (final report)*, 2013, http://www.scottishrefugeecouncil.org.uk/policy_and_research/research_reports/integration_research

5   M Gillespie, *Trapped: destitution and asylum in Scotland*, 2012, http://www.scottishrefugeecouncil.org.uk/policy_and_research/research_reports

6   M Shisheva, G Mulvey and G Christie, *Refugees in Scotland After the Referendum*, 2012, http://www.scottishrefugeecouncil.org.uk/policy_and_research/research_reports

Nineteen

Perspectives on gender equality in Scotland

Angela O'Hagan

On the brink of the last Scottish referendum in 1998, it seemed that, following numerous calls, equality would be central to the 'new politics' of Scotland and present in the new institutions and the new approaches to tackle poverty, inequality and social justice that were emerging. Women's representation was prominent on the political agenda following the highly visible 50:50 campaign led by the STUC women's committee. Indeed, 47 women were elected as Members of the Scottish Parliament – a breakthrough level of 37 per cent. The establishment of an equal opportunities committee in the Scottish Parliament and an Equality Unit within the Scottish government (then the Scottish Executive) all pointed to an institutional commitment to advancing equality for all in Scotland.

In 2000, the newly formed Scottish Women's Budget Group proposed gender budget analysis as one of the new approaches to doing things differently from Westminster.[1] This proposal met with early support from the first Finance Minister, Jack McConnell, who committed the Scottish Executive to pursuing this alternative process.[2] In 2001, Henry McLeish, as First Minister, pledged a 'more open, inclusive budgeting process, which actively seeks to inform and involve people outside the immediate political process of budget-setting'.[3]

These bold statements of political support characterised Scotland as a pioneer in equality analysis in the budget process in the early years of devolution. However, a more laggardly slump in political action and commitment occurred during the second and third terms of the Scottish Parliament. Then, in 2009, the Scottish government produced the first Equality Budget Statement.

The Equality Budget Statement is the outcome of a decade of push and pull, and is a significant development in policy making in the Scottish government. However, this progress requires enduring political commitment if Scotland is not to fall behind developments elsewhere. For example, Gipuzkoa (one of the four county-level governments or *diputaciones* comprising the Basque Country autonomous region in Spain) produced an analysis of its full budget for 2014/15 based on the theoretical framework of the 'capabilities approach', as developed by Amartya Sen and Martha Nussbaum.[4] This approach to wellbeing budgeting looks to the government budget as a lever, capable of delivering changes in the economic, social and physical wellbeing of citizens. Wellbeing gender budgeting has also been gaining purchase at local and regional government level in Italy in recent years, with examples in the city of Modena, the district of Bologna, and the regions of Lazio and Piedmont.[5] The autonomous community of Andalucía in Spain has applied gender budget analysis since 2005, changing the way the government produces its budget, requiring all spending departments to identify and rank policies and programmes as 'motors for change' for their contribution to advancing gender equality. Outcomes have been slow to materialise, but a significant shift in how policy is made has been achieved, and at its core is the pursuit of women's equality and women's social, economic, and political advancement.

Over the last thirty years, different approaches have emerged to gender budget analysis globally. At its core, it is an attempt to reconfigure the budget process into a more open, democratic and transparent one that underpins spending and revenue proposals that support political goals to transform the status quo by reducing inequalities and creating greater equality between women and men across their different and distinct economic, ethnic and social contexts.

In looking for alternative foundations for Scotland's future, we could do worse than consider the propositions from feminist thinker and political activist Marilyn Waring. She proposed that the national budget should reflect the economic and environmental wellbeing of a nation, demonstrating concern for paid and unpaid labour, care for children and the elderly, health improvement and provision of adequate housing.[6] In Scotland, there has been some progress towards a budget process that reflects these concerns and the need for alternative approaches to defining and securing economic wellbeing for all.

Recently, there have been changes in thinking around the centrality of equality to economic development and wellbeing in Scotland. In 2012, the Scottish government acknowledged the impetus behind the Women's Employment Summit as:[7]

> ... the current pressures on women's employment and the limitations of economic models which fail to reflect the contribution of women's paid and unpaid employment.

Arguably, this amounts to a shift in political discourse, echoing calls for greater alignment between social and economic wellbeing, as evident in statements such as:[8]

> Equality is fundamental to a modern democratic society. It is essential to economic growth and to social wellbeing and to realising our ambitions for a successful sustainable country in which all can flourish.

As to how this narrative translates into policy and spending is another matter. Do we have a gender-aware budget in Scotland? No, not yet. Is gender equality a shared political priority in Scotland? Perhaps. Equality between women and men may be articulated as a shared political goal, but it is not a reality in the content of public policy as evidenced in, for example, the Modern Apprenticeship scheme, where men significantly outnumber women in publicly funded training programmes, and both sexes continue to be channelled along gender-stereotyped occupational areas.[9] The pay gap stubbornly endures, with women's full-time average earnings 13.3 per cent, and part-time earnings just under 34 per cent, less than those of men. According to Close the Gap, the difference in (mean) full-time weekly earnings between women and men working full time in Scotland is £108.30 per week.[10]

Have there been sustainable changes in policies and processes within Scottish government and public authorities? Well, that would be a yes and no answer. Changes in the budget process to date have not gone far enough in embedding gender analysis of public spending and public policy proposals. As for changes in the way public authorities and government make policy decisions and put equality outcomes centre stage, evaluations of the public sector equalities duties produced by the Equality and Human Rights Commission in 2013 reveal a generally poor level of performance and response to the potentially transformative approach to public policy making introduced in the 2010 Equality Act.[11]

This less than desirable level of policy change has, it can be argued, not been for the want of trying. An Equality Strategy was widely consulted on in the early days of devolution and produced in 2000.[12] This was premised on the concept of mainstreaming equality throughout the policy process – including the budget. The strategy took a broad-based approach to 'equalities', across what are now known under the legislation as 'protected characteristics'. This expansive approach of equal treatment was intended to address issues for distinct communities of interest and group identities, but without appearing to advantage or prioritise any particular group or set of interests.

Concerns with socio-economic and health inequalities dominated major policy platforms such as Closing the Opportunity Gap. This focus on socio-economic indicators has continued within the broad sweep of the National Performance Framework targets since 2007, and their focus on 'tackling significant inequalities' has, arguably, resulted in specific impacts and consequences for particular groups being overlooked or bypassed. The absence of quality data informing policy options and evaluations in the first instance, and of robust equality impact assessment measures, has contributed to a less nuanced and intersectional approach to public policy analysis. In its responses to Scottish government draft budgets and in parliamentary evidence, the Scottish Women's Budget Group has argued that the social justice narrative conflated equalities objectives and ignored or rendered invisible the impact on women of major policy and spending decisions.[13] Recent analysis by the Scottish government has identified the significant impact of UK government welfare reforms on women,[14] but this understanding has not been carried into specific policy responses.

There is plentiful evidence and analysis that the current gender-blind dismantling of the benefits and taxation system is affecting, and will continue to impact more on, women than men.[15] The collision of public sector reform, economic recession and welfare reform all impact significantly on women in Scotland, but as yet there is a lack of specific and integrated policy response. Analysis from Women in Scotland's Economy (WiSE), among others, consistently highlights the imbalance affecting women's income and employment through the recession, recovery and reform of public services.[16] There are legal requirements to assess, mitigate and eliminate this imbalance and detrimental impact. There is also evidence of the failure of government at all levels in Scotland and the UK to conduct effective equality impact assessments, develop and use accurate data, and develop meaningful equality outcomes.

Why is this mismatch occurring? Why is it ongoing? Arguably, it is a consequence of the failure to put gender equality central stage as a legitimate political and economic goal, and of relegating equality to being a desirable secondary outcome of other primary policy objectives.

Contributors to this book have argued the case for sustainable, adequately paid employment as a principal response to embedded poverty. In addition, the WiSE Research Centre has argued that childcare is one area of the economy requiring increased and sustained investment, generating jobs in construction through increasing physical infrastructure, in employment for women and men as skilled childcare workers, increasing access to employment for parents seeking work or to remain in paid employment, and thereby increasing family incomes, distribution of spending across local economies, and investment in children's welfare and development.[17] Childcare is not a 'women's issue', it is an economic and social issue which cuts across training, education, employment, economic development, welfare and taxation policy. Recent changes by the UK government to working tax credit and proposals for universal credit and access to childcare vouchers are contributing to greater pressure on family income and budgets.[18] There is substantial evidence that the high costs of childcare in Scotland have a negative effect on already poor families' access to work, study and training.[19] A 'transformational change to childcare', as signalled by the Scottish government,[20] is possible, and of interest to politicians and the voting public in the lead-in to the independence referendum in 2014. The lessons are there from across Europe to be learned and applied to transform childcare provision and access in Scotland, regardless of the constitutional arrangements (see Chapter 25).[21]

The referendum and the prospect of constitutional change hold great promise, but at present it is one of 'jam tomorrow'. The bread is cut pretty thinly in 2014. Gender equality must be made more central to the vision and ambition of Scotland regardless of the constitutional arrangements. Other countries have taken bolder steps. Following economic and constitutional upheaval in Iceland, economic and social wellbeing are at the heart of the finance ministry's mission and a central tenet of the constitution.

Now and into our future, government in Scotland, of whatever hue, can draw on innovation from elsewhere, can choose to make the public sector equality duties work effectively, and can draw on the international levers from the European Union and the United Nations for the progressive realisation of social and economic rights. A future Scotland can, and should, create and direct public spending to policies that eliminate poverty and disadvantage based on discrimination and unequal treatment predicated on the basis of gender and the status of being a woman or a man.

Notes

1   Scottish Women's Budget Group, *Independent Budget Review Response from Scottish Women's Budget Group*, 2000, http://www.scotland.gov.uk/Resource/Doc/919/0102241.pdf

2   J McConnell, Contribution to Budget Scotland Bill (Stage 1) debate, Wednesday 26 January 2000, http://www.scottish.parliament.uk/parliamentarybusiness/28862.aspx?r=4205&i=27351&c=0&s=equality%20budget

3   Scottish Executive, *2002/03 Annual Expenditure Report*, Scottish government, 2001, p1

4   M Nussbaum, *Women and Human Development: the capabilities approach*, Cambridge University Press, 2001

5   T Addabbo, 'Gender Budgeting in the Capability Approach: from theory to evidence', Conference Paper, Counting on Women: gender, care and economics, May 2011, pp24–26, Women in Scotland's Economy Series Conference, 2012

6   M Waring, *If Women Counted: a new feminist economics*, Harper and Row, 1988

7   Scottish government, *Equality Statement Scottish Draft Budget 2013/14*, Scottish government, 2012, p6

8   Communities Analytical Services Division, *The Gender Impact of Welfare Reform: equality and tackling poverty*, Scottish government, 2013, p4

9   J Campbell, A McKay, S Ross and E Thomson, *How Modern is the Modern Apprenticeship in Scotland?*, Briefing Sheet 3, Women in Scotland Economy Research Centre, Glasgow Caledonian University, 2013

10 Close the Gap, *Working Paper: gender pay gap statistics*, 2014. Calculations based on ONS Provisional Results Annual Survey of Hours and Earnings 2013, Table 3.

11 Equality and Human Rights Commission (Scotland), *Measuring Up: monitoring public authorities performance of the Scottish specific duties*, 2013

12 Scottish Executive, *Equality Strategy: working together for equality*, Scottish Executive, 2000

13 Scottish Women's Budget Group, www.swbg.org.uk

14 See note 8

15 J Campbell, S Ross and A McKay, *Scotland and the Great Recession: an analysis of the gender impact*, Briefing Sheet 4, Women in Scotland's Economy Research Centre, Glasgow Caledonian University, 2013; Women's Budget Group, *The Impact on Women of the Coalition Spending Review 2010*, 2010, http://wbg.org.uk/RRB_Reports_4_1653541019.pdf; D Sands, *The Impact of Austerity on Women*, Policy Briefing, Fawcett Society, 2012; Scottish government, *The Gender Impact of Welfare Reform*, 2013, http://www.scotland.gov.uk/Topics/People/welfarereform/analysis/welfarereformanalysisgenderimpact

16 A McKay, E Thomson and S Ross, *Where are Women in Scotland's Labour Market*, Briefing Sheet 2, Women in Scotland Economy Research Centre, Glasgow Caledonian University, 2013

17 J Campbell, D Elson and A McKay, *The Economic Case for Investing in High-quality Childcare and Early Years Education*, Briefing Sheet 5, Women in Scotland's Economy Research Centre, Glasgow Caledonian University, 2013

18 UK government, *Tax-free Childcare Consultation*, https://www.gov.uk/government/consultations/tax-free-childcare

19 Save the Children, *Making Work Pay: the childcare trap*, 2011, http://www. savethechildren.org.uk/sites/default/files/docs/Making_Work_Pay_Scotland_bri efing _1.pdf

20 Scottish government, *Scotland's Future: your guide to independent Scotland*, 2013, http://www.scotreferendum.com

21 I Naumann, C McLean, A Koslowski, K Tisdall and E Lloyd, *Early Childhood Education and Care Provision: international review of policy, delivery and funding*, Scottish government, 2013

Section Six

Perspectives from
Europe and beyond

Twenty
Perspectives from Europe and beyond

Gill Scott

Looking outwards

Demands for constitutional and territorial reform have become far more prevalent across Europe and North America over the last twenty years. The significant amendments to the UK devolution acts and the referendum in Scotland in 2014 have occurred at the same time as moves towards greater political independence within multi-plural and multi-national states elsewhere. In Spain, Catalonia's sovereignty movement is currently bolstered by a parliament with a majority of pro-independence parties, and over the last decade numerous amendments have been made to the statutes of the autonomous regions of Catalonia and the Basque Country. In Canada, referendums on Quebec secession have occurred and attempts made to amend the Canadian constitution to recognise Quebec as a distinct society. Since at least 2007, Belgium has seen a growing possibility of a break up or fundamental changes to the federal system. Wherever they occur, they have far-reaching implications, not just for governance but also for inter-regional and intra-regional patterns of poverty and anti-poverty policy.

In many of these situations, demands for constitutional reform have been accompanied by demands for the separation of an existing welfare state from national boundaries. So, for example, in Canada, sovereignty debates have been accompanied by the provinces taking over responsibility from the federal government for increasing areas of social provision; in Spain, sovereignty debates have accompanied an increase in the power over the standards of services available to their citizens that autonomous regions exercise; in Belgium, the most recent state reform included proposals on how to integrate social security in a multi-layered government structure; and increasing constitutional power in Scotland has occurred alongside increasing divergence in welfare provision. So changes and divergence in welfare as well as in claims for transfers of more power to

Scotland are not unique.[1] Indeed, Béland and Lecours' study of national-ism and social policy in Scotland, Quebec and Flanders highlights the importance of social policy as an instrument of territorial differentiation in struggles over political autonomy.[2]

Political and social directions and the value of comparative analysis

There is a range of reasons for a rise in the claims for combining social and territorial justice. Key are the dissatisfactions with the extent and use of power in national and sub-national political arenas and a belief that a dom-inant and centralised government does not, or will not, meet the welfare needs of citizens at sub-national level. There are two outcomes to this: a desire to look at alternatives for power redistribution and a desire to look at alternatives for meeting the needs of citizens. For this book on poverty in Scotland and the significance of the 2014 independence debate, it is not so much a question of what sort of political settlement would allow Scots to make decisions about things that matter to them (although this is obviously seriously important), but more what sort of social welfare would meet the more social democratic views of Scots and how can poverty be addressed? The two questions – of sovereignty and socially just welfare – are not automatically the same, but they are crucial and intertwined. In practice, comparison with other countries has been used in developing ideas for these two questions – both about the political struc-tures that would give Scots greater power over decisions affecting them and also about the sort of society that people want. In the discussion of Scotland's future and claims for independence, the examination of how other nations address welfare and poverty reduction has become an important tool. Comparative study helps to remind us that the British wel-fare state is not the only model of welfare that has been adopted across the developed capitalist world of Western Europe and North America. It serves to remind us that other models of welfare can be more effective, whether judged in terms of income maintenance, social support or the reduction of social and economic inequalities.[3]

Since an independent or more devolved Scotland would no longer be part of the British welfare state in the same way as at present, ideas for future directions are needed and experiences from other countries could help.

Choosing which society to draw on, however, is not without its difficulties, and changes over time. In 2006, when Alex Salmond argued that Scotland could draw on the experiences of Iceland and Ireland in an 'arc of prosperity', he little knew that the arc would become more one of austerity, and that economic growth was not an automatic answer to poverty reduction. When the Calman Commission started work in 2008, it drew heavily on what was seen as a positive Canadian experience of federalism to examine how the Scottish government's expenditure could be made more responsive and 'independent' – just before the Parti Quebecois gained power and the Canadian experience looked more complex than it had seemed. At the moment, it is the Nordic countries and their welfare system and the Spanish autonomous regions of Catalonia and the Basque Country that appear most often in discussions of transferable policies and structures of governance. Whichever model is looked to, what we have to remember is that, while lessons can be learned from other countries, comparison is never simple and the following chapters remind us of exactly that.

What can other countries tell us about the relationship between different political cultures and addressing poverty?

In this section, writers from different countries and regions examine how strategies for poverty reduction have developed nationally and sub-nationally and whether territorial politics have affected the strategies and their impact.

Two long-federated nations, Germany and Canada, are included and provide interesting examples of how innovative anti-poverty policy and sovereignty can go hand in hand. The chapter on Germany shows how a federal system attempts to maintain common living standards at the same time as decentralising power. With increasing disparities in poverty between north and south, the commitment and ability to retain common standards within a decentralised political system is shown to be stretched. The chapter highlights how, while federal law and limited financial support has encouraged *Länder* to introduce sufficient childcare to decrease poverty levels, strained federal and local resources are producing a postcode lottery of provision and give cause for concern. It shows that the 'transformational shift' in childcare described as future policy by the SNP may not be quite as easy to achieve as many hope.

The essay on Canada provides evidence on the need to get commitment on anti-poverty strategy at all levels if the flexibility of sub-national anti-poverty strategy, as well as national commitment to a good national minimum level of welfare, is to be developed. Like Scotland, many Canadian provinces have chosen to pursue a child poverty strategy and provide regular reports to their parliaments on measures taken to progress. But unlike the UK, Germany or even Norway, the commitment is not mirrored by a national one and many families fall through the net in provinces because their sovereignty is greater than the Länder in Germany or the devolved nations of the UK. So while Quebec may never secure independence, it has a form of 'independence lite' that allows it to raise any taxes it wants, and remain prosperous while implementing policies such as universal childcare for seven dollars a day, at the same time as British Columbia has an ever-increasing rate of poverty and declining public services.

The chapter on poverty and social security in Belgium reminds us that social security and federalism are not necessarily happy bedfellows. Recent state reform there has had to balance the case for the principal redistributive instruments of social security continuing to be organised at the highest tier of government, alongside arguments in favour of greater powers for sub-national entities. Bea Cantillon's conclusion is that the solution adopted is not necessarily a stable one that will serve all Belgians equally and will need careful handling by politicians in the decades to follow. It is a significant point to make as Scotland moves towards greater independence on social security matters. Spending on social security would probably be assigned to Scotland easily in the case of a 'Yes' vote in the country, and that would be popular when attitudes about welfare differ considerably between Westminster and Holyrood. But the chapter reminds us, as do reports from the Institute for Fiscal Studies[4] and the Scottish government's Expert Working Group on Welfare[5] that there are still many questions to be asked about cost and priority differences in the future, whether social security is devolved in a similar pattern to the situation in Northern Ireland or with greater powers given to Scotland.

The two autonomous regions within Spain reported here – Catalonia and the Basque Country – highlight differences that can emerge in anti-poverty policy despite similar demands for national identity and power. The Basque Country is shown to have been able to address poverty at the same time as the demand for independence has declined, while Catalonia highlights the central concern with territorial justice in the region alongside a reduction in commitment to social justice. This raises the question of whether welfare policies automatically improve in moves towards independence and highlights the continuing need to keep the inequality and insecurity this book has profiled in the gaze of politicians and the public.

As mentioned, the decision to include a chapter that considers the lessons that could be learned from the experience of Nordic states is not surprising. The Nordic model is certainly attracting considerable international interest as a way of creating the conditions for a flexible and competitive economy with adequate welfare provision. The Nordic countries consistently top the international rankings for education and training, gender equality, innovation and competitiveness and the SNP, as well as those promoting the 'Common Weal' model, hold up the Nordic model as one an independent Scotland should follow. However, as the chapter included here reminds us, we should perhaps not look for a wholesale adoption of the model in Scotland. The chapter forces us to be more questioning: not everyone benefits, and although social exclusion of the young unemployed is partially addressed, it is not a perfect model.

In sum then, drawing on lessons from elsewhere needs to be done carefully and critically. In fact, the chapter on Ireland argues that Scotland can learn as much from what other countries have not done insofar as it reminds us that relying too heavily on economic growth to reduce poverty and looking to Europe may never allow the poverty reduction that most in Scotland want to be attained. It is clear that most people in Scotland want a well-funded, efficient welfare system, with good-quality public services that meet the needs of all. Looking at other independent nations and federal states provides a picture of what can be achieved and the pitfalls that are to be avoided. The following chapters give a glimpse of how important this is.

Notes

1   B Cantillon, *Belgian Social Federalism: quo vadis?*, Research Paper 2, David Hume Institute, 2013; M Keating, *The Government of Scotland: public policy making after devolution*, Edinburgh University Press, 2010; J Mclean, J Gallagher and G Lodge, *Scotland's Choices: the referendum and what happens afterwards*, Edinburgh University Press, 2013; N McEwen, *Nationalism and the State: welfare identity in Scotland and Quebec*, Peter Lang, 2006

2   D Béland and A Lecours, *Nationalism and Social Policy: the politics of territorial solidarity*, Oxford University Press, 2008

3   A Cochrane and J Clarke, *Comparing Welfare States*, The Open University, 1993, p2

4   D Phillips, *Government Spending on Benefits and State Pensions in Scotland: current patterns and future issues*, Institute for Fiscal Studies, 2013

5   Scottish government, *Expert Working Group on Welfare Report*, 2013, http://www.scotland.gov.uk/Publications/2013/06/8875/0

Twenty-one

Catalonia: from the fight against poverty to the fight against poor people

Miquel Fernández

This chapter contends that there has been a significant shift in emphasis in how the problem of poverty is conceived and addressed in Catalonia. At the current time, a growing demonisation of people experiencing poverty is evident, which sits alongside a general mood in favour of nationalism. Support for both comes from neoliberal responses to financial pressures exacted on the state. Although far from intertwined or an inevitable coupling of interests, these dominant moods reflect the contemporary reality of Catalonia. It is particularly noteworthy for Scotland, where welfare debates have largely been seen as central to the independence debate, as it shows that political self-determination is not intrinsically socially progressive.

After the end of the regime of dictator Francisco Franco, Catalan society pursued a progressive goal of ending poverty. Dozens of campaigns against poverty and in favour of labour, social services and affordable housing established the socio-economic framework for a Catalan welfare state.[1] However, in the decade following 1996, Catalonia took a neoliberal turn and, instead, pursued the enrichment of the few at the expense of the majority. Although GDP rose by three points during the decade, the *Gini* co-efficient rose in a similar proportion.[2]

More recently, this situation has worsened as the pursuit of neoliberal goals that were initially merely unfavourable to people experiencing poverty has been succeeded by social policies that are explicitly hostile towards them. Fiscal pressure is used as an argument for the necessity of scaling back on social protection expenditure, although, as it will be argued here, the underlying motivations may be more ideological in nature. For example, the ruling conservative party, the CiU (Convergència i Unió), has stripped back the support that was available through the RMI programme to those receiving less than €400 a month;[3] indeed, Catalan Minister of Enterprise and Employment (Conseller d'Empresa i Ocupació) Francesc

Xavier Mena cancelled the RMI programme in 2012. Citing unproven concerns over fraud in the administration of the scheme, this decision adversely affected more than 7,000 of the very poorest Catalan families.[4]

More generally, conditions for the poorest people in Catalonia have worsened markedly in recent years. Although fiscal pressures may partly account for the difficulties faced, responsibility also rests with the Catalan government, which has primary responsibility for public security (health, housing, labour market and education). Since 2008, the population living with poverty has increased dramatically.[5] The Catalan *Sindic de Greuges* (regional ombudsman) denounced the increase of child malnutrition in Parliament.[6] More than one-quarter of children live in poverty (there was a child poverty risk rate of 26.4 per cent in 2011) – an increase of nearly nine percentage points in just three years (from 17.6 per cent in 2008). In response, the governing CiU said that the ombudsman was 'alarmist' and prevented its health and education spokespeople from responding in Parliament.

Thus, the debate concerning the independence of Catalonia from the Kingdom of Spain and the debate concerning the financial crisis have been prominent on recent institutional political agendas in Spain, but have not automatically been connected. Officially, from Catalonia, the process towards statehood has begun, following several meetings between the current government of Catalonia (*Generalitat de Catalunya*), the President of Catalonia (Artur Mas) and the President of Spain (Mariano Rajoy). Since the beginning of these meetings in February 2012, Rajoy refused to take part in any negotiation because the Catalan government demanded exclusive competences to collect taxes. Such arrangements have been made elsewhere in Spain – for example, the special fiscal pact of Euskadi and the Chartered Community of Navarre with Spain. Faced with this impasse (no further negotiatations with Rajoy), Mas and his government declared they are now pursuing independence.[7]

The political and economic context in which these events are occurring is revealing. The 'financial crisis' has been used to justify the privatisation of large areas of the already diminished Iberian welfare state. So while wealthy Catalans and Spanish continue to increase their profits through privatisation (and, it might be argued, also from abuses of the tax system), the Catalan government has become the first of the autonomous communities to make cuts in public spending. Paradoxically, this disinvestment, which began in autumn 2011, came amid scandals of a very different nature, especially the *Palau de la Música* case and other incidents of white collar crime. A recent study stated that the intended savings from cuts in education and public health in Catalonia in 2011 were not sufficient to counterbalance one-sixth of the fraud committed by those in power: public disinvestment of €2.7 billion against the embezzlement of €16 billion by the state administration.[8] While for the Catalan government tax evasion of great fortunes is considered elusive, the cuts in social spending are considered necessary, desirable and achievable.

The independence cause could have adopted (and could yet adopt) a socially progressive response to the challenges faced. However, instead, it has positioned itself – with almost universal public acceptance – as the champion of new strategies for the *punitive management of poverty*, at the heart of which is the demonisation of people experiencing poverty. These strategies have been implemented in the US, have some support in the UK, but are less common in continental Europe. Such punitive policy against the poor, however, is camouflaged by a caring and patriotic veneer that functions to allow a systematic assault against vulnerable sections of the population.

It might be argued that the punitive management of poverty has been necessary in order for the powerful to divert attention away from the socially regressive policies that are disadvantaging people experiencing poverty (such as tax exemptions for heritage assets, the reduction in taxes for the upper classes, inheritance and tax amnesties, as well as the flagrant cuts in health, education and subsidies[9]). Uniting against a common cause (the errant and undeserving poor) is a repressive mechanism of control through which rapid increases in social insecurity and public disorder can be managed. In this context, justificatory rhetoric from afar has been imported into Europe – referred to by the sociologist Wacquant as 'American penal judiciousness'.[10] This provides an ideological and policy framework that justifies the persecution and imprisonment of the poor. It dismisses the social democratic concept of 'rehabilitation' as naive.

Solutions to the 'problem of poverty' are redefined within this framework. The concern is not to improve the potential of the welfare state to be socially progressive. Increasingly divisive groups among those experiencing poverty blame their situation on others who experience poverty (rather than the socio-economic structures that work in the favour of the most advantaged). For example, the problem of petty crime is addressed by imposing strict regulations on street activities. Such restrictions have increased exponentially and, as a result, virtually any informal work or leisure practice on the street is problematised (including those through which the poor may legitimately pursue income to ameliorate the intensity of the poverty they experience). Increasingly, the problems associated with poverty are left in the hands of charitable organisations.

At the same time, a consensus is emerging regarding the delegitimation – by law – of several kinds of inhabitants. This smacks of primordial nationalism. In this sense, 'immigrants' are labelled by definition and the varied assortment of people and practices as 'uncivic', and remain excluded from the concept of the 'ideal community citizen'.[11] This conspires to maintain people in a permanent state of segregation in which a full range of punitive measures can be systematically implemented. In response to the demonisation of immigrants and concerns that are expressed about their entitlement, social protection for all (immigrant and non-immigrant alike) is threatened.

The management of poverty and criminality – through charitable surveillance and the penal system – has become increasingly the domain of powerful industries.[12] The Spanish Catholic organisation Cáritas Diocesana has an annual budget of €250 million and this continues to increase.[13] Although a planned privatisation of prisons is now uncertain because of the 'financial crisis', the Interior Department of the Spanish government is nevertheless trying to 'improve the external control of penitential institutions with private security'. Evictions continue while bank bailouts are arranged, unemployment continues to rise, and insecurity and decreasing wages are a daily reality for hundreds of thousands of Catalans.[14] This coincides with the penalisation of all disorderly conduct, increased punishment, substitution of administrative faults for penalties, and building new penal facilities or CIEs (immigration detention centres).[15] The persecution of those involved in prostitution, pickpockets, street vendors, drink vendors, buskers and other 'undesirables' (all considered in equal terms) is considered a necessary part of the neoliberal management of poverty. The undesirable elements in society may face the option of accepting any employment under any conditions, 'here or in Lapland',[16] and refusal to do so could result in a prison sentence.

Politically, the neoliberal solution is for the majority of a population who are suffering the cuts to unite around a primordial nationalism, which reproduces and complements the soothing effect of charitable rhetoric and practices. The 'true poor' – as defined by our institutions – can count on Christian 'handouts' and citizens' charity: if they behave 'correctly' and subscribe to the project of the 'new state of Europe'. It will not be necessary for them to go to prison; they will be able to live – certainly with some difficulties – on the charity of 'good citizens'.

In 2012, the first year of the financial cuts, the Medal of Honour of the Catalan Parliament (the highest honorary distinction of the Catalan Parliament awarded to personalities and institutions who are creditors of exceptional recognition) was jointly awarded to the two 'souls of the country', Omnium Cultural and Càritas Diocesana. The former is a cultural association focused on the protection of 'language, culture and country', long associated with sustaining Catalan national identity in the Franco years. The latter is an agency of the Catholic church, dedicated to the coordination of beneficence. That these 'two souls' of Catalonia are claimed to 'symbolise that national and social aspirations are inseparable'[17] is a chilling triumph of neoliberal rhetoric and the defeat of solidarity in the quest to tackle poverty in contemporary Catalonia.

Notes

1   O Salido and L Moreno, 'Welfare and Family Policies in Spain', *Política y Sociedad*, 44(2), 2007, pp101–14

2   See *Statistical Distribution of Personal Income and Risk of Poverty in Catalonia 2005*, http://www.idescat.cat/cat/idescat/publicacions/cataleg/pdfdocs/edrirp 05.pdf and *Pobresa, Desigualtats i Exclusió Social a Catalunya*, http://www20. gencat.cat/docs/economia/Documents/Arxius/doc_16846585_1.pdf

3   *Renda mínima d'inserció* (RMI), literally 'minimum insertion income'.

4   See 'Més de 7.000 famílies esperant el PIRMI', http://www.eldebat.cat/cat/ viewer.php?IDN=100888

5   In 2011, 42.7 per cent of the population were under the poverty line before social transfers. In 2004, 36.9 per cent of the population were in this condition.

6   See *Report on Child Malnutrition in Catalonia August 2013*, http://www.sindic. cat/site/unitFiles/3505/Informe%20malnutricio%20infantil%20castella.pdf

7   ABC.es 'Rajoy y Mas, dos encuentros oficiales y dos reuniones secretas', ABC, 4 January 2012

8   The main source of data is provided by the Technical Union of the Ministry of Finance (GESTHA). The analysis was published in an article by the current deputy of the Catalan Parliament d'Unitat Popular-Alternative d'Esquerres (CUP-AE). See D Fernández, 'Silenci, aquí es defrauda: 16,000 milions d'euros anuals', *La Directa*, 8 November 2011

9   All these measures have been taken in both Catalunya and in the rest of the Spanish state, whether these governments were conservative or progressive. In fact, the first act of privatisation of public health was initiated by the first socialist president after the Civil War, Felipe González in 1986.

10 L Wacquant, 'La represión penal promovida como nuevo valor 'de izquierda'', *Las Cárceles de la Miseria*, Alianza, 2000, pp132–45

11 M Domínguez Sánchez, 'Crítica del Ciudadanismo', in *IX Congreso Español de Sociología*, Barcelona, Grupo de Trabajo de Sociología Política, Ponencia mimeografiada, 2007, pp1–9

12 Only the Spanish Catholic organisation Cáritas Diocesana has an annual budget of €250 million increasing every year. See L Daniele, 'Los donativos privados a Cáritas aumentan un 3.5%; los públicos caen un 2.9%', ABC, 23 October 2012. The privatisation of prisons is now uncertain because of the 'financial crisis', but note that 'the Interior Department of the Spanish government tries to improve the external control of penitential institutions with private security' – see 'Interior contrata a 95 exescoltas para vigilar 21 cárceles', *El País*, 15 August 2013

13 See note 12

14 Data from January 2012 – 19.8% of the Catalan population live below the poverty line, according to the indicator AROPE (At risk of poverty or social exclusion) of the European Union. In this sense, child poverty reached 24 per cent and there are over 50,000 malnourished children according to the latest report from the *Sindic de Greuges* (Catalan ombudsman).

15 The crisis scenario changes this logic in an unknown way until today. The call for higher criminal penalties is accompanied by an economic need to reduce the unsustainable size of the prison population, 'groping' the possibility of an amendment to the criminal law in a clear efficiency-based sense. See I Rivera Beiras, 'Algunas notas sobre el debate epistemológico de la cuestión punitiva,' *Revista Española de Sociologia*, 15, 2011, pp103–7 and Forero and Jimenez, 'La Cárcel Española en (la) Crisis. Mano dura y escasez. ¿Hacia la esquizofrenia punitiva?', *Indret Revista para el Análisis del Derecho*, awaiting publication. On the other hand, note that the last prison built was Puig de les Basses in 2011, but has not yet opened. Catalonia has exclusive jurisdiction in this matter. In the case of the CIE the Spanish state has jurisdiction in Catalonia. The Catalan government announced that the inauguration of Puig de les Basses prison would be in 2014, as soon as the government budget of this year has been approved. But after this public statement, the Catalan government has said there is not enough budget for building the prison in 2014. An editorial of the most influential newspaper of the Spanish Kingdom, *El País*, says that this is a strategy employed by Mas in order to blame Rajoy and to convert the delayed budgets in 'sovereignist fuel'. See Editorial, 'Propaganda. Artur Mas convierte la prórroga de los Presupuestos de 2012 en combustible soberanista', *El País*, 8 August 2013

16 The leader of the employer's representative, the Spanish Confederation of Business Organisations (CEOE), José Luis Feito, proposed that the unemployed should stop collecting unemployment benefits as soon as the first offer of employment is refused. Feito said that 'an unemployed person should take any job even if it was in Lapland; if you do not agree you do not receive unemployment benefits.' 'CEOE afirma que "hay que aceptar trabajos aunque sean en Laponia"', *Europa Press*, 20 February 2012

17 S Hinojosa, 'Un país amb dues ànimes', *La Vanguardia*, 11 September 2012

Twenty-two
Social policy against poverty in the Basque Country
Fernando Fantova

Introduction

This brief chapter provides some basic information about the development, instruments and effects of the anti-poverty policies implemented in the Basque Country, seen in the context of the empowerment process carried out in this autonomous region over the last thirty years.

It also aims to offer a critical and constructive overview of these policies, as well as to explain how they interact with the structuring strategies in that region, in order to enable some of the lessons learnt to be extrapolated to other contexts.

The autonomous region of the Basque Country

The Basque Country (or *Euskadi* as the Basques call it) is an autonomous region with a population of 2,174,000 located in Spain, a member state of the European Union (EU). Castilian Spanish is the common language spoken by the whole population, although half of those over the age of 16 also speak *Euskera* (the Basque language).

Unlike most other autonomous regions in Spain, the Basque Country (like Navarra) establishes and collects its own taxes and then pays an agreed sum (reviewed and updated periodically) to the central government. Some experts have calculated that the Basque Country is over-funded at a rate of about 60 per cent per capita in comparison with the mean level found in other autonomous regions in Spain.[1] All the major political parties in the Basque Country defend this system, affirming that it is not a privilege, but rather a shouldering of greater responsibility and risks.

The autonomous region of the Basque Country has a health service and education system, as well as an employment service and a police force (in compliance with the basic common legislation for Spain as a whole). It also has exclusive devolved power in the field of social services. However, the pension and unemployment benefit services are integrated within the Spanish national social security department. This pays care allowances or non-contributory benefits (retirement pensions, unemployment benefit and disability pensions) that have a major impact on the fight against poverty.[2]

Of the population of the Basque Country, 21.1 per cent is aged 65 or over. This percentage is higher than in any of the other 28 EU states. The birth rate is 9.7 births per one thousand inhabitants per year, as opposed to 10.7 in the EU. Life expectancy at birth is 79 years for men and 85.7 years for women, figures which are, again, higher than in any other EU state. Foreign immigrants account for 6.9 per cent of the Basque population (the figure for Spain is 12.1 per cent). The per capita GDP is 132 (with 100 being the mean for the EU), and the unemployment rate is 15.46 per cent (approximately half the mean rate for Spain as a whole). Per capita expenditure on social protection is €6,320 (a little over the EU mean of €6,209). Therefore, we find ourselves in the position of having a relatively older, more industrialised and richer society than those around us.[3]

Currently, the two political parties with the most seats in the Basque Parliament are committed to Basque nationalism (one has moderate Christian Democrat roots and the other is a radical left-wing party which was historically linked to the terrorist activities of ETA, active until 2011). The other two parties, which have fewer seats, are the two main parties active in Spain (socialists and conservatives).

Anti-poverty policies over the last thirty years

Structured public policies for fighting poverty in the Basque Country were first introduced through the *First Comprehensive Plan for Fighting Against Poverty in the Basque Country*,[4] which was drafted following the first *Survey of Poverty and Social Inequality*.[5] The Basque region then became the first autonomous region in Spain to establish a public income guarantee system, with a subjective (enforceable) right to a periodic subsistence benefit from very early on. Up until that time, almost all economic aid to the poor was provided by the Catholic charity Cáritas and other voluntary organisations, as well as any other pre-existing social welfare or aid organisations.[6]

This change in policy stemmed from the confluence of a number of different factors: the existence of an economic surplus in the Basque government coffers, growing social awareness by those in government at the time (the Basque Nationalist Party) and the influence of experiences, such as the French RMI (minimum guaranteed income), and the recommendations of the common European institutions.[7]

From that time onwards, successive laws have been enacted to further structure and restructure the fight against poverty in the Basque Country through guaranteeing income (1990, 1998, 2000, 2008 and 2011). In general, these laws have enjoyed widespread political support, based mainly on agreements signed between the Basque Nationalist Party (PNV) and the Basque Socialist Party (the Basque wing of the Spanish Socialist Party). Another party which has played a key role in this process is *Eusko Alkartasuna*, a party which ended up joining the radical nationalist left-wing coalition. The conservative Popular Party has, in general, also supported these policies.

The modification to the law approved in 2000 mainly came about as the result of a popular legislative initiative, promoted by social movements and trade unions, which collected over 82,000 signatures and which constituted the first initiative of its kind in the history of the autonomous region of the Basque Country.[8]

The first decade of the twenty-first century saw a major improvement in benefit access levels. This evolution is linked to a growing acceptance of immigrants' rights to access the system (including illegal immigrants), the application of employment stimulus packages, the increase in pension payments to pensioners and the substantial progress made in relation to minimum guarantees.

This piece of legislation is based on the Basque Country's exclusive devolved power in the field of 'social aid', although some clashes have occurred with the central Spanish government, especially when a supplement for small social security pensions was introduced as part of this policy, and it was to come out of the Basque budget.

It is striking that the 2008 modification was made possible by a consensus between Basque nationalists and Spanish socialists, despite the fact that the political context at the time was not an easy one, since the modification was proposed towards the end of a term of office in which the political agenda had been dominated by a proposal by the PNV to organise a referendum based on the Basque Country's right to decide (right to self-determination). A new law prohibited the radical nationalist left from participating in the 2009 elections (due to its collusion with ETA terrorists) and a pact was made between the two Spanish parties (the

Popular Party and the Socialist Party) to oust, for the first time ever, the PNV from its seat of power in the Basque government.

Currently, benefits are set at 88 per cent above the minimum professional wage, although in 2012 they were cut by 7 per cent, a reduction that will hopefully be recovered in the future once the economic situation improves. Depending on recipients' housing requirements, the size of their family and other circumstances, the sum in question can be as high as 200 per cent of the minimum wage. In this sense, the situation in the Basque Country is far superior to that of the majority of Spain's other autonomous regions, and this has led to some criticism from certain sectors (employer organisations, for example), with claims that amounts are too high and act as a disincentive for people to look for work. The coverage rate for all recipients (both direct recipients and users) per 1,000 inhabitants is very high in the Basque Country (71) when in other regions it reaches figures as low as 2.89 in Extremadura or 3.17 in Murcia.[9] In 2010, the Basque Country accounted for 42 per cent of all expenditure in Spain related to these programmes, despite the fact that it had no more than 2.6 per cent of the population estimated to be living in poverty. Today, due to much greater cuts in other regions, the data for the Basque Country are undoubtedly even more favourable, with data for 2012 indicating public expenditure on these programmes of over €432 million.

As regards the impact of these actions, we should highlight that, at least until the middle of 2012, the poverty rate remained similar to those recorded during earlier years, characterised by a much higher level of economic growth in the region. Moreover, this rate is clearly lower than that recorded from 1986 to 1996 (the period before the economic crisis and recession). Largely thanks to its protection system, the situation in the Basque Country is clearly different from that of the rest of Spain, even when we take into account other areas of comparable economic development, such as Catalonia. Unlike this last region, which currently has comparatively high poverty rates within the European context, the Basque Country is at the other extreme, and is counted among those regions with the lowest risk of poverty.[10]

Furthermore, and as stated earlier, the unemployment rate is not as serious in the Basque Country as it is in Spain as a whole. However, this was not the case in 1988, prior to the establishment of the income guarantee policy, when the Basque Country's unemployment rate was 2.7 per cent higher than the Spanish mean, 3.7 per cent higher than in Catalonia and 6.7 per cent higher than in Madrid.[11] Again, this could indicate that the minimum guaranteed income policy has had some influence.

Currently, nearly 60,000 households receive benefits and income support. Nevertheless, the latest change to the law (2011) established stricter access criteria (as the result of a proposal by the Popular Party, accepted by the Socialist Party). The main difference is that while previously, recipients were only obliged to have been registered with a town council for one year before applying for benefits, they are now required to have been on the register for three years and to prove actual residence (although not legal residence).[12]

Since its return to power in 2012, the PNV has been striving to maintain the income guarantee system with no cutbacks, arguing that social policy is vital to the future of the region. In 2013, the two issues dominating the political agenda are the economic recession and social policy. Thus, the debate on a new political status for the Basque Country has been postponed until the end of the current term. This stands in sharp contrast to the situation in Catalonia, where the referendum on self-governance is top of the agenda, and the social cutbacks being implemented are far greater than those being introduced in the Basque Country.

Data provided by the Basque government's Immigration Observatory in June 2013 reflect an increase in social unrest about, for example, the payment of social benefits to illegal immigrants:[13]

> Almost six out of every 10 people interviewed (57.6 per cent) said they believed that the arrival of more immigrants would make it harder for the native population to access social aid. Concern has increased significantly – in 2008, this percentage was 41.6 per cent.

Nevertheless, so far at least, these social murmurings have yet to find or articulate a stable technical or political voice in the public debate.

The truth is, however, that we do not know how long the current economic recession is going to last, nor can we foresee the social and political phenomena that may occur in the near future. The comparatively better economic situation in the Basque Country than in the rest of Spain, the nationalist or communitarianist elements existing in the articulation of social cohesion and the political commitment to maintaining the basic pillars of the income guarantee system and social policy in general, together form an unstable trio which may, nevertheless, begin to fall apart at any moment.

Conclusions and lessons learnt

The Basque Country has used its devolved powers to develop a noticeably more robust and ambitious anti-poverty policy than the other autonomous regions in Spain, and indeed the central government itself. This policy has, in general terms, enjoyed a broad consensus among the region's leading political parties, and has never been the subject of large-scale controversies or corrections. Even in moments of intense political tension caused by debates on national identity (and particularly in relation to the terrorist acts committed by ETA), the fight against poverty has remained a firm regional policy and a clear area of consensus.

Alongside other social and cultural policies and initiatives to foster economic and industrial expansion and research, development and innovation activities, the fight against poverty has become a hallmark of Basque society – a society that enjoys a high level of cohesion and which has a more competitive economic model than the majority of other Spanish autonomous regions. It is perhaps important to point out here that the Basque Country is characterised by firm family and community values and a strong sense of solidarity, with definite Christian roots (common to all parties to a certain extent), which may partly explain the emergence of certain other phenomena also, such as the large-scale co-operative movement located in Mondragón.

Whatever the case, we can see it is vital to improve co-ordination between the minimum income guarantee policy and other social policies (social services, pensions, employment), and it is necessary to recuperate and reinvent the role of the family and community networks in social protection and development at different scales. It is also very important to strengthen continuous (and accurate) assessment, participatory governance (with the third sector) and effective management (making efficient use of technology), to ensure that policies designed to fight against poverty avoid the risks of clientelism and paternalism, and are as flexible and stimulating as possible.[14]

Notes

1   Á De la Fuente, *La Financiación Territorial en España: situación actual y propuestas de reforma*, CEOE, 2010, p2

2   M Laparra, 'El sistema de garantía de ingresos mínimos en España: un 'sistema' poco sistemático', en G Jaraiz, *Actuar Ante la Exclusión: análisis, políticas y herramientas para la inclusión social*, Fundación FOESSA/Cáritas Española, 2009,

p177

3 Eustat (Basque Statistics Institute), *The Basque Country in the UE-27*, Basque government, 2012, http://www.eustat.es/document/epubs/publicaciones/euskadienlaue27_ce/files/3dissue.swf

4 Basque government, *Primer Plan Integral de Lucha Contra la Probeza en el País Vasco*, Vitoria-Gasteiz, 1988

5 Basque government, *Encuesta de Pobreza y Desigualdades Sociales*, Vitoria-Gasteiz, 1986

6 Basque government: *1984–2008: 25 años de estudio de la pobreza en Euskadi*, Vitoria-Gasteiz, 2008

7 I Uribarri, 'Historia y futuro de las rentas mínimas en Euskadi', in *Cuadernos de Trabajo Social*, 25(1), 2012, p75

8 G Moreno, 'Veinte años de rentas mínimas de inserción autonómicas: el caso vasco dentro del contexto español y europeo', in *Revista de Fomento Social*, 2010, pp471–90

9 CCOO (Comisiones Obreras), *Pobreza y Rentas Mínimas en España y en la Unión Europea*, 2013

10 Basque government, *Encuesta de Pobreza y Desigualdades Sociales 2012: principales resultados*, Vitoria-Gasteiz, 2012, http://www.gizartelan.ejgv.euskadi.net/r45-docuinfo/es/contenidos/informe_estudio/epds_2012/es_epds2012/adjuntos/EPDS_2012es.pdf

11 L Sanzo, *Nuevas Propuestas Para Nuevos Tiempos*, 2012, p15, http://www.nodo50.org/redrentabasica/textos/index.php?x=998

12 Basque government, *III Plan Vasco de Inclusión Activa*, Vitoria-Gasteiz, 2012

13 Basque Immigration Observatory, *Barómetro 2012: percepciones y actitudes hacia la inmigración extranjera*, Vitoria-Gasteiz, 2013, p34, http://www.ikuspegi-inmigracion.net/documentos/barometros/2012/bar_2012_cas_ok.pdf

14 L Moreno, *La Europa Asocial*, Península, 2012

Twenty-three
Poverty, social security and Belgian federalism
Bea Cantillon

Introduction

How can a bipolar and heterogeneous federation reconcile devolution of powers in the field of social security with safeguarding social solidarity? For the negotiators of the sixth Belgian state reform (following a regime crisis and a painful federal government formation which took over a year and a half to achieve), this is a difficult policy puzzle.

Income redistribution that is realised through the mechanism of social security is interpersonal in nature: from the healthy to the sick, from the employed to the incapacitated, from youngsters to the elderly, from rich to poor. Mechanisms of horizontal, vertical and inter-generational solidarity generate income redistribution between individuals facing different risks and income situations. Hence, social security is, much more than taxation, an extremely important instrument that can be used to guarantee fundamental social rights, to redistribute income and to combat poverty.

To the degree that social risks are spatially unequally divided and/or that the regional capacity to contribute to social security schemes varies, systems of interpersonal redistribution produce financial flows between regions in a country on the basis of carrying capacity (wages) and needs (social risks). This makes social security the instrument *par excellence* to homogenise socio-economic differences in a country. With the insurance principle and built-in solidarity mechanisms, social security organises inter-regional income transfers that automatically correct for (regional) shifts in capacity and needs caused, for example, by diverging ageing rates.

For the first time in Belgian history, the negotiators of the most recent state reform (in 2011) could not ignore the question of social security. Further devolution of power necessitated splitting the branches of social security, as it accounts for about 70 per cent of the total expenditure of the federal budget. The previous state reforms had already transferred important social powers and their associated resources to the communities and regions. However, extending the same splitting logic to the interpersonal transfer system of social security is much more difficult because the delicate balance that has been established in the social security system between insurance and solidarity is so important in the fight against poverty. As splitting parts of social security entails a narrowing of the solidarity circle, worse social protection is looming – first for those who live and/or work in the least fortunate regions (Brussels and Wallonia) and later (due to mechanisms of downward social and fiscal competition) possibly also for the more fortunate in the prosperous regions. However, there was a strong argument in favour of greater powers for sub-national entities. So, how did the negotiators of the sixth Belgian state reform unravel this puzzle?

Poverty and inter-regional transfers

For a considerable number of years now, there has been a constant financial flow from the Flemish to the Walloon region and, since the 1990s, also to the Brussels capital region.[1] This inter-regional solidarity follows important socio-economic differences between Flanders, Wallonia and Brussels: Flanders is doing better both in terms of economic growth and labour market performance. The inter-regional differences are less obvious with regard to demographic features: all regions are facing an ageing population. This trend, however, appears to be more pronounced in Flanders as the share of people aged 65 and over has grown faster than in Wallonia over the past decade. There are, moreover, significant differences between the northern and the southern parts of the country with respect to life expectancy. On average, the life expectancy at birth is two years higher for the Flemish than for Walloons.

These social and economic differences between Flanders and Wallonia are reflected in the composition of disposable household income: 64 per cent of disposable per capita income in Flanders is generated through work, with 28 per cent coming from social security, compared with (respectively) 57 per cent and 34 per cent in Wallonia.[2] It has been estimated that in the hypothetical absence of social security transfers, average household income would increase in Flanders by around 7 per cent, whereas it would decrease in Wallonia by, on average, approximately 4 per cent.[3] This translates into a sharp increase in the theoretical poverty risk in Wallonia, from 13 per cent to around 18 per cent. So federal social security is a strong instrument for reducing poverty in Wallonia and Brussels and, by extension, in the country as a whole.

On which tier should social security be organised?

Redistribution by social security is best organised at the highest possible level: inter-regional transfers avoid unwanted competition between regions that could lead to social dumping, while expanded 'risk pooling' can better resist the consequences of economic and demographic shocks. That is the reason why in all welfare states (also in big and heterogeneous countries such as the US, Canada, Australia and Germany), the most important inter-personal solidarity streams are established at the highest national level. Moreover, social security enhances both social and economic cohesion, crucial for the stability of federal states. Social security programmes are also important for maintaining economic and monetary union and, hence, for the creation of economic cohesion. Most importantly, while Flanders has the financial resources and fiscal capacity to pursue its own social security policy, the same is certainly not the case for the other sub-states.[4]

But, for reasons of efficiency, legitimacy and resilience, interpersonal (and the resulting inter-regional) transfers should neither be caused by policy (or non-policy) in one particular region, nor deprive these regions of the necessary space to develop policy that is required by local opportunities, needs and preferences. Neither do they lead to policy deadlocks as a result of diverging political preferences in the constituting regions. Moreover, in an asymmetric bipolar federal state, regional redistributive systems run into problems of legitimacy. While it is more difficult to find support for solidarity and redistribution at the more heterogeneous federal tier compared with more homogeneous sub-national tiers,[5] bipolar asymmetry and legitimacy deficiencies reduce the willingness of the wealthier region to show solidarity towards the poorer region. Maintaining a major federal transfer system, therefore, enhances Flemish pleas for confederalism. From this, it follows that recognising the (Flemish) struggle for decentralisation of matters related to social security is of vital importance in securing Belgian federal legitimacy.

From the viewpoint of social adequacy (ie, which system offers the best guarantees of the best possible social protection for as many people as possible), social redistribution is better organised at the highest possible tier of government. But at the same time, considerations of political legitimacy, efficiency and innovative potential need to be taken into account. The result is that neither splitting nor maintaining the status quo of a centralised social security system are viable options for the future of Belgian social security. A more nuanced and solution is needed.

The sixth state reform and Belgian social security: ambiguous premises

The negotiators of the sixth state reform assumed three 'captive' premises and rationales:

- splitting (parts of) social security, while maintaining solidarity through inter-regional transfers;
- creating so-called homogeneous packages of power; *and*
- rendering the sub-national entities accountable.

The resulting state reform agreement explicitly starts from the principles of national solidarity and interpersonal redistribution. These principles are guarded by keeping replacement incomes with the strongest potential for redistribution at a federal level and for the parts of social security that are transferred to the regions – child benefits, elderly care, labour market policies and parts of healthcare – the resources are distributed through federal grants, based on a demographic allocation formula. This is not an easy process.

Why mature systems of social protection are difficult to split

A developed and mature social protection system, such as Belgian social security, has a complex institutional and financial architecture, relies on complex governance structures and consequently requires considerable expertise in its implementation. It is therefore hard to disentangle, and transferring competences fully to sub-national entities is an expensive and politically risky operation that requires a vast investment of time and money.

In fact, this means that it is presumed that a similar degree of solidarity can be organised by means of inter-regional transfers with (potentially conditional) allocations. Moreover, it is also presumed that inter-regional transfers would be 'more transparent' than those implemented through social security. But are both presumptions correct?

The interpersonal redistribution of social security automatically corrects for (regional) shifts in capacity (wages) and needs (due to, for example, a different ageing rate in the regions concerned; relative changes in morbidity and the birth rate; schooling; and structural and cyclical shifts in the labour market). An inter-regional transfer ideally would take the same factors into account. However, the statistical apparatus and awareness of possible relevant divergences in socio-demographic and economic trends always lag behind social reality.

More fundamentally, inter-regional solidarity in Belgium will have to be enforced in a battle between the weaker 'them' (Wallonia and Brussels) and the stronger 'we' (Flanders). It is unlikely that the result of this process will be as generous as the solidarity generated by insurance and enlightened self-interest:[6]

> ... thinking explicitly about inter-regional solidarity, focuses attention on regional identities. Would this help in keeping the inter-regional solidarity intact? ... Feelings of a shared fate are not only necessary for creating strong social insurance institutions, they are also influenced by the existing institutions.

Therefore, trading interpersonal for inter-regional solidarity almost inevitably means a less 'broad' solidarity in practice.

The fiction of homogeneous policy packages

Traditional discourse on institutional reform often refers to the need to create 'homogeneous power packages'. Even though there are good examples of inefficient distribution of powers, it is an illusion to think that in an increasingly layered social policy it is possible to achieve homogeneity: numerous limitations exist that are imposed by the broader international framework and there is inevitably a strong entanglement of different policy domains (such as social benefits, taxation, work, education, family and care).

The Belgian sixth state reform has indeed added a little 'homogeneity'. The transfer of powers concerning labour market policy, healthcare and child benefits result in a (further) 'intertwining' of powers. This will obviously require more co-operation and co-ordination. At least in the transition phase (which will take a long time in view of the complexity of the operation), the sub-national entities will be dependent on the federal administrations for the implementation of their policies.

Accountability versus autonomy

The third rationale for rearranging powers in the field of social security is 'accountability'. This principle has been interpreted in various ways, from 'autonomy' to 'accountability to the whole'.

In the case of social security, the first interpretation of accountability obviously runs into the above-mentioned obstacles of splitting and the homogenisation of power packages. Fundamentally, autonomy cannot be detrimental to the general interest nor stimulate the sub-national entities to design policies that are detrimental to other sub-national entities. For example, the situation in which a sub-national entity develops policies that aim to attract the highly educated at the cost of other sub-national entities must be avoided.

The second interpretation is more recent. The argument goes that when sub-national entities exert a real influence, within their existing powers, on the expenses of federal social security, shared financial responsibility and a desire to design policies that benefit the general interest result in efficiency gains. This is because when sub-states are responsible for social policy as a whole, except for social security, they can develop divergent policy paths (as is clearly the case for activation policies and education policy in Belgium).

The idea that with forms of accountability it would be possible 'to preserve Belgian solidarity while favouring efficiency' enjoys some intellectual and political support. Rendering sub-national entities accountable with a *bonus malus* system (ie, a system with rewards and penalties) runs, however, into the difficulty of finding relevant assessment criteria: cyclical unemployment, for example, is determined by factors that lie outside the influence of federal, as well as regional, policy. Imposing a penalty for substandard regional performance, moreover, runs into the objection that it could cause a downward spiral, whereby in times of rising unemployment and an increased need for activation, the resources to do so would decrease. Hence, for the time being, there are no traces of direct forms of accountability in Belgian social federalism. Does this mean that the new distribution of powers cannot lead to greater accountability and more efficiency? Obviously not. Spending freedom entails that the sub-national entities 'will feel the consequences of their actions (or their policy) themselves'.[7] If, for instance, they develop successful employment policies that decrease the number of 'target groups' for which reductions in social contributions are necessary, they will be able to use the resources that are made available for this purpose for other policy purposes.

This, however, yields a danger for the general (federal) interest or for another sub-entity. As it is clear that unemployment insurance must remain a federal matter, one will have to make sure that active labour market policies maintain a certain degree of homogeneity. It is indeed clear that a common social insurance can only exist with (relatively) homogeneous implementation rules. Also, agreements will have to be reached on tax reductions to avoid overly divergent wage costs for companies with Walloon, Flemish and/or Brussels employees.

Conclusion

In Belgium, the largest and most important poverty reducing mechanisms remain inter-personal and federal. However, child benefits and elderly care will be split, while the existing interpersonal solidarity will be traded for – less generous – inter-regional solidarity. This means that solidarity will become less broad.

A homogeneous transfer of child benefits and elderly care is anticipated but, at the same time, in other areas a further 'intertwining' of powers will take place. Some important levers of employment policy will be transferred with the view of rendering sub-states accountable, even though there are no direct (dis)incentives to induce the communities and regions to design policy that favours the 'general interest'. Regions and communities will penetrate some decision-making bodies of the federal social security system and many co-ordination platforms are anticipated to strengthen co-operation in a landscape that will undoubtedly become much more complex.

Taken as a whole, the sixth state reform will move Belgium in the direction of a social federalism with shared costs, shared decisions and shared implementation. In a bipolar, by definition non-hierarchical, system, this holds great dangers. 'Shared' in this setting means *de facto* veto rights. If, however, the transferred powers are handled responsibly, the social partners retain an important role in the system's management, and the constitutional court takes a strong stance in the protection of fundamental social rights, it is not impossible that a basis will develop on which a durable and inclusive layered system of social security could develop.

This is a shortened version of a paper, *Belgian Social Federalism: quo vadis?*, written for the David Hume Foundation in 2013.

Notes

1   J Van Gompel, *Financiële Transfers Tussen de Belgische Gewesten*, Mimeo, 2004
2   B Cantillon, S R Veerle De Maesschalck and V Gerlinde, 'Social Redistribution in Federalised Belgium', *West European Politics*, 29(5), 2006, pp1034–56
3   See note 2
4   B Cantillon, 'The Paradox of the Social Investment State: growth, employment and poverty in the Lisbon era', *Journal of European Social Policy*, 21(5), 2011, pp432–49
5   M V Pauly, 'Income Redistribution as a Local Public Good', *Journal of Public Economics*, 2, 1973, pp35–58
6   B Cantillon, *Belgian Social Federalism: quo vadis?*, Research Paper No.3, David Hume Institute, 2013
7   F Vandenbroucke, 'Two Dilemmas in Institutional Reform: the Pieters dilemma and the Cantillon dilemma', in P Popelier, B Cantillon and N Mussche, *Social Federalism: how is a multi-level welfare state best organized*, Re-Bel Initiative, 2011, http://www.rethinkingbelgium.eu/rebel-initiative-ebooks/ebook-9-social-federalism-how-is-a-multilevel-welfare-state-best-organized

Twenty-four
Nordic states
Carolina Stiberg

Norden: consensual parliamentary democracies

The countries that constitute Scandinavia are Norway, Sweden and Denmark. Finland and Iceland also count as Nordic countries, and all five nations are reliant on a welfare model built on equality, respect for human rights, justice, democracy and good administration. Scandinavia consists of three constitutional monarchies with multi-party parliaments that are predominantly social-democratic. Finland and Iceland are characterised by strong parliaments, but rather than a monarch, these states are ruled by a president.[1]

Initially, it was Sweden that inspired the creation of the 'Nordic welfare model', a nation that was seen as a 'social laboratory', with an 'ultra-modern' view of society.[2] It could be argued that, to some extent, the progress and success of the Swedish, or Nordic, model was not entirely due to reform and socio-economic changes on a governmental level, but rather an instinctive sense of pragmatism adherent to the Swedish people. This positive image of the Swedes as a peaceful folk, with a strong trust in their government and a close tie to both solidarity and individualism has been suggested by scholars to be one of the greatest aspirations for other countries to follow.[3]

In 2008, the Scottish government published the paper *Achieving Our Potential: a framework to tackle poverty and income inequality in Scotland* as an attempt to outline a 'fresh approach' to strategies, and to illustrate successful examples of 'good practice'[4] in relation to tackling social injustices.[5] On numerous occasions, the Nordic countries, in particular Finland and Norway, are mentioned as nations which:[6]

> ... have combined high levels of economic growth with significantly lower levels of income inequality than Scotland. They have shown that greater Solidarity (*sic*) is not just an outcome of economic growth, but a driver of that growth.

The framework paper demonstrates one of many instances when the SNP government has explicitly used the Nordic countries as a model to learn from and to follow, particularly in its discussions of an independent Scotland. It further mentions that the most appealing aspects of the Nordic model to the SNP government are the high levels of 'equality of income and significantly lower rates of poverty'.[7]

An egalitarian view and the importance of fairness are two strong aspects of the model that Scotland does indeed share with the Nordic countries. Nevertheless, this welfare model is not without flaws – it has been under pressure both internally and externally. Vulnerable groups within the societies, such as the young unemployed, are disadvantaged to an extent, which is stirring social and political concerns that cannot be met by the current system.

In general, there appears to be a strong desire to break the cycle of welfare dependency in the Scandinavian countries. Their welfare system is based on universalism, and its very core is constructed around the enablement and rehabilitation of people – especially the younger generations. The social issues touched on above are, naturally, not unique to the Nordic countries, and this chapter will examine how early intervention could inhibit poverty from taking root.

Utopia or dystopia? Poverty in the Nordic region

Being among the most prosperous industrialised countries in the 1980s, the Nordic countries had good records of economic development and their main concerns were 'the comprehensiveness of social security systems, institutionalised social rights and [...] solidarity accompanied by universalism.'[8] The Nordic model has also been called *social democratic*, with a clear support for a mixed economy that combines private and public ownership. The preconditions for such a model to occur include a strong and organised working class, along with mobilised trade unions cooperating with the social-democratic parties.[9] This idyllic picture is, however, quite complex and changeable.

The years 1989 to 1991 saw an upheaval in the Nordic countries, which served as a turning point, undermining the strong position of the Nordic model.[10] Sweden went through its deepest recession since the Depression. The public debt doubled, together with ever-increasing unemployment during the following three years.[11] It could even be argued that the welfare state was itself declining, with middle-class lifestyles evolving alongside individualism. This, in turn, eroded the popular status of the welfare state, and the Nordic model began to be questioned and challenged, both politically and socially, by policies of liberalisation and deregulation.[12] The most recurring topic of debate was, and still is today, how to sustain the generous welfare system yet still decrease the ever-rising income taxes.[13]

Nevertheless, poverty rates in the Nordic countries still remain some of the lowest in Europe. At the current time, unemployment is estimated at 9.1 per cent in Sweden, 4.3 per cent in Denmark and 3.4 per cent in Norway. In terms of youth unemployment in this region, Sweden holds the top position with figures at 23.7 per cent.[14] This nation is becoming increasingly segregated, with the most exposed groups living in communities bordering larger cities. Immigrants and young people experience the highest rate of unemployment and are the groups who are most dependent on social security and benefits. This became pertinently clear in May 2013 when riots broke out in Husby, a suburb of Stockholm. Initially, the riots started as a reaction to the killing of a 69-year-old man who was shot after threatening the police. Yet regardless of what instigated them, the aftershocks that followed sprang from a general frustration and feeling of social injustice among the locals.[15] This issue has been confirmed by numerous scholars, such as Dr Mary Hilson, who conceded the fact that the Nordic countries should by no means be seen as some form of utopia completely void of social exclusion, poverty, inequality or poor health. In fact, she pointed out that these problems are very much present and acute in Scandinavia, much as they are in the UK, and politicians would be wrong to overlook this when discussing policies from which to draw lessons.[16]

However, when it comes to using the Nordic model as an inspirational tool, the SNP's preferred country of choice has always been Norway because of the many similarities this particular nation shares with Scotland: the small size of population (nearly five million inhabitants); the historical bonds with the Vikings; and the fishery and oil industries. Norway, with its little over one hundred years of independence, has been described by Scottish politicians as 'one of the most successful social democracies in Europe, if not the world'.[17] The country's achievements in terms of high life expectancy, a superior education system, stable GDP per capita and gender equality are all favoured topics, but most preferred of all is the matter of North Sea oil resources and how these have enabled Norway to prosper, despite its size.[18]

The argument that the Nordic model is positive and uniform is still rather strong, yet the issue lies, in particular, with the problem of its adaptation. Even though many, on the social democratic left in particular, look at the Nordic countries as a blueprint for reform, at the same time it has been argued that the Nordic model is indeed nothing but a utopia, serving as an objective which, in truth, is unfeasible and inapplicable. Extended criticism of the model claims that these countries are associated with nothing but 'melancholy, conformity and control',[19] thus presenting a dystopia, an undesirable model for others to follow. Yet, regardless of its qualifications, historical accounts have shown that the Nordic model has served as a 'transitional tool' for newly independent countries, for example within the Baltic region. However, due to the scope of this chapter, the focus is primarily on the Scandinavian countries.

Tackling poverty through policy

Known as a 'public service' system, the Nordic welfare model is ruled by the principle of universalism, which allows a considerable percentage of the population to access health and social care services since these are publicly funded from tax revenues. It is a system which arguably promotes higher levels of social equality.[20] Nevertheless, having a strong social insurance system was not what made the Nordic model stand out in the post-war era, but rather the ambitious vision that the Nordic countries had for their welfare states, and their governments' conviction that they were capable of creating a better society. In addition to this, proficiency and professionalism have always been high priorities within the Nordic welfare state, an extension of which throughout the healthcare, social services and education fields has been an essential policy goal in these countries.[21]

Arguably, it is these features of the Nordic countries which attract foreign politicians the most: the promotion of female labour participation, universal daycare and universal student loans along with a strong emphasis on children's rights, creating a:[22]

> ... harmony between the model and the principles of the market – that the basic unit of society is the individual and a central purpose of policy should be to invest in human capital and maximise individual autonomy.

These examples highlight the successes – family poverty is particularly low in these countries – but there are, however, significant concerns about growing poverty and insecurity among young adults.

As shown earlier, youth unemployment is an issue which has become particularly problematic in the Nordic region. In May 2013, the four Nordic prime ministers met in Stockholm to discuss how to tackle this increasingly prominent root of poverty. According to the statistics presented at this meeting, Norwegian youth unemployment is currently 8.6 per cent, Danish is 14.1 per cent and Finnish is 19 per cent.[23] The reason why these figures are so diverse has been pointed out by researchers as being mainly due to Norway's favourable economic climate, as well as the fact that Norway and Denmark both operate a particular traineeship system which enables young people to integrate more efficiently into the labour market.[24]

During the meeting, Finance Minister of Sweden, Anders Borg, focused mainly on issues such as ongoing globalisation, population growth and technical development, which are putting pressure on the employment market. The reasons behind this, he claimed, are partly due to the Asian, South American and African markets expanding, and with them, so does the range of inexpensive labour and manufacturing. Nevertheless, the blame should not be put on external factor first and foremost; employers in general are sceptical about employing young, inexperienced people.[25] Making youth unemployment one of the governments' top priorities could thus enable more young people to enter the labour market, and subsequently tackle social issues and unrest at an early stage.

Scandinavian lessons for Scotland beyond the referendum

Regardless of how the Nordic model, in itself, has been contested or to what extent it is declining, the concept of *Norden* appears to remain stable and resilient to external pressure. The five independent countries still co-operate internationally today, constructing a framework that remains unchallenged, possibly due to their shared culture and identity, and which has been maintained intact despite internal structural fluctuations and political disruption. The Nordic countries' autonomy is a force to be reckoned with, especially on an intellectual and academic level, and, with the creation of the Nordic Council after World War Two, this autonomy was displayed as a model to follow in terms of international co-operation.[26]

Nevertheless, the reason why the Nordic countries can invest four times as much in their education is, naturally, due to their high tax rates, both in terms of income tax and VAT. This has been considered by many as a major issue in terms of adopting the Nordic model in Scotland, as was discussed in the Common Weal paper, launched as a response to this by the Jimmy Reid Foundation. The Common Weal project admits that progress necessitates increasing tax rates, yet simultaneously claims that an independent Scotland could still be richer, fairer and more progressive without necessarily having to increase income tax rates.[27]

It has been suggested that Norway, with its 100-year-old parliament, is an impeccable example of how Scotland could benefit from seceding from the UK, especially in terms of how successful Norway has proved to be as a nation, following the country's peaceful separation from Sweden. Relying on a mixed economy which is structured through both government intervention and free market activity combined, Norway has enjoyed sustained economic expansion since the 1990s. The petroleum industry is the most significant contributor to Norway's wealth, and the country is the third largest exporter of oil, which is the reason why the Norwegian government founded the Petroleum Fund in 1990.[28] The fund works on an investment basis, with oil and gas revenues being paid into it and later invested internationally – a mechanism designed to act as a buffer for the economic fluctuations which frequently occur within this industry, as well as enabling future generations to benefit from reserves which soon might be spent. On a more general note, the quality of life in Norway is reported to be remarkably high, gaining a top position ranking in the UN Human Development Index of 2004, where measures such as life expectancy, educational attainment and income are calculated and evaluated, followed by Sweden in second place. The UK lags some way behind, ranking 12th.[29]

In terms of tackling the rising trend of increased rates of youth unemployment, there is much to learn from some Nordic countries. Drawing lessons from Denmark and Norway, where well-developed traineeships allow young people to enter the labour market directly from university, thereby making them more attractive for employers, Scotland could equally follow and adopt this initiative. The need for improved opportunities for young people has already been identified by several policy-making institutions, such as Skills Development Scotland, an organisation focusing on meeting the skills needs of employers in Scotland.[30]

The challenges surrounding tackling poverty require a complex policy mix, and the ultimate solution might lie in drawing from best practices and lessons learnt from other countries. This chapter has briefly discussed the importance of early intervention and pointed out some issues that may be addressed by enabling young people to gain better access to education and facilitating their entry to the labour market. By expanding companies' flexibility in terms of employment practices and co-operating with organisations, such as universities, young people would be able to move straight from finishing their degree to finding a profession. This has proved to be an efficient policy in countries such as Norway, with its trainee programmes, and Denmark, with its flexible work market and employment policies. With the rise in poverty levels and an ever-aging population, it could definitely be argued that Scotland's future depends on the prosperity of the younger generation, and this is a collective responsibility shared by companies, policy makers and governments alike, required for this generation to thrive in a Scotland beyond the independence referendum.

Notes

1 M Hilson, *The Nordic Model: Scandinavia since 1945*, Reaktion Books Ltd, 2008, p51

2 J Andersson and M Hilson, 'Images of Sweden and the Nordic Countries', *Scandinavian Journal of History*, 34(3), 2009, pp219–28

3 See note 2

4 Author's citation

5 Scottish Executive, *Achieving Our Potential: a framework to tackle poverty and income inequality*, Scottish government, 2008

6 See note 5

7 See note 5

8 M Hauotto, *Nordic Social Policy: changing welfare states*, Routledge, 1999, p12

9 See note 8

10 See note 1, p186

11 H Mouritzen, 'The Nordic Model as a Foreign Policy Instrument: its rise and fall', *Journal of Peace Research*, 32(1), 1995, p15

12 See note 8, p23

13 'The Swedish Model: adjusting to a changing world', *Svenskt Näringsliv Online*, 2012, http://www.svensktnaringsliv.se/english/about-sweden_46257.html

14 'Ungdomsarbetslöshet – Internationellt', *EkonomiFakta Online*, 2013, http://www.ekonomifakta.se/sv/Fakta/Arbetsmarknad/Arbetsloshet/Ungdomsarbetsloshet-i-EU

15 O Carp, 'Upplopp och Bränder i Husby', *Dagens Nyheter Online*, 20 May 2013, http://www.dn.se/sthlm/upplopp-och-brander-i-husby

16 M Hilson, 'Meeting of Nordic Horizons: the revolution will be Nordic', Parliamentary interview, Scottish Parliament, 27 October 2011

17 A Neil, '100 Years of Norwegian Independence: a study and comparison with Scotland', Press Release, 9 June 2005, http://www.alexneilmsp.net/index.php? subaction=showfull&id=1118312047&archive=&start_from=&ucat=1&

18 See note 1, p184

19 See note 1, p179

20 See note 1, p87

21 See note 8, p54

22 L Tragardh, 'The Swedish model is the opposite of the Big Society, David Cameron', *The Guardian Online*, 10 February 2012, http://www.guardian.co.uk/commentisfree/2012/feb/10/swedish-model-big-society-david-cameron

23 See note 14

24 See note 14

25 N Efendic, 'Arbetslösheten Biter Sig Fast', *Sveriges Dagblad Näringsliv Online*, 16 May 2013, http://www.svd.se/naringsliv/nyheter/sverige/arbetslosheten-biter-sig-fast_8177990.svd

26 See note 1, p187

27 T Gordon, 'A new blueprint for an independent Scotland', *The Sunday Herald Scotland Online*, 5 May 2013, http://www.heraldscotland.com/politics/referendum-news/a-new-blueprint-for-an-independent-scotland.20985084

28 See note 17

29 See note 26

30 R Clark, 'New incentive to employ young people', Scottish government, 26 August 2013, http://news.scotland.gov.uk/News/New-incentive-to-employ-young-people-352.aspx

Twenty-five

Poverty and childcare: lessons from the German model

Lisa Hauschel

Germany's federal structure

The correlation between sufficient childcare provision and low poverty levels has long been acknowledged.[1] Consequently, childcare has been on the political agenda in both Germany and Scotland: in Scotland, in the form of the Children and Young People (Scotland) Bill and, in Germany, with the recent establishment of childcare as a legal right for all children from the age of one. A crucial difference between childcare provision in the two countries is the level of government support. In Britain, 25 per cent of childcare costs are covered by the state; in Germany it is up to 80 per cent.[2] In his keynote speech to the SNP 2013 spring conference, First Minister Alex Salmond promised a seismic shift in childcare with independence:[3]

> 'Our ambitions for childcare are the hallmark of our approach to social and economic policy [...] I believe a transformational shift towards childcare should be one of the first tasks of an independent Scotland.'

This chapter seeks to outline what lessons can be learnt from the German model of childcare. In order to provide some context, the first part attempts to explain both Germany's political organisation, with a focus on the country's federal structure, as well as the nature and scale of poverty. The second part is concerned with an analysis of two much-debated family policies in order to shine a light on how the redistribution of services towards a better provision of childcare can help tackle poverty, especially among single mothers. It concludes with some lessons to be learned for Scottish childcare provision.

German federalism was established in 1949 in an attempt to decentralise political power. The basic law and supplementary legislation stipulate a highly structured relationship between the federation and the 16 constituent states – the *Länder*. The federal government holds responsibility for foreign affairs, defence, migration, citizenship, currency, transport and some aspects of policing. All other matters fall under the legislative power of the Länder and their distinct governments. Yet, federal intervention is justified wherever it is deemed necessary to preserve 'equivalent living conditions' throughout the country.[4]

German federalism requires a high degree of intergovernmental co-ordination to ensure common living standards. Since the 1980s, this has become increasingly difficult due to the emergence of a north-south divide, with the north suffering from economic decline in traditional industries and the south enjoying economic success in high-tech manufacturing and an expanding service sector.[5] Economic divergence has not only caused the Länder to pursue different, sometimes conflicting, policy interests (resembled, for instance, in significantly varying childcare costs), but has also led to greater financial transfers from the economically stronger south to the less well performing north. While the ethos of co-operation and solidarity still prevails to a great extent, Länder governments in prospering areas have criticised the existing federal system for their inability to pursue regional interests by making greater use of their own resources.[6]

The nature and scale of poverty in Germany

While many other European countries suffer record high unemployment rates and austerity measures as a consequence of the 2008 financial crisis, the German economy is marked by robust growth and, according to the Federal Agency for Civic Education, its strongest employment figures in more than 20 years.[7] However, despite being the world's fourth largest economy, Germany's poverty rate is higher compared with countries with a considerably weaker economy: in 2010, one in six Germans (15.8 per cent) was living in poverty.[8] Although this number is lower than both the OECD average and UK figures, the 2010 poverty rates of Germany were higher than those of neighbouring countries, such as the Czech Republic (9.8 per cent) or France (14 per cent).[9]

Looking at the distribution of poverty in the Länder, a north-south divide again is evident. There are considerably fewer people living in poverty in the southern Länder, such as Bavaria (11.3 per cent) or Baden-

Württemberg (11.2 per cent) than there are in the north, especially in Berlin (21.1 per cent) and Bremen (22.3 per cent).[10]

The risk of poverty is greatest among lone parents. According to the Federal Statistical Office, 37.1 per cent of single-parent households are living below the poverty line.[11] Additionally, women are more likely to fall into poverty than men, which is mostly due to the fact that women, especially mothers, are more likely to take up part-time employment or take time out of the labour market.

Efficient or outdated? Germany's family policy in focus

Unemployment remains the main reason for poverty in Germany.[12] As mentioned above, the group most at risk of poverty are single mothers. This is broadly due to an increased difficulty in finding a job-life balance, facilitated by childcare barriers, insufficient training opportunities and a lack of adequate social benefit transfers. In an attempt to address this problem, family policy was put high on the agenda of all political parties prior to the September 2013 national elections. The German government's annual expenditure on promoting children and families amounts to €200 billion – almost two-thirds of the federal budget.[13] A 2011 OECD publication shows that 'countries that do well on family outcomes devote about half of their public spending on family benefits'.[14] However, the effectiveness of the German government's family policies becomes questionable considering Germany's low birth rates and relatively high poverty rates. Five years ago, the German government ordered an extensive and independent cost-benefit study of its family policies. The final report, *Overall Evaluation of Benefit Payments to Married Couples and Families*, published in 2013, reveals that significant areas of family policy are in need of reform, as the most expensive measures fail to target groups that are most in need of support, such as lone parents.[15] It is easy to lose track of the nearly 160 benefits, tax credits and social services that the German government provides. Two of these family services in particular have been criticised heavily for not being targeted at the groups most in need of additional support.

First, 'tax splitting' for married couples allows partners to lower their tax burden by pooling and then dividing their earnings to calculate individual income tax. This allows a married couple to save up to €15,694 in income tax payments a year, and costs the government €20 billion. The report concludes that tax splitting is especially ineffective in terms of poverty prevention, as it incentivises the partner with the lower income to work less. If a couple divorce, this can leave the lower earner, usually a woman, worse off in the long run as the time spent out of work will likely have a negative impact when s/he returns to the labour market.

Second, the continuous increase of the monthly child benefit allowance, which both the previous and the current government have used to win voters over the past decades, has been criticised for being targeted at the wrong families. Every child that lives in Germany, regardless of its socio-economic background, is entitled to a monthly amount of €184 which, in some instances, is paid until the child turns 25. Unlike Scotland, the allowance is further increased for every additional child in an attempt to stimulate birth rates. The total cost for the state is €40 billion a year, an amount which will increase if German Chancellor Angela Merkel stands by her election promise to raise the monthly allowance. While there is consensus about the value of child benefit allowance as a social protection measure, critics have argued that a further increase is not beneficial for two reasons. First, the allowance is ineffective in supporting poorer families, as the money is offset against unemployment and welfare benefits, thus failing to offer additional support for low-income families. Second, critics argue that increasing the monthly allowances disincentivises parents from taking up employment.

Both of these services fail to target low-income families, and promote a traditional family model of the male breadwinner and the female homemaker – a family picture which, according to government-commissioned experts, is outdated and should not form the basis of modern policy making.[16] The report concludes that in order to support low-income families better and create higher work incentives for parents, costly services that are targeted at the wrong groups in society need to be reconsidered in favour of more effective and financially sustainable measures, like the extension of flexible and affordable childcare opportunities.

The last section of this chapter will discuss how the 'transformational shift' in childcare provision that Scotland's First Minister has promised is already underway in Germany, and how this, in turn, can help to inform the childcare debate in Scotland.

Lessons for Scotland

The federal structure of Germany has significant consequences for the provision of childcare. Under federal law, the Länder are responsible for childcare regulation in their respective local authority areas. Yet, traditionally the federal government has offered some financial support to the state governments.[17] The different approaches to childcare provision make it impossible to draw general conclusions, as different aspects such as cost, flexibility and, indeed, quality vary from *Bundesland* to *Bundesland*, and sometimes even from city to city. How substantial these variations are was revealed in a 2009/10 study that compared childcare provision in Germany's hundred largest cities. Similar to the existing 'childcare lottery' in Scotland, costs, for instance, range from a yearly amount of €0 to €2,500 depending on factors such as parental income and the ability to set costs off against tax liability. On average, a median-income family has to pay a yearly €814 for the childcare provision for one child[18] – a sum considerably lower than the average cost of childcare in Scotland, which amounts to approximately £4,368 (€5,124) per year.[19] However, the study also found that the cost of childcare in the northern *Bundesländern* is greater than in the south. In Lübeck, the second largest city of the northern state Schleswig-Holstein, the average cost of childcare for a low-income family is €1,716, 7 per cent of the yearly income. In contrast, Heilbronn in Baden-Württemberg provides free childcare for families from all socio-economic backgrounds. A main reason for this variation lies in the differing economic strength of the Länder, but arguably the force of political will is likely to be a key factor.

The 2013 national elections have stirred the debate about childcare once again. In 2008, the German government and the Länder authorities announced the introduction of a new childcare law, *Kinderförderungsgesetz* (*KiföG*), which entitles all children who have reached the age of one to a full-time (10 hours/day) place in a nursery. Costs vary from free provision for low-income families to a yearly amount of up to €2,500, subject to different laws for each of the Länder. Previously, only three- to six-year-old children were legally entitled to a place. The new law became effective on 1 August 2013 and, arguably, surpasses the Scottish government's recent proposal to increase the provision from 475 hours per year to 600 hours annually for three- and four-year-olds and looked-after two-year olds. Nonetheless, the enforcement of the law confronted many of the federal states with severe problems: a lack of qualified staff, an insufficient number of new spaces, and a struggle to finance the development of new nurseries, to name only a few.

With regard to the recent changes in childcare provision in Germany, there are two lessons, in particular, that may help to inform the debate around childcare in Scotland. First, in spite of the problems that were encountered with the implementation of the new childcare law for younger children, it is likely to have a positive long-term effect, especially for vulnerable groups such as lone parents. According to a government report, mothers with children between the ages of one and three who have found a nursery place work 12 hours more a week than mothers whose children are not enrolled in a nursery. The benefits of greater labour force participation are twofold: families have an average gross income gain of almost €700 a month, and the state benefits from tax and social insurance payments.[20]

The new law also addresses the quality of early years development with a particular focus on language promotion and integration. Under the 'early chances initiative', the state has made €400 million available to nurseries to enable a fair start for children from all backgrounds by promoting speech development. Additionally, funding has been made available for 600 local initiatives to develop early years education, and to guarantee a 1:5 nursery staff/child ratio by 2015.[21] While it is still too early to assess the success of these initiatives, critics have warned that the rushed development of sufficient childcare places to abide with the new law has left a significant gap in the number of well-trained staff to guarantee high-quality childcare.

The second lesson from the German experience concerns flexible childcare. A report on atypical working hours by the Federal Statistical Office reveals that, in 2012, 25 per cent of all employees worked after 6pm and on weekends.[22] Inflexible opening hours of nurseries constitute a big problem for those parents. The German government is receptive to the call for more flexible childcare. Under 'the charter for family-conscious working hours', companies commit themselves, albeit voluntarily, to guarantee family-friendly working conditions for their employees. Additionally, new nursery models such as 24-hour kindergartens or workplace nurseries are not only promoted in the government's manifesto but also heavily subsidised, which has led to a rise in private investors who promote childcare as a commercial pursuit. In conclusion, it can be said that, for Germany, a country in which childcare was traditionally provided primarily on a part-time basis and rarely used as an instrument to facilitate greater female employment, these developments, although still in their fledgling stages, can be seen as a step in the right direction to tackle poverty. Alex Salmond has tasked the Council of Economic Advisers to analyse the impact of Scotland moving towards the childcare provision that is commonplace across Europe – a glance at Germany may help to bring about the 'transformational shift' he has promised.

Notes

1 Barnardo's, *Paying to Work: childcare and child poverty*, 2012, http://www. barnardos.org.uk/ptw_childcare_and_child_poverty.pdf

2 L Riddoch, 'Gender may sway referendum vote', *The Scotsman*, 2013, http:// www.scotsman.com/news/lesley-riddoch-gender-may-sway-referendum-vote-1-2855465

3 SNP Spring Conference 2013 address, http://www.snp.org/speech/2013/mar/first-minister-alex-salmond-gives-his-spring-conference-2013-address

4 Deutscher Bundestag, *Grundgesetz für die Bundesrepublik Deutschland*, 1949, section 2: 'Der Bund und die Länder', http://www.bundestag.de/bundestag/aufgaben/rechtsgrundlagen/grundgesetz/gg_02.html.

5 B Benoit, 'Germany's north-south split', *Financial Times*, 2007, http://www.ft.com/cms/s/0/798fc53e-6532-11dc-bf89-0000779fd2ac.html#axzz2bffwKM40

6 A Gunlicks, *The Länder and German Federalism*, Manchester University Press, 2003

7 Bundeszentrale für politische Bildung, *Arbeitslose und Arbeitslosenquote*, 2013, http://www.bpb.de/nachschlagen/zahlen-und-fakten/soziale-situation-in-deutsch land/61718/arbeitslose-und-arbeitslosenquote.

8 Statistisches Bundesamt, '15,8% der Bevölkerung Deutschlands waren 2010 armutsgefährdet, EU-weit waren es 16,9%', 2013, https://www.destatis.de/DE/PresseService/Presse/Pressemitteilungen/2013/03/PD13_121_634.html.

9 See note 7

10 Bundeszentrale für politische Bildung, *Armutsgefährdungsquoten nach Bundesländern*, 2013, http://www.bpb.de/nachschlagen/zahlen-und-fakten/soziale-situation-in-deutschland/158610/armut-nach-bundeslaendern

11 Statistisches Bundesamt, *Armutsgefährdungsquote nach Sozialleistungen in Deutschland nach dem Haushaltstyp*, 2013, https://www.destatis.de/DE/ZahlenFakten/GesellschaftStaat/EinkommenKonsumLebensbedingungen/Lebe nsbedingungenArmutsgefaehrdung/Tabellen/ArmutsgefQuoteTyp_SILC.html

12 Deutscher Bundestag, *Lebenslagen in Deutschland – Vierter Armuts- und Reichtumsbericht*, 2013, http://dip21.bundestag.de/dip21/btd/17/126/1712 650.pdf

13 BMFSFJ, *Ehe- und familienbezogene Leistungen insgesamt*, 2013, http://www. bmfsfj.de/BMFSFJ/familie,did=158318.html

14 Office for Economic Co-operation and Development, *Doing Better for Families*, 2011

15 H Bonin and others, *Zentrale Resultate der Gesamtevaluation familienbezogener Leistungen*, 2013, http://www.diw.de/documents/publikationen/73/diw_01.c.428680.de/13-40-1.pdf

16 See note 14

17 BMFSFJ, *Gute Kinderbetreuung*, 2013, http://www.bmfsfj.de/BMFSFJ/Kinder-und-Jugend/kinderbetreuung.html

18 Institut der Deutschen Wirtschaft Köln Consult, *Kindergarten-Monitor 2009/2010*, 2010, http://www.insm-kindergartenmonitor.de/files/Endbericht_Kindergarten monitor.pdf

19 Children in Scotland, *The Cost of Childcare in Scotland: a special report*, 2011, http://www.childreninscotland.org.uk/docs/CIS_Costofchildcarereport_FEB2011_001.pdf. The weekly average of £84 was multiplied by 52 (weeks) to get a yearly figure.

20 BMFSFJ, *Kinderbetreuung hat Positive Effekte*, 2013, http://www.bmfsfj.de/BMFSFJ/familie,did=197418.html?view=renderPrint

21 See note 16

22 Statistisches Bundesamt, *Arbeitszeit, Ausgleich von Beruf und Privatleben*, 2013, https://www.destatis.de/DE/ZahlenFakten/Indikatoren/QualitaetArbeit/QualitaetArbeit.html?cms_gtp=318944_slot%253D3&https=1%20

Twenty-six
Poverty in Ireland
Dr Mary P Murphy

Introduction

This chapter first outlines the Irish political context, and then addresses the nature and scale of poverty in Ireland. It follows with an assessment of Irish anti-poverty policy, before concluding with lessons and recommendations for Scotland.

The Irish political context

Ireland's relatively strong commitment to tackling poverty has to be understood in the context of its 'Celtic Tiger' model, based on a 'low-tax, service-poor equilibrium'.[1] Irish political, economic and social policy responses to the 2008 crisis remain loyal to this low tax formula. 'Austerity' translates into managing the fiscal deficit through cutting expenditure rather than raising taxes.

In September 2008, the Irish state adopted a strategy of bailing out all national banks, and the total sovereign debt rose to unsustainable levels. This ultimately led to the loss of sovereignty to the troika of the European Commission, European Central Bank and the International Monetary Fund in November 2010, and a reinforced emphasis on expenditure cuts.

In the Irish 2011 general election debate, political parties differed on how to manage austerity. The new 2011 coalition government of Fine Gael and Labour produced a political compromise that continued to favour cuts over tax increases, but also included 'a triple lock' to protect public sector pay, baseline adult social welfare rates and income tax levels. The focus of expenditure cuts, therefore, shifted towards frontline services, with a consequent impact on those most reliant on public services, especially women with children.

This macro-economic framework sits uneasily with the Irish national target to reduce 'consistent poverty' to 4 per cent by 2016 and to 2 per

Figure 26.1:

Progress towards the previous national poverty target 2005–2010

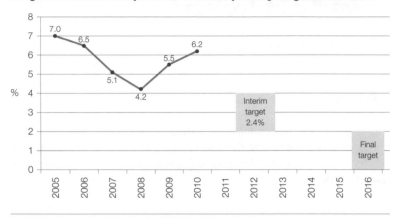

Source: http://www.welfare.ie/en/downloads/2012_nptbriefing.pdf, p12

cent or less by 2020 (from a baseline rate of 6.2 per cent in 2010).[2] Sub-targets include reducing the differential in consistent poverty between children and adults, and reducing the concentration of people in consistent poverty who are in jobless households. Ireland's contribution to the European Union (EU) target of reducing poverty by 20 million is to remove a minimum of 200,000 Irish people from the risk of poverty by 2020 (2010 baseline). However, as Figure 26.1 and the discussion below show, at both EU and Irish levels, economic and austerity targets remain far greater political priorities, and Irish anti-poverty targets show regressive progress.[3]

The nature and scale of poverty in Ireland

The latest poverty data is for 2011 and does not capture the last two years of the crisis.[4] From 2009 to 2011, consistent poverty increased from 5.5 per cent to 6.9 per cent and relative poverty increased from 14.1 per cent to 14.9 per cent. Income inequality also increased – the *Gini* co-efficient rose from 29.3 per cent to 31.3 per cent and the S80/20 rose from 4.3 per cent to 4.9 per cent. Particularly disturbing is the increase in levels of deprivation, which increased by 50 per cent to 25 per cent of the population. Fifteen per cent of those in work experience deprivation (twice as many as in 2009), but unemployed and lone parents continue to be hit the hardest, the latter experiencing a deprivation rate of 56 per cent.

Although the income support system remains relatively effective in lifting many out of poverty, much of the increase in poverty and inequality can be directly attributed to rising unemployment, which grew from a pre-crisis low of 4.2 per cent in 2006 to a high of 15.1 per cent in 2011 and has now declined to 2.4 per cent in early 2014. Long-term unemployment represents 58.4 per cent of the claimant count. However, not everyone out of work is captured in official unemployment counts – lone parents and women working in the home are not formally counted, nor are the growing numbers of under-employed. The International Monetary Fund calls the extent of Irish under-employment 'staggering'. Low work intensity is a structural problem – 23 per cent of all households are jobless, many with dependent children.

Generational injustice is a growing concern. There is clear evidence that austerity measures are falling on families with children, particularly lone-parent families with children (90 per cent of whom are women). Pensioners enjoy the lowest risk of poverty, but have experienced no cut in the basic state pension. From 2009 to 2011, consistent child poverty increased from 8.7 per cent to 9.3 per cent, and child deprivation rose from 25 per cent to 32 per cent. The 0–17-year-old age group comprises 27 per cent of the population, but 35 per cent of those experiencing deprivation. At 19.7 per cent, Ireland's child poverty is the fifth highest in Europe.[5] Ten per cent of people in Ireland are living in food poverty, with increased use of food banks and reports of hungry children attending school. Youth unemploy-ment is 26.4 per cent and would be significantly higher were it not for net emigration – in 2011, 88 per cent of all emigrants were aged between 15 and 44, with 43 per cent being in the 15–24 age group. Despite such high levels of emigration, one-third of young men under 25 are unemployed, with 18.4 per cent not in employment, education or training (the fourth highest in the EU). Yet austerity budgets have halved jobseeker assistance for those under 25.

Assessment of Irish anti-poverty policy

Ireland has historically been innovative in its approach to fighting poverty. The 1995 Irish National Anti-poverty Strategy was a model for EU social inclusion strategies, and pioneered geographical, partnership and equality strategies to empower local communities and communities of interest.[6] Sharp declines in consistent poverty were attributed to massive decreases in unemployment (from 18 per cent in 1988 to 4.2 per cent in 2006) and from 2001, significant increases in Irish social welfare payments (by-products of populist electoral budget cycles during the years of the Celtic Tiger).

However, employment-based anti-poverty strategies ignored the significant numbers of working-age adults dependent on disability, lone parent and carer's social welfare payments. There was a failure to streamline or integrate public employment services and income supports, and to develop a coherent activation strategy. Expenditure on active labour market measures was significant, but much of this was invested in measures which offered poor progression, poor-quality public employment services were politically protected from reform. Rather than investing in upskilling and enabling working class Irish people to participate in a buoyant labour market, mid-2000s labour shortages were managed by attracting employment-ready migrants.

Jobs are often an effective route out of poverty, but a persistent group of social welfare claimants experience significant employment and poverty traps. These are less to do with the level of payments and more to do with the structure of supplements (private rented housing and primary healthcare provision) and rules governing transition from work to welfare. These impact most on families with children. In addition, the in-work income supplement for families, family income supplement, has poor take-up. Unlike its equivalent in many EU countries, it is administered through the social welfare, rather than the tax, system. Those with poor educational qualifications and low skills remain trapped in low paid and casual employment.

Since the crisis, there has been a structural shift in the quantity and quality of available employment opportunities, so that male part-time unemployment has doubled from 6 per cent to 12 per cent (over 50 per cent involuntary). Light-touch employment regulation also allows the growing use of temporary staff and atypical employment relations. A significant part of the labour force is low paid (16.6 per cent for men and 24 per cent for women). A series of cuts in 2009 and 2011 to the duration of jobseeker benefit, levels, eligibility and entitlement criteria, as well as one-parent family payment income disregards, make it harder for low-paid workers to augment poor wages with income supports. It is more likely that people will be trapped in casual employment with no access to social protection.

Ireland continues to struggle to implement comprehensive activation strategies. There is a clear mismatch between the targets of activation (the jobseeker claimant count) and those in jobless households (people with disabilities, lone parents, carers and partners). Reforms in child income supports and adequate childcare services are both needed to enable parents to access jobs, but the Celtic Tiger period saw an over-reliance on cash payments and a related lack of investment in services like childcare and early childhood education.[7] While universal cash payments remain crucial, there is room for a realignment of expenditure towards better targeting of cash payments and investment in services. There appears to be little political capacity, however, to build support for such needed reforms.

The European Anti-poverty Network argues that Ireland has failed to mainstream anti-poverty measures into key policies (health, education, refugee and asylum policy).[8] While Ireland was an early innovator, poverty and equality-proofing tools and impact assessment processes were never embedded into budget and policy planning processes. Previous investment in civil society, social capital and community development has been pared back to levels which threaten the services' viability. Key agencies, including the Combat Poverty Agency, the Equality Authority and the Irish Human Rights Commission, have been either closed or run down. Lack of meaningful engagement with communities living in poverty means a serious disconnect between policy and practice, and a failure to appreciate the cumulative impact of budget cuts.

Lessons for Scotland

Scotland can learn most from what Ireland did not do. Economic growth is never enough – a sustainable tax base is needed to underpin a long-term investment approach to social expenditure. Investment in early childhood, education and preventative social policy can reap significant social dividends.

Lone parents endure very high risks of poverty, but remain outside mainstream labour market strategies. Full employment and activation supports need to extend to all working-age adults, and the focus needs to be on the quality, as well as quantity, of employment and on a well-regulated labour market that delivers decent work. Work must pay; a core priority remains to resolve poverty traps. Integrating tax and welfare systems is a challenge for all anti-poverty strategies. Work only pays when there are decent jobs that pay a living wage. Employment protection legislation, wage policy and in-work benefits need to be aligned to ensure that new forms of atypical work are not tomorrow's poverty and unemployment traps.

Anti-poverty strategies, proofing tools and geographical strategies are not fads; they need to be mainstreamed into all budgetary strategies, preferably by legislation. Employment will never be the only route out of poverty. Irish experience shows that income supports or social transfers are crucial. Maintaining public support for adequate income supports is vital. Scotland has a proud record of leadership in equality and rights institutions. These, together with civil society institutions, need to be sustained at national and local levels and supported to keep poverty visible on the political agenda.

Finally, Irish anti-poverty targets are clearly being sacrificed on the altar of European economic and monetary union. This is diluting progressive Irish support for the EU project. Scotland needs to lobby for Europe 2020 social targets to be integrated into EU mainstream economic governance. A strong social Europe is vital for Scotland, and maybe, particularly important if the independence vote is 'Yes'.

Notes

1   S Dellepiane and N Hardiman, 'Governing the Irish Economy: a triple crisis', in N Hardiman (ed), *Irish Governance in Crisis*, Manchester University Press, 2012, p11
2   The term 'consistent poverty' describes someone whose income is below the at risk of poverty threshold (60 per cent or below the national average annual income) and who cannot afford at least two of 11 agreed deprivation indicators, such as: two pairs of strong shoes; a warm waterproof overcoat; buying new, not second-hand, clothes; and eating meat, chicken, fish or a vegetarian equivalent every second day.
3   Department of Social Protection, *National Anti-poverty Targets Review*, 2013, http://www.welfare.ie/en/downloads/2012_nptbriefing.pdf
4   Central Statistics Office, EU SILC 2011, 2013
5   See note 4
6   European Anti-Poverty Network, *Submission to Department of the Taoiseach on National Reform Programme*, 2013
7   OECD, *Doing Better for Families*, 2011
8   See note 6

Twenty-seven

Anti-poverty policy and political sovereignty in Canada

Gill Scott

Introduction

Canada has a number of things in common with the UK that make it a useful country to turn to when issues of territorial politics and welfare are discussed. Both countries saw their developed economies rocked by the economic crisis of 2008. Central government has been challenged by sub-national governments over its capacity and desire to reduce poverty. Both countries face a rising tide of poverty and insecurity that has a territorial dimension. And welfare has been a key component of national and sub-national identity construction.[1] In Canada, this has shown itself particularly in the relationships between the province of Quebec and the Canadian federal government, but it is by no means the only province where it is the focus of inter-governmental tension.

Constitutionalists and policy makers alike in Scotland have turned to Canada in their discussions of how to give greater control over revenue and increase accountability for welfare.[2] Suggestions for devolving a proportion of income tax to Scotland (for example, in the Calman Report[3]) were based on the Canadian experience. Debates over welfare and the nature of social justice that come with fiscal power, however, go beyond debates about the mechanics of fiscal union.[4] Welfare policies in both the UK and Canada have been affected by austerity measures and neo-liberal policies from central governments now for over a decade, but measures to reduce poverty and insecurity and enhance a social justice vision of a new Scotland were key features defining devolved government in Scotland from its very beginning. In Canada, similar claims for legitimacy based on welfare from provincial governments have a long history.

This chapter examines the way in which anti-poverty programmes have been a core feature of policy and fiscal debate between federal and provincial governments in Canada and highlights some of the key impacts. In doing so, it attempts to show how significant sub-national policy making, within a much more devolved system than Scotland is at present, is in addressing poverty.

Why look to Canada?

State-provided social services, or social entitlements, and the political struggles surrounding them are central features of Canadian citizenship. Together with hockey and cold winters, social programs have helped to define the Canadian national identity.[5]

This may be a claim that is used largely to distance the country from the US and showcase the sort of values that many Canadians feel makes their country unique. It certainly is the case that, until the 1990s, national minimum standards on employment insurance, health and pensions were supported by most Canadian citizens, and supported by provincial and federal governments, largely through support of the process of 'equalisation' managed through federal and provincial negotiations. Equalisation refers to transfer payments made by the federal government to less wealthy Canadian provinces to equalise their ability to generate tax revenue. The formula is based solely on revenues, not on need in any of the provinces, although payments help guarantee reasonably comparable levels of healthcare, education and welfare. There currently is a high degree of political tension over the calculation of equalisation payments, based to a significant extent on the fact that provincial identities and interests are key factors in Canadian politics. In fact, Canada is among the most decentralised federations in the developed world. Each of the ten provinces maintains a closely guarded independence over its own jurisdiction and taxation. Provinces set minimum wage levels, education and health services are governed at provincial level, and social assistance is a provincial responsibility. In fact, Canadians pay more in taxes to their provincial and local governments combined than to the federal government. Resistance to social policy centralisation is a key marker of provincial/federal relations: Quebecois nationalist struggles highight how often social policy control and autonomy are connected. Federal programme spending (including on pensions, foreign policy and defence) is less than provincial programme spending and has declined significantly since the

1990s. The result is a variation in social policies and measures addressing poverty, which are often tied to territorial politics[6] and intense 'inter-state' politics over relative contributions to and benefits from federal equalisation funds.[7] As such, it is worthy of examination for a Scotland where social policy has moved up the agenda quite markedly and where there is a growing inter-relationship between anti-poverty policy and demands for national autonomy and self-government.

Poverty and insecurity in Canada

At first sight, Canada would not appear to be the first country that policy makers and poverty analysts would look to for ideas. After all, data from the OECD on income inequality and poverty from the mid-1980s to the mid-2000s show that, among comparison nations, Canada, the US and the UK are distinguished by their relatively high poverty rates. The following table, for example, provides a pretty dismal picture of child poverty in the mid-2000s in Canada compared with other OECD nations.

Table 27.1:
Percentage of children living in relative poverty, with less than 50 per cent of national median household income, 2008

	%
Denmark	3.7
Iceland	5.7
UK	12.5
Australia	14.0
Greece	12.1
Canada	15.0
Germany	8.3
USA	21.6

Source: Adapted from OECD Family Database: Child Poverty, Table CO2.2, Poverty rates for children and households with children 2008, OECD, 2012, http://www.oecd.org/els/soc/CO2.2%20Child%20poverty%20-%20update%20270112.pdf

Nevertheless, a more nuanced view of the history of Canadian anti-poverty policy shows that policy at both federal and provincial level can make a difference to the experience of poverty. In 2010, before taxes and transfers, the relative income poverty rate in Canada was 26 per cent. After taxes and transfers, it reduced to the OECD average of 11 per cent.[8] Compare this with the US where before tax and transfers the poverty rate was 28 per cent and after taxes and transfers it was 17 per cent. Between 1981 and 1990 Statistics Canada shows a long-term, albeit modest, decline in the measure generally used as an indicator of poverty – the 'after tax low income cut-off', particularly for seniors. From the mid-1990s, the reductions in poverty that started in the 1980s were cut short by an economic downturn and by the restructuring of federal public policy – by cuts in cash benefits and reductions in social programmes that took place under the Liberal government led by Jean Chretien.[9] Where economic expansion took place, the result was increased income for higher income families, while the earnings of poorer families stagnated and social transfers fell.

The introduction of the federal child tax credit in 1998 made a difference – federal child benefits are estimated to reduce the poverty rate of all Canadian families with children under 18 by at least 6 per cent,[10] but there are still significant differences across the provinces and the restructuring in the 1990s put greater pressure on provinces to fund and manage poverty reduction. The OECD in 2008 noted striking increases in income inequality and poverty rates from the mid-1990s in Canada, but there is no comprehensive federal anti-poverty plan, and official poverty measures do not exist at national level.[11] It is the capacity of provincial governments to raise and spend at the sub-national level, as well as the refusal by many of them to accept the austerity packages and neo-liberal policies at federal level that has ameliorated a picture of rising poverty at local level. The result is that the rate and distribution of poverty varies significantly by province: poverty rates among the provinces in 2010 ranged from 11 per cent in British Columbia to 3.9 per cent in Prince Edward Island.

Obviously, some differences will be due to varying rates of economic growth between provinces, but variations in poverty do not match them or the existence of non-renewable natural resources, such as oil, in any direct fashion. The difference can perhaps be better explained in terms of commitment to, and pursuance of, anti-poverty policies.

Provincial differences, sovereignty and anti-poverty policy

Most Canadians have a strong identification with the province in which they live, and social policy acts as an important mechanism of territorial identity building, as well as mobilisation against federal government. Nowhere is this seen more clearly than in Quebec, where, like Scotland, there is a strong relationship between social policy, nationalism and nation building.[12] Ethnicity and language have been important dimensions of the Quebec separatist debate, but the development of pensions, healthcare and childcare were very significant definers of Quebec identity between the 1970s and late 1990s. More recently, there has been a focus on anti-poverty policies. Quebec was the first province to develop a law for poverty reduction in 2002 and initiate a Poverty Action Plan in 2004. By 2012, all provinces and territories, with the exception of British Columbia and Saskatchewan, had poverty policies in place or were in the process of developing them[13] and two provinces, Quebec (2002) and Ontario (2009), have enacted anti-poverty legislation that, in theory, ensures government accountability in those provinces.

Each provincial strategy differs according to local need, but sets objectives, targets and mechanisms as well as the key areas they target, such as housing, early childhood development initiatives, employment programmes, income supplementation and place-based initiatives. As Quebec was the first and has the most developed strategy, it is worth looking at in a little more detail. Quebec's stated goal in the 2002 Plan was 'to progressively make Quebec, by 2013, one of the industrialised nations having the least number of persons living in poverty.' It established a provincial strategy to combat poverty and social exclusion (a term seldom used in Canada) and accompanied it with a fund. Key features included fully indexing employment assistance (similar to the UK's jobseeker's allowance), improving access to affordable housing, providing better access to early intervention and early childhood education (a day's childcare costs only CAD$7), investing in community initiatives, as well as coordinating with First Nations' (Aboriginal) governments within the province and federal government. Results had to be reported every three years and consideration for specific needs, such as gender, age, ethnicity, disability and regional discrepancy, were built in to the strategy. Following the provincial government's evaluation of the 'success' of the first Poverty Action Plan, using measures agreed at the beginning of the Plan, the government released its second Poverty Action Plan in 2010 – a plan for 2010 to 2015. Between 1999 and 2009, Quebec's poverty rate dropped by 40 per cent, and while economic growth was a major factor at the time, the Plan has been seen as at least a partial success and a buffer for the poor against the impact of the economic crisis of 2008 – that is, in the good times the Plan ensured that the rates of poverty reduction were greater than would have been expected, and in bad times the poor have been protected more than otherwise might have been the case. Not all, however, agree with the provincial government's evaluation. Canada Without Poverty, a national anti-poverty organisation, concluded in 2012 that:[14]

> In many respects Quebec has blazed the trail for action on poverty in Canada with its robust Act legislating the government's responsibility to combat poverty, its definition of poverty as encompassing of social exclusion, and its commitment to universal child care. However… civil society organisations have questioned whether government actions have been adequate to address poverty in the province, with particular concern around income support.

That concern about income support is one that resonates in every province, particularly for working-age adults – who, as in Scotland, appear to be likely to be poorer today than they were three decades ago.

Provinces differ. While in Quebec and Ontario, for example, there is a growing awareness that, as work becomes a less guaranteed route out of poverty, more effective income support measures are needed, particularly for lone parents, disabled people, First Nation communities and working-age single adults. Such concerns are not evident in every province and highlight the role that sub-national level government plays in a highly decentralised nation. British Columbia has consistently had the highest rate of poverty in Canada: it does not have a plan to reduce or eliminate poverty; it has the highest rate of child poverty in the nation despite years of strong economic growth and record low unemployment; the gap between the rich and poor has been growing; and it has the worst record of affordable housing in Canada. Such a situation raises the issue for us in Scotland of what happens when inter-governmental action to maintain a minimum of income, health and housing is missing, or at least under pressure. Some have argued that greater decentralisation will produce just such a race to the bottom.

Lessons for Scotland

Social policy acts as an important mechanism for national and provincial mobilisation against the federal government in Canada. A similar picture exists in Scotland today – a focus of mobilisation against the UK government. The situation in Canada, however, can be viewed in two ways. Provincial autonomy/sovereignty provides the space to develop carefully crafted anti-poverty policy, such as that in Quebec (population: eight million) and Ontario (population: 13 million). We could therefore see an example of how a poverty strategy could be strengthened. But we can also see how, without the continuation of co-operation on social welfare and social policy at national level, the pathway being followed by Canada's third largest province, British Columbia (population: five million), is also a possibility. With Scotland's past history of social democracy and public support for public services and a measure of equality, the model of decentralisation from Canada drawing on British Columbia or on Quebec is one that provides lessons on what not to do, as well as what to do. It also reminds us that tensions between national and sub-national levels of government are significant factors in the development of anti-poverty strategies.

Notes

1   N McEwen, *Nationalism and the State: welfare and identity in Scotland and Quebec*, Peter Lang, 2006; I McLean, J Gallagher and G Lodge, *Scotland's Choices: the referendum and what happens afterwards*, Edinburgh University Press, 2013

2   I McLean, J Gallagher and G Lodge, *Scotland's Choices: the referendum and what happens afterwards*, Edinburgh University Press, 2013; I McLean, *Calman and Holtham: the public finance of devolution*, 2010, http://163.1.40.43/Research/ Politics%20Group/Documents/Working%20Papers/2010/Calman_and_Holtham_ %282%29.pdf

3   Commission on Scottish Deveolution, *Serving Scotland Better: Scotland and the United Kingdom in the 21st century* (The Calman Report), 2009, http:// www.commissiononscottishdevolution.org.uk/about/index.php

4   M Mendelson, *Is Canada (still) a Fiscal Union?* Caledon Institute of Social Policy, 2012, http://www.caledoninst.org/Publications/PDF/998ENG.pdf

5   L Harder, 'Whither the Social Citizen?', in J Brodie and L Trimble (eds), *Reinventing Canada: politics of the 21st century*, Pearson Education (Canada), 2003, pp175–88

6   N McEwen, *Nationalism and the State: welfare and identity in Scotland and*

Quebec, Peter Lang, 2006

7   A Lecours and D Béland,'Federalism and Fiscal Policy: the politics of equalisation in Canada', *Publius*, 40(4), 2010, pp569–96

8   Statistics Canada, *Income in Canada 2011*, 2012

9   D Raphael, *Poverty in Canada*, Canadian Scholars Press, 2012; Citizens for Public Justice, *Poverty Trends Scorecard*, 2012, www.cpj.ca

10 D Hay, *Poverty Reduction Policies and Programs in Canada*, Canadian Council on Social Development, 2009

11 Organisation for Economic Co-operation and Development, *Growing Unequal: income distribution and poverty in OECD nations*, 2008, http://dx.doi.org/10.1787/422076001267

12 A Béland and A Lecours, 'Federalism, Nationalism and Social Policy Decentralisation in Canada and Belgium', *Regional and Federal Studies*, 17(4), 2007, pp405–19

13 Canada Without Poverty, *Poverty Progress Profiles*, 2012, http://www.cwp-csp.ca/poverty/poverty-progress-profiles

14 See note 13

Section Seven
Conclusion

Twenty-eight
Imagining a different welfare state?

Gerry Mooney

Few of us could have predicted that the debate around Scottish independence would also become a debate about the kind of welfare state we
would like to see in place in Scotland – and in the UK as a whole. That the
issues of welfare, childcare, equality, fairness and social justice have come
to occupy a central position within the wider constitutional debate is of
course to be welcomed. It provides a space, a badly needed space, for
discussion of the ways in which poverty and disadvantage can best be
addressed. It allows for the development of new ways of thinking, for new
ideas to emerge, and it affords an opportunity to challenge the punitive
and anti-poor thinking and policies that have become so characteristic of
the current UK coalition government.

The referendum may have given it impetus, but Scotland was ready
for this debate. Since 2010, the UK coalition government has embarked
on one of the most radical benefit-cutting programmes of any UK government in history. As we have seen across the essays in this book, the context is one that is shaped by the twin processes of UK government
austerity-driven welfare reform alongside the not unrelated desire for some
degree of more Scottish autonomy over welfare provision.

Before we get carried away by thinking that the battle to position
progressive thinking at the heart of debate has been won, all that has happened, important that it is without doubt, is that a space has been opened
up for discussion – and this volume is seeking to make a contribution to
that discussion. However, there is nothing intrinsically 'progressive' (or,
indeed, regressive) about independence. There is, likewise, no inevitability
that a future welfare system that is largely devolved to Scotland, or a fully
independence-based Scottish welfare state, would be any more (or less)
progressive or underpinned by (or devoid of) a social justice approach
than a UK welfare state. Part of the argument advanced by proponents of
the union (Chapter 10) is that independence could lead to the erosion of
the existing welfare entitlements and solidarities:[1]

> The progressive story of the UK is one of common endeavour to build a just, tolerant open society where our collective resources can be shared… The idea of a state pension… means that if you retire in Lerwick your pension is paid by tax contributions of a young worker in Liverpool.

On the other hand, part of the argument advanced by proponents of independence is that it will provide an opportunity to redress the recent erosion of welfare entitlements and solidarities:[2]

> …we will pursue a Scottish tax and economic policy to boost jobs, growth and social justice. Westminster governments, rejected at the ballot box in Scotland, will no longer be able to inflict the poll tax or the bedroom tax on the most vulnerable people in our society.

The idea of Britishness as being 'cemented by the common endeavour of… building the welfare state'[3] was a crucial part of the defence of the union made by leading New Labour politicians in the context of the establishment of devolution for Scotland in 1999. Likewise, in 2009, the then Labour-controlled Scotland Office in its submission to the Commission on Scottish Devolution (the Calman Commission) argued that:[4]

> All parts of the UK regard the provision of healthcare as a fundamental part of what it means to be a citizen – devolution has responded to local needs, but it has not altered this fundamental feature of our citizenship.

However, the New Labour UK government together with its successor, the Conservative-Liberal Democrat coalition, have shared a commitment to 'reforming' welfare which, in important respects, altered the nature of that shared UK national purpose through welfare citizenship by promoting conditionality and, more recently, by diluting provisions. Today, following recent trends in UK welfare provision – as well as the impact of 15 years of devolution – it is arguably much more difficult to advance the argument that the UK government (and by stint of that, the union) remains the defender of the welfare state, despite claims (mainly coming from the Labour Party) that a 'social union' built on welfare remains a fundamental element of the union.

This is, of course, a fundamentally different understanding of the idea of a 'social union' from that advanced by the SNP: of post-independence cultural and social ties in which Scotland could act as a 'beacon of progressiveness'[5] for the rest of the UK. And this is a beacon in which a

Scottish welfare system comes to occupy centre stage, underpinned by 'shared values':[6]

'... where we have the power we have chosen a different path. A path that reflects Scotland's social democratic consensus, our shared progressive values – our priorities as a society. Now Labour and Tory dismiss these gains as the luxuries of a something for nothing country – really? Personal care for older people, free tuition for young people, to be cast aside as something for nothing? This is not a something for nothing country but a something for something society and this party shall defend that social progress made by our parliament. ... with even just a taste of independence we have been able to deliver fairer policies than elsewhere in these islands. With a measure of independence on health, on education and on law and order we have made Scotland a better place.'

'Progressiveness', 'social union', 'solidarity', 'social justice' 'citizenship': though such language has come to be prevalent in the constitutional debate, much of it remains vague, ill-defined and contested.[7] Most of the political parties in Scotland claim to be in favour of social justice, of some kind of another; few articulate precisely what they understand this to mean. Social justice of the kind that is often associated with the post-1945 Keynesian welfare state is rarely advanced today by the main political parties, including both the Conservative Party and the Labour Party. Underpinned by a social democratic understanding of society and the causes of social problems, the post-1945 vision has arguably been diluted, hollowed out and ideas of social democracy and solidarity largely replaced by ambiguous commitments to fairness.

Nonetheless, the idea of social justice and social democracy remain politically important in the Scottish context, not least as the two main political parties, Labour and the SNP, lay claim to be the inheritors and protectors of a uniquely 'Scottish' social democratic tradition. This claim is fuelled by a narrative of Scottish distinctiveness and Scottish difference; the assertion, or assumption, that there is a unique set of national attitudes that reflect a commitment to egalitarianism and social justice.

The idea of Scotland as underpinned by a set of distinctively progressive Scottish values should also be viewed with caution. Most evidence from social attitudes surveys suggests that attitudes to poverty and welfare in Scotland are only marginally more welfarist than England as a whole, and are no more welfarist than some parts, such as the north of England. In relation to poverty, for instance, research has shown that when it comes to measuring the basic necessities of life that are essential for participation in society, Scots do not have a different standard from other areas of the UK. On a UK-wide basis, there is a general consensus about the same kind of acceptable social minimum below which people should not be allowed to fall.[8] Thus, there is contested evidence for the claims that a more socially just welfare system would necessarily be established in Scotland. But nonetheless, the idea that Scottish attitudes and 'Scotland' is markedly more progressive and socially just than the rest of the UK is a powerful story and generates much political capital.

What is the 'progressive' welfare state to which people in Scotland seemingly aspire or yearn? That there is support in Scotland for publicly provided services and for a somewhat ill-defined, but generally 'progressive', welfare system has not prevented job losses across the public sector in Scotland or deterioration in some services. On the other hand, it might be argued that there was little alternative, given the depth of the cuts to the Scottish block grant – with limited other sources of revenue available to the Scottish government under devolution as presently configured. Further, anti-poor narratives are evident in Scotland (evidenced not least by the hugely controversial BBC Scotland series *The Scheme*, broadcast in 2010) and cannot readily be dismissed as the preserve of people, places and politicians outside Scotland.[9]

In Chapter 1 we highlighted that 'welfare' was integral to the early debates around devolution. It was asserted that a Scottish Parliament would be able to generate, in the words of the first First Minister Donald Dewar, 'Scottish solutions for Scottish problems', and many of these were problems that social welfare policies could address. As we have seen throughout this volume, policies from both the UK and Scottish governments have made a difference at various points since the late 1990s, not least in relation to child poverty, though we have also highlighted that some of these gains are now in serious danger of being eroded. Scotland remains a society scarred by widespread problems of poverty, disadvantage and inequalities of different kinds. And as different contributors here have pointed out, there is much to be done to address such deep-seated, and long-standing, problems. Having the tools to tackle the problem is key to success.

Looking ahead

Whatever the outcome of the independence referendum, it is widely agreed that the status quo is not an option, and that there will be further constitutional change. Advocates of 'devolution plus', 'devolution more' or 'devolution max' recognise that further devolution to Scotland will take place; it has also been advocated that this may involve some devolution of welfare matters along with more fiscal devolution on the back of the Scotland Act 2012. While much of this remains vague and uncertain, the future direction of welfare in Scotland will be different, not least because the country is undergoing significant demographic change. That the two main political parties in Scotland, the Labour Party and the SNP, describe themselves as social democratic – in some way or another – also means that there is *potential* for a welfare system in Scotland that differs from the current UK model. But this is only potential and again there is no inevitability that Scottish means better than UK.

Caution here is in part driven by the concern that there are, as yet, no clear plans for the funding of any future welfare state in Scotland – devolved or independent.[10] What role would be given to the market or to for-profit companies, for instance, in delivering welfare or in-work activation programmes? How far will trade unions and campaigning organisations be given scope to play central parts in the development of new ways of thinking and doing? Further, there has been little discussion of citizenship rights in any future Scotland. Surely a meaningful discussion of citizenship is central to configuring the future state of welfare in Scotland? At the time of writing, a Scottish government expert working group is considering and consulting on 'the medium- and long-term options for a welfare system in an independent Scotland', but it remains to be seen to what extent such issues will be addressed.[11]

In the constitutional debates, competing and contested claims to 'national interests' are often voiced. There has been much talk, for instance, about independence being in 'Scottish national interest' or that staying within the union is likewise in 'Scotland's best interest', that is the '[UK] national interest'. Focusing on the national or nation – in its different meanings in the Scottish/UK context – has at least two potentially significant dangers: of marginalising or overlooking issues of oppression and exploitation; and of accepting the inevitability of market-driven solutions to a range of social and economic problems. Claims – claims that are hugely contested of course – can be made that 'nation', when deployed in a

Scottish context, is more 'inclusive' than at a British or UK level. But this is also very contentious and can also draw attention away from the fundamental social divisions that characterise Scotland as much as other parts of the UK. In such ways, tackling social issues such as poverty come to be seen as a corollary of economic growth and prosperity; 'flexible' labour markets and low corporate taxation are the means to achieve global economic competitiveness for Scotland – and are therefore also in the national interest. While there are other economic models that do not follow the flawed neoliberal paradigm, these models also advance claims of the national interest and, again then, are susceptible to similar limitations and problems.

At times, the debate about Scotland's constitutional future has been couched in terms of territorial justice, 'national' justice even – that is, Scotland as a country taking charge of its own affairs, of guaranteeing that Scotland would have a government for which it voted and not, as is currently the situation, a UK Conservative-Liberal Democrat coalition government that commanded only 35 per cent of the popular vote in Scotland at the 2010 general election. That the debate has gradually become more a question of social justice offers the possibility of avoiding the dangers of an over-emphasis on nation and territory. Key here are the dissatisfactions with a lack of power in national and sub-national political arenas and a belief that the UK government does not, or will not, meet the welfare needs of its citizens. There are two outcomes to this: a desire to look at alternatives for power redistribution and, second, a desire to look at alternatives to meeting the needs of citizens. For this edition of *Poverty in Scotland*, the significance of the independence debate is not so much a question of what sort of political settlement would allow Scots to make decisions over things that matter to them (although this is obviously seriously important) but more what kind of social welfare arrangements would meet the seemingly more social democratic outlook of much of the population – and how can poverty and disadvantage be addressed?

New ways of thinking about welfare in Scotland

From the left in Scotland, we can identify at least two perspectives on the future of welfare, which differ in terms of their demands for greater power and autonomy for Scotland (independence versus 'devolution max'), but which share demands for greater social justice. The Jimmy Reid Foundation's Common Weal project[12] and the Red Paper Collective's

Class, Nation and Socialism: the red paper on Scotland 2014[13] largely agree on the need to recognise the extent of social and economic inequality and the need for political change. The Common Weal discussion paper argues for the need to draw direct lessons from the success of the Nordic nations in political governance, a balanced economy and social democracy (although, as we saw in Chapter 24, it is important to have a critical approach to the welfare systems of the Nordic states), and imagine it as the norm for a future independent Scotland. Common Weal papers also stress issues of social inequalities and social divisions of class, gender and race in the Scottish context. Likewise, class features prominently in the work of the Red Paper Collective, which argues that a historical analysis of class and political change highlights the need to look beyond the current constitutional debate and examine how to extend democracy and community self-management within a political movement devoted to reducing inequalities across the UK. The Collective rejects independence but supports a more federal UK with greater powers for Scotland, something that does not command support among the main UK political parties. This partly reflects the different constitutional alternatives that were outlined in Chapter 9 (status quo, 'devolution plus', 'devolution max' or full independence), but also highlights the need to develop ideas about policy directions in a future Scotland.

A manifesto for a different kind of welfare state

The Calman Commission on Scottish Devolution in 2009 recommended that the Scottish Parliament should be able to propose amendments to the housing benefit and council tax benefit systems in Scotland, not least because they are closely connected with areas of policy that are fully devolved. Recommendation 5.19 in the Calman Report proposed that:[14]

> There should be scope for Scottish Ministers, with the agreement of the Scottish Parliament, to propose changes to the Housing Benefit and Council Tax Benefit systems (as they apply in Scotland) when these are connected to devolved policy changes, and for the UK Government – if it agrees – to make those changes by suitable regulation.

There was recognition too that the Scottish government had a legitimate interest in the delivery of policies underpinned by the reserved benefits system in Scotland. For the SNP Scottish government, however, such proposals did not go nearly far enough and failed to give the Scottish government a substantive role in policy making in these key areas.

In 2009 in *Your Scotland, Your Voice: a national conversation*, the Scottish government identified several key principles for a fully Scottish welfare system which would work to eradicate poverty and reduce income inequality in Scotland:[15]

- a fair and transparent benefits system, sympathetic to the challenges faced by people living in poverty and providing confidence in the security of their income;
- support systems working in harmony to support those who can move from poverty through work, with financial benefits for working that are significant and sustained;
- transitional support into employment should be transparent, responsive, quick and effective, so successful employment is not undermined by financial uncertainty;
- for those that cannot work, benefits must provide a standard of living which supports dignity, freedom and social unity.

The challenge, as ever, is how these goals are to be realised. There is some recognition here that there are real barriers to work and, more importantly, that work does not always pay a living wage. While individuals, families and whole communities are all too frequently blamed for not being in paid employment, a lack of affordable and adequate childcare, poorly paid jobs and, indeed, a lack of jobs represent significant barriers to employment. Scotland is also no different from many other societies in being dependent on a huge amount of unpaid caring work, primarily done by women, for the sick, elderly and, of course, children. How can this be recognised and rewarded as socially necessary and hugely valuable work?[16]

The issue of childcare has already been flagged by the Scottish government as a key plank in its vision of a future Scottish welfare system. In the independence White Paper published in November 2013, there is a commitment to the provision of childcare in a future independent Scotland, initially amounting to 30 hours of childcare per week for all three- and four-year-olds, as well as vulnerable two-year-olds, and then expanding to include all children from one to school age:[17]

> We will in our first budget: provide 600 hours of childcare to around half of Scotland's two year olds. Those whose parents receive working tax credit or

child tax credit will benefit by the end of the first Parliament: ensure that all three and four year olds and vulnerable two year olds will be entitled to 1,140 hours of childcare a year (the same amount of time as children spend in primary school) by the end of the second Parliament: ensure that all children from one to school age will be entitled to 1,140 hours of childcare per year.

This has the potential to revolutionise the ability of many women to take up meaningful employment. However, it also requires some imaginative thinking about the ways in which these 30 hours are to be delivered. Critics from the 'Better Together' campaign, among others, argue that there is scope within the existing devolution settlement for the Scottish government to do more about meeting childcare needs now. (There are, of course, parallels here with the situation in Germany, which was discussed in Chapter 25).

As we saw in Chapter 1, the increasing economic and financial vulnerability of a growing section of the working population on the back of irregular and poor-quality employment, pay freezes, low pay and deteriorating terms and conditions of employment is a further reminder that a work-first approach to poverty is insufficient. The growing numbers of working poor in Scotland, as elsewhere in the UK, represent a serious challenge to policy makers. A low-wage, high unemployment and high under-employment economy is not the basis for a sustainable welfare system.

The Jimmy Reid Foundation and Oxfam Scotland are among the most vocal to call for a fully 'reformed' economy, one which operates for the benefit of the majority and not for the privilege of the few.[18] High-value jobs founded on at least a living wage for all are among the key principles here. Freedom of organisation for workers is also a key route for not only tackling inequalities at work but also for the generation of ideas about new ways of working.

A reformed welfare system can develop alongside a reformed economy. This should not be one driven by negative stereotypes and the stigmatisation of those experiencing poverty, but one that is grounded in human rights and the understanding that people's welfare should come first in any progressive society. This involves recapturing and rescuing the notion of 'welfare' itself, bereft of the negative connotations that have characterised it since the early days of the Thatcher governments in the late 1970s and early 1980s. Social welfare and social security, and not the 'dis-welfare' and social insecurity of contemporary UK government policy making, must become the foundation principles of any new system in

Scotland, enshrined in a social contract of rights and responsibilities for citizens and for all levels of government. Such rights should also be extended to all areas of work and employment.

As was highlighted in Chapter 13, alongside such collectivism, universalism should also be a founding principle. Taken together, such principles immediately remove the 'us' and 'them' divisions between benefit recipients and the rest of society. We all have a collective interest in social welfare and we all collectively benefit from the security that such social provision offers.

The Scottish Campaign on Welfare Reform has made the case for a human rights-based approach as the building block of a new welfare system for Scotland.[19] Welfare becomes, through such an approach, the means by which people come to participate in and engage with society. This also involves the users of welfare in the design and implementation of welfare and public services. With such principles cemented into the foundations of a new system, dignity and respect for all can replace stigmatisation and the lack of recognition of the contribution that everyone can make to society. Such an approach can be applied whatever the outcome of the constitutional debates.

The independence White Paper and social welfare

While this volume remains neutral on the question of Scotland's constitutional future, nonetheless the publication in late 2013 of the Scottish government's blueprint for independence, *Scotland's Future*, marks a significant moment in the independence debate and provides an important focal point.[20] Welfare is one of the key areas of contention that is likely to figure prominently in the independence debate leading up to the September 2014 referendum. The task set for the White Paper was less to put forward concrete manifesto commitments and more to establish the terrain of independence. It highlights a number of the areas in which an independent Scotland would be markedly different from a devolved Scotland within a UK context. Here, for instance, the proposal to abolish the 'bedroom tax' (which, as was discussed in Chapter 1) acts almost as a proxy for a wider theme about a sense of fairness and social justice that would underpin an independent Scottish welfare system. But *Scotland's Future* also points to areas of policy making that might not be that different in an independent Scotland from the rest of the UK, but which would be more in tune with Scottish needs and better able to address them. Key areas of economic policy are in particular highlighted as cases in point.

Designing an appropriate system of benefits and social protection is an important task for any modern independent nation state and the White Paper clearly sets out the broad principles that the Scottish government claims would guide its long-term approach in an independent Scotland. Many of these are relatively uncontroversial and cannot be seen as necessarily or uniquely 'Scottish'. For us, the importance of this document is that social welfare is placed centre stage in the proposals for an independent Scotland and appears to be driven by a set of principles that will help generate a more inclusive and equal society. As noted earlier, there are ambitious proposals for 1,140 free hours of childcare for all Scottish children from one to school age – plans that are portrayed by the Scottish government as 'transformational'. Elsewhere there is a commitment to, once again, uprate working-age benefits and tax credits and allowances in line with inflation (in contrast to the current UK government's 1 per cent cap on uprating). There is an aspiration to provide a standard of living that enables dignity and respect for those who cannot work, and commitment to uprate a Scottish national minimum wage in line with inflation (although, disappointingly, there was no commitment to aim to align this with the living wage). The vision for tax and welfare policy in an independent Scotland suggests that these will be better integrated with employment, education and health services.

Other headline proposals – some of which were long trailed before the White Paper – include abolishing the bedroom tax and benefit cap, and cancelling the implementation of universal credit (which the UK government plans to introduce to replace a number of working-age benefits and which, in late 2013, was being rolled out in Inverness). Taken together, these proposals represent a substantial departure from the recent direction of travel for the UK benefits system. *Scotland's Future* calls for a benefits system which 'fosters a climate of social solidarity'; is critical of attacks by the UK government on the benefits for disabled people and the unemployed; and argues for a social security system which allows dignity and participation in society for all. In other contexts, such proposals and sentiments are hardly radical, but set against the arguments and policies advanced by the UK coalition, they represent a sea change from the policy-making context that underpins social welfare currently.

Scotland's Future also contains a wide range of possible future policy interventions around labour market regulation, including strengthening employment protection through action on minimum terms and conditions, maternity and paternity rights, and a stronger role for unions and collective bargaining. Elsewhere, there is recognition that in-work poverty is a major issue as a result of under-employment and low wages. All of this should be welcomed by those who wish to see a new approach to combatting poverty. Likewise, proposals to tackle fuel poverty, which is a growing issue in Scotland and across the UK, to improve health outcomes, in part by a more preventative approach involving the tackling of poverty, and to address the consequences of poverty for educational attainment and other educational problems are also forward looking and to be welcomed.

Critics have pointed out that the proposals set out in the White Paper are largely uncosted and make numerous assumptions about the future health of a Scottish economy which cannot be certain. Further, it also reaffirms the SNP's commitment to a shared system of financial regulation, to 'fiscal discipline' and to securing 'credibility with the financial markets', which critics (on the left in particular) are wary of on account of its commitment to some kind of neo-liberal economic model, with low corporation tax and a dynamic free market economy. In much the same way, the White Paper advances that an independent Scotland with low business taxes and enhanced economic competitiveness would provide the basis for economic growth, rising living standards and a 'successful and secure Scotland'.

Many of the claims made and arguments advanced in the White Paper will be contested and subject, no doubt, to widespread and intense debate. *Scotland's Future* has raised important issues for all of us who are concerned with poverty and disadvantage in Scotland and elsewhere in the UK. As a vision for a more equal Scotland with lower levels of poverty, there is little doubt that it is far more palatable than anything on offer policy wise from the current Westminster government.

Conclusion: towards the good society?

Scotland has undergone significant change across the past few decades. In some respects, it is a very different place from when the first edition of *Poverty in Scotland* was published in the early 1990s. But there are also continuities with the past that should not be ignored. Scotland remains a hugely unequal society by any measure; it is characterised by wide and growing inequalities, marked social divisions and is scourged by the prevalence both of extreme poverty – *and of extreme wealth*. The independence White Paper contains no proposals for a far-reaching redistribution of income and wealth through a much fairer tax regime. Nor are there any clear political or ideological commitments to challenging privilege and vested interests. The making of a good society – the good Scottish society – necessitates that such issues are addressed.

This does not mean that we are making any assumptions about Scotland's constitutional future, or the likelihood of a distinctive and separate Scottish welfare state. There is much that can be done now to tackle poverty and inequality – if the political will is there to do so. The full powers of the existing devolution settlement have yet to be deployed. However, the tone of the debate in Scotland, in no small part due to the independence question, is different from that taking place elsewhere in the UK, where a culture of permanent austerity seems to be the only vision on offer. Yet Scotland, as we have seen, is not immune from the increasingly harsh public attitudes, degrading stereotypes and hostility that demonise those in need and fuel a culture of animosity towards people experiencing poverty and disadvantage. Where are the voices of people in poverty and those who are disadvantaged and oppressed in the debate about Scotland's constitutional future?

Whatever the outcome of the independence referendum, Scotland will be a very different place. There will also be different relationships between Scotland, England, Wales and Northern Ireland, either through a different kind of union or, with independence, new international relations between Scotland and the other countries in the British Isles. But our hope in this very different Scotland, in the very different British Isles, is that there will also be new ways of addressing poverty and inequality. In looking forward to the independence referendum and beyond (the subtitle of this book), we recognise and argue that issues of poverty and inequality cannot be reduced to issues of constitutional change alone. Yet we also recognise that the constitutional future of the UK has, on the back of the Scottish independence debate, provided a much welcomed forum and opportunity for us to explore the makings of a new welfare system. One of the things that we would welcome is that, in Scotland at least, 'welfare' has regained some of its more positive meanings and connotations. *Scotland's Future* talks about social security in a future independent Scotland, and it is important that this is recaptured and understood as a necessary feature of any good society.

Finally, as we seek to recapture (and re-think) notions of social security and welfare from their largely pejorative and negative usage of the past three to four decades, we look back and look forward. There are important lessons to be learnt from decades of failed attempts to tackle poverty, as well as decades of political unwillingness to address the root causes of poverty and inequality. We understand that poverty and inequality do not happen by some natural or accidental process – but reflect conscious political decisions and ideological visions. However, our imagination should not be constrained by the past. Too often it feels that the vision for the future welfare system is one premised on a return to some mythical 'golden age' welfare state of the past, pre-Thatcher era.

In this book the contributors have opened up new ways of thinking about the issues that surround the discussion of poverty in Scotland. We are also learning from other countries that other ways of doing things are possible. All of this feeds our imagination of what a future Scottish society and a future welfare state could possibly be like. The task in the independence debate and beyond is to seek to develop new ideas, new understandings and new policies, and to challenge inequality, poverty and disadvantage in all its diverse forms.

Notes

1 D Alexander, 'Let's work together, not walk away', *The Third Way Magazine*, October 2013, http://bellacaledonia.org.uk/2013/10/08/lets-work-together-not-walk-away/

2 A Salmond, Preface to *Scotland's Future* (independence White Paper), Scottish government, 2013

3 G Brown and D Alexander, *New Scotland, New Britain*, The Smith Institute, 1993, p19

4 Scotland Office, *Government Evidence to the Commission on Scottish Devolution*, 2008

5 A Salmond, Hugo Young Lecture, London, 25 January 2012, http://www.the guardian.com/politics/2012/jan/25/alex-salmond-hugo-young-lecture

6 A Salmond, Speech to the SNP Conference, Perth, 19 October 2013

7 See G Mooney and G Scott (eds), *Social Justice and Social Policy in Scotland*, Policy Press, 2012; G Mooney and G Scott, 'Poverty and Social Justice in the Devolved Scotland: neoliberalism meets social democracy?', *Social Policy and Society*, 8(3), 2009, pp379–89; G Hassan, 'The Myths and Potential of Social Justice in Scotland', in J Derbyshire (ed), *Poverty in the UK: can it be eradicated?* Joseph Rowntree Foundation/*Prospect Magazine*, 2013, pp52–55, http://www.prospectmagazine.co.uk/wp-content/uploads/2013/11/jrf_web.pdf

8 M Gannon and N Bailey, *Attitudes to the Necessities of Life in Scotland: can a UK poverty standard be applied in Scotland?* PSE Working Paper: Analysis Series No.5, 2013, http://www.poverty.ac.uk/sites/default/files/attachments/

WP%20Analysis%20No.5%20-%20Attitudes%20to%20the%20%27necessities
%20of%20life%27%20in%20Scotland%20%28Gannon%20Bailey%20Nov13%
29.pdf

9 See *Poverty in Scotland 2011*, Chapter 9, on misrepresentations of poverty in Scotland and also specifically on *The Scheme* programme. For a fuller critique of *The Scheme*, see also A Law and G Mooney, '"Poverty Porn" and '*The Scheme*: questioning documentary realism', *Media Educational Journal*, 50, Winter, 2011/12, pp9–12

10 The SNP claims that independence will bring about economic growth and that, together with revenues from North Sea oil and renewable energy industries, the economic basis of a future Scottish welfare state can be secured.

11 Further information about the work of the expert working group can be found at http://www.scotland.gov.uk/Topics/People/welfarereform/EXPERTWORKING-GROUPONWELFARE

12 See http://reidfoundation.org/wp-content/uploads/2013/05/The-Common-Weal.pdf

13 P Bryan and T Kane (eds), *Class, Nation and Socialism: the red paper on Scotland 2014*, Glasgow Caledonian University Archives, 2013

14 Commission on Scottish Devolution, *Serving Scotland Better: Scotland and the United Kingdom in the 21st Century, Final Report, Executive Summary*, 2009, http://www.commissiononscottishdevolution.org.uk/uploads/2009-06-12-csd-a5_final-summary_ibook.pdf

15 Scottish government, *Your Scotland, Your Voice: a national conversation*, 2009, p62

16 A McKay, *Welfare to Work or a Welfare System that Works? Arguing for a citizens basic income in a new Scotland*, David Hulme Institute Research Paper No.5, February 2013

17 Scottish government, *Scotland's Future* (independence White Paper), 2013, Chapter 5, http://www.scotland.gov.uk/Publications/2013/11/9348/9

18 See M Danson and K Trebeck (eds), *Whose Economy? An introduction*, Oxfam, 2011, http://policy-practice.oxfam.org.uk/publications/whose-economy-seminar-papers-complete-series-188809

19 Scottish Campaign on Welfare Reform, *A Manifesto for Change*, 2013, http://povertyalliance.org/userfiles/files/campaigns/SCoWR_manifesto_2013.pdf

20 See note 17